Better Self Defense Omnibus

Neal Martin

ISBN-10:1507770332
ISBN-13:9781507770337

Self Defense Tips Everyone Should Know

INTRODUCTION

"Self defense is not about learning a whole bunch of cool physical tricks. Self defense is an attitude that is backed up by a few very simple practical strategies and tactics. There are no guarantees and it is as much about acknowledging your limitations as it is about developing your strengths."

Neal Martin

There is a lot of bad information out there on self defense. Look around YouTube and the myriad blogs and websites that exist on the web and what you will find are an awful lot of people who proclaim to know all about good self defense, but in fact haven't got a clue what they are talking about most of the time, and indeed the information they are putting across to people could potentially do more harm than good.

If you are new to self defense and have never done any kind of training before then it can it seem that most of the fighting systems and arts out there look really effective for self defense. A quick trawl through YouTube will reveal countless videos of people teaching what appear to be really cool and useful moves that could work against a real attacker.

The truth about most of these cool moves is that they are little more than neat little physical tricks, like magic tricks designed to wow spectators and people who don't know any different.

And most people *don't* know any different. To know what works and what is really useful in a physical confrontation requires one to have some kind of experience in these things (or to have at least trained with other people who have). Most people don't have that experience because most right thinking people tend to avoid violence like the plague.

Others, like me, actively sought out violent situations in order to know them better and to find out the best ways of dealing with them. I went into the bouncing game for precisely that reason. I wanted experience and I wanted to see what worked. And what I found was, the vast majority of the information being taught as self defense simply had no bearing whatsoever on real life.

You see, self defense is not about learning a whole bunch of cool physical tricks. Self defense is an attitude that is backed up by a few very simple practical strategies and tactics. There are no guarantees and it is as much about acknowledging your limitations as it is about developing your strengths.

This book will not teach you how to do all those physical tricks beloved of martial artists and self defense practitioners the (web) world over. Instead this book will give you something far more valuable. It will give you a sound game plan and the tools to help you develop the right attitude which will not only help you take responsibility for your personal safety, but also help you prevail in any conflict situation.

The information I have chosen to include in this book is designed to be of real practical value. There is next to no theory in it. I want to give you information that you can use right away to formulate your own self protection game plan, information that is going to help you prepare yourself mentally and physically should you ever have to defend yourself in a conflict situation.

All the information in here is taken from my thirty odd years of experience in the martial arts and self defense worlds, and also the practical experience I gained from working doors for many years.

Read each chapter and let the information sink in. Let it color your developing attitude towards your own personal safety. To stand any chance of developing a good game plan you have to start thinking in a certain way. At points in the book I will explicitly explain this attitude. At other times you will have to read between the lines for yourself.

I have no doubt that by the time you are finished this book you will be far better equipped to protect yourself and your loved ones than what you were in the beginning, as long that is, as you put what I tell you into practice. Even if you don't, you will still find a change in attitude, and sometimes, that's all it takes.

So let's crack on and take a look at some self defense fundamentals first of all, beginning with the most important thing: how to take responsibility for your own personal safety.

1: TAKE RESPONSIBILITY FOR YOUR OWN PERSONAL SAFETY

"I don't even call it violence when it's in self defense; I call it intelligence."

Malcolm X

Making a full commitment to taking responsibility for your own personal safety is paramount when it comes to self defense.

One of the main barriers to personal safety that many people have in today's society is that they believe they have no need for any kind of self defense skills or general self protection game plan.

There is no doubt that there is much violence in the world and that it is never far away from our own doorstep. If you watch the news or read the newspapers on a regular basis you would be forgiven for thinking that our society is more violent than it actually is. Even though there is much violence in today's society, the times in which we live are actually not as dangerous and violent as many believe they are, despite the impression that the mainstream media puts across. As hard as it is to believe, the levels of criminal violence in our society are less than what they were in recent years and beyond. Yes, there is still much violence out there, but not as much as people generally believe.

I'm reminded of the late great comedian and social commentator, Bill Hicks, talking on stage about the news media and how it paints a vivid picture of this truly frightening and horrible world filled with death, violence, war, famine, destruction, disease etc. on a daily basis. And then you look out your window and...nothing, just the sound of silence or crickets chirping in the background. To quote Bill: "Where is all this shit happening?!"

My point here is that the world is not as horrible and violent as some would have you believe. Lots of self defense instructors out there have a vested interest in making people believe that the world is a scary place, that you could get mugged or raped or killed at any time.

While this may be true to an extent, the world is nowhere near as bad as these unscrupulous instructors would have you believe. That's just marketing, scare tactics to try and get people to sign up to their classes and expensive courses, nothing more.

So am I saying that the world in which we live is some kind of peaceful paradise where violence and street crime don't exist? Of course not. Obviously these things exist. What I'm saying is that you need to maintain a healthy psychological attitude towards all the bad in the world. Acknowledge that it exists, but at the same time don't let it affect your life in any adverse way. Don't allow fear or paranoia stop you from living your life to the full.

At the same time, it would be foolish to think that violence will never cross your path. The risk of violent confrontation still exists, yet many people choose to deny this fact, and therefore don't see the need for any kind of self defense training.

Some of the reasons people overlook self defense training are:

- A fear of the unknown (don't like to try new things)
- They possess a defeatist or negative attitude - I can't do it!
- They think the police will protect them- they won't!
- They live a very sheltered lifestyle, walking around with an "it can't happen to me" attitude.
- They think it requires too much effort—laziness, in other words!

- They are naive or oblivious to the real world.
- They believe God will protect them.
- They claim they don't have the time or are too busy to look into self defense training.

When looked at, none of the above reasons hold any water. The most important reason from that list to reconsider is the fact that some people think the law or other people in general will save them if anything happens to them.

No! The law will not save you. Why would you think the police are going to be there if something happens? Have you ever called the police out anyway? How long did they take to respond? Exactly.

Only you can take responsibility for your own personal safety, and it is something that you *absolutely* must do. You must have the attitude that if something happens, no one will be there to save you, so you have to learn how to save yourself.

There is terrific strength to be gained from making this mental shift. No one likes to feel reliant on anyone else. There is nothing worse.

Becoming self-reliant, especially in regard to your personal safety, will not only give you an increased sense of confidence, but more importantly, should you find yourself in a situation where you must defend yourself or risk injury or death, you will react swiftly and forcefully, because you know that it is up to you to do so, that no one will magically appear to save your ass.

You have to save your own ass!

I really can't stress enough how important this is: take responsibility before you do anything else. Everything else you do in regards to self defense must come from that initial decision.

By committing to taking responsibility for your own personal safety you are also making a secondary commitment, which is this:

That you will never be anybody's victim.

You must tell yourself that you have the inalienable right to live your life in peace and that no one has the right to threaten that peace in anyway. If someone does threaten you in a physical manner then it is your duty to stand up for yourself and defend against any physical violence that comes your way.

If you don't install this belief from the start then you will never be sure about your actions in a self defense situation. You are drawing a line in the sand, knowing full well that if anyone crosses it you will react swiftly and forcefully to drive them back over it again.

We will go more into this subject later on in the book.

In the meantime, take a look at the practice drill suggestion below. There will be suggested practice drills in each chapter of this book and they are designed to help you focus and give you action steps that will greatly improve your self protection skills. Once you read a chapter, try out the practice drill. It is essential that you do more than just read about things, you must apply the advice I give you in some practical way, otherwise you will be no better equipped to defend yourself than you were when you first began reading this book.

Sit down and think about what your personal safety means to you and how far you are willing to go to protect yourself and your loved ones. Think about the fact that you can't rely on anyone to save you if you are in trouble, and then make the firm decision that you will take full responsibility for your own safety from now on. Keep reminding yourself of this decision daily until the belief is firmly ingrained in your mind.

2: MAKE A GAME PLAN

"Every fighter has to go in there with a game plan."

Rau'Shee Warren

When it comes to your personal safety it is useful to have some kind of game plan in place, a set of instructions if you will, that will help you get through a situation, in this case, a physical altercation.

Going blind into any kind of difficult situation is not the best plan of attack. After all, you wouldn't climb into the boxing ring to fight and just hope for the best. You would already have figured out what your approach to the fight is going to be, how you are going to fight and what to do if things go a certain way.

Self defense is no different. You need to plan ahead and decide what steps you are going to follow should you find yourself in a situation where someone is being hostile or violent towards you.

Having a game plan in place will give you the biggest chance of success and of handling the situation in the right way. You can't be thinking about what you are going to do while the situation is unfolding. It's too late then, and you won't be able to think clearly because of the massive stress you'll be under.

What you need is a self protection game plan put in place. A basic set of instructions that you can follow in most sets of circumstances.

In one sense, this whole book is a self protection game plan, just a very detailed one. In this chapter however, I want to give you an overview of what a good self-protection game plan should be all about. Then in the succeeding chapters, I'll go into more detail on the various aspects of that game plan. So let's look at the overview first.

Awareness And Target Hardening

Awareness should be bedrock of your self-protection gam plan. After all, it is by being aware and "switched on" to your environment that you can avoid most trouble in the first place. Awareness makes it possible for you to spot trouble from afar or sense impending danger. The quicker you pick up on that danger, the more options you will have to deal with it and avoid it altogether. Your options become severely narrowed when trouble is right on top of you. We'll discuss awareness in further detail in the next chapter.

Target hardening is a term that simply refers to making yourself a less easy target for criminals and those who would wish you harm. It's about how you present yourself to the world, how you carry yourself, how you interact with other people and the signals you put out to other people, especially those that may be after their next victim, like street predators. Again, we'll discuss in more detail later.

Avoidance And Escape

It should be your goal to avoid trouble as much as possible, to keep yourself out of situations that may pose a danger to you.

Should you find yourself in trouble then your main priority should be to escape the situation wherever possible. There is no merit in staying in a dangerous or life threatening situation if you don't have too, unless of course you have no choice. Sometimes you just can't escape or you must stay to protect third parties, such as a loved one.

Situational Control And Verbal De-escalation

If you find yourself trapped in a situation and all avenues of escape are temporarily blocked then you must begin to take control of the situation as much as possible. If faced by a would-be assailant then you need to use your contact management skills to control your personal space and make it difficult for the other person or persons to attack you.

At this stage of the game, your priority should be to try and talk the other person down, to verbally de-escalate the situation. Many times, if you are confident and assertive enough, you can defuse a situation without recourse to physical violence. More on this later.

Pre-Emptive Action

Sometimes, no matter what you do or say, a situation cannot be defused by verbal de-escalation and it will quickly become clear (through your aggressors actions and body language) that an attack is imminent. In this case, your best course of action is pre-emptive action, i.e. you hit your attacker first before they hit you. This may sound like a brutal or even thuggish course of action, but believe me, it is almost always the best course of action and it will nip the situation in the bud before it escalates any further.

Don't worry if you can't see yourself doing this. Later in the book I will show you exactly how you can get the right mindset that will allow you to take pre-emptive action whenever necessary.

The plan here is to hit and run whenever possible. You should always be thinking about escaping the situation at the earliest opportunity. Hitting your attacker will give you that opportunity, buying you time to make your escape.

That in a nutshell is a basic self-protection game plan. In a high stress situation like a physical altercation you won't have time to think too much, that's just the way it is. The more prepared you are, the more options you will give yourself and thus the greater your chances of prevailing in an attack situation.

Now, in the remaining chapters of this book, I'm going to go into a bit more detail about the concepts and principles laid out in this game plan, plus a whole lot more.

Let's do this!

3: AWARENESS (TAKE A LOOK AROUND ONCE IN A WHILE!)

It has become a bit of a cliché in self defense circles to say that awareness is the bedrock of good self defense; that self defense starts with awareness. Every self-protection instructor in the world now pays glib homage to this statement whenever they teach people (especially newcomers), before moving swiftly on the really cool physical stuff that everybody pays their money for.

I don't mean to suggest here that the concept of awareness in self defense isn't an important one. It is, obviously. It is very important.

There is usually a problem though, in the way that awareness is taught, if indeed you could be said to be teaching awareness. For the most part awareness isn't taught, it's merely relayed to students in the manner of a lecture, which usually means dry and boring. You generally don't take stuff in very deeply when it is relayed in such a non-impactful way.

I hope to make enough of an impression on you here that you take in just how important having good awareness skills are. Not only that, but you become motivated to take action and actively practice being aware in your daily life.

Just by being more aware in your daily life, by stepping it up even a little bit, you will get a lot more out of the experience of life. That in itself should motivate you to be that bit more aware every day.

Our main focus here though, is awareness as it pertains to self defense, and there are three different levels to that: *situational awareness*, *self-awareness* and *threat awareness* (or threat recognition). Let's look at self-awareness first of all.

Self-Awareness

Unless you make a habit of getting into fights with dogs or grizzly bears or cute hamsters in pet shops that bite your finger when you try to pick them up (bastards!), then you would likely agree that when we practice self defense, we practice it with people in mind. That means we deal with other people and their behavior every day. It would seem to make sense then that the more you know about people and how they act and why they do certain things, the better your interactions with others are going to be.

The more you know and understand about yourself, the better you will be able to understand about other people and their behavior, because you can empathize with them and also quite often predict their behavior.

It's therefore in your interests to be more self-aware and to try and understand why you are the way you are and why you do the things you do all the time. The more self-aware you are, the better you will be able to deal with people, even when they are being aggressive and violent.

A good level of self-awareness will allow you to be conscious of your strengths so that you can play to them better, and this includes in conflict situations. You will also know your weaknesses, which again will help you because you will know what about you needs developing.

Being self-aware will also reduce the chances of you behaving like an insensitive asshole and winding people up all the time. People who do this are quite often barely even aware that they are doing it. They just crash through life, oblivious most if the time of the damage they are doing.

A high level of self-awareness leads to good self-control and self-monitoring. You will think before you act (most of the time). These are all good things for helping you to avoid or defuse conflicts before they get physical.

Studies have also shown that those with good levels of self-awareness are more capable of handling their feelings and emotions, especially in times of stress. This is a good thing, especially considering just how highly stressful conflict and physical altercations can be. In such pressurized circumstances, the more self-control you can exert the better.

> ## EXERCISE
>
> *Reflect on a time when you found yourself in conflict with someone, or a time when you had to physically fight someone, a time when your feelings may have influenced your thoughts and behaviour. Did you feel in control of the situation? Did your emotions affect your level of confidence in this situation or how you perceived others? Emotions can prompt action and inaction, intervention and withdrawal. Write your thoughts down or discuss this occasion with a friend.*

Discovery of the self is an on-going, continuous process which, at times, can be painful as hidden aspects are slowly uncovered. When confronted with difficult situations such as violent conflicts, we are expected to behave in a certain way, although feelings of vulnerability and uncertainty may challenge our perceived abilities. Being more self-aware can help us to cope in such circumstances, helping us to respect our fears, anxieties and concerns, and prompting questions about how these could be overcome.

Self-awareness is quite a deep subject as you can see. It also has many applications for self defense. Get to work on it.

Situational Awareness

Situational awareness is all about being tuned in to your surrounding environment. It's about being aware of what's going around you.

We lead such stressful and busy lives these days that it is easy to walk around in a very "switched off" state, where all of our attention is directed towards what is going on inside our head (or on the screen of our iPhones!), rather than to what is going on around us.

When you're switched off it can be hard to detect changes in your environment or notice things that are out of place or not quite right. You could be walking into danger and you wouldn't even know it until it was too late.

To maintain situational awareness you must be switched on at all times. To be switched on is not to be in a state of hyper vigilance that borders on paranoia and makes you suspicious of everything. Instead, to be switched on is to be in a state of *relaxed alertness*, which means you go about your daily business as usual but you maintain your awareness always.

This is mostly an unconscious process that runs in the background of your mind, meaning you can go about your business while still maintaining a good level of awareness.

Obviously, if you find yourself in unfamiliar environments, or environments that are known to be trouble spots, then you would up your awareness levels, but again, not to the point where you become wound up tight and jump at the slightest noise or movement. You are still relaxed, but your senses are on high alert.

Maintaining a switched on state in your daily life will help you avoid trouble, because a lot of the time, you will notice trouble well before it is on top of you and it is too late to do anything about it. You will spot potentially troublesome people and groups of people in time to either avoid them or keep a close eye on them. You will notice dodgy looking areas up ahead so you can take a different route and avoid them. And if trouble does come suddenly and unexpectedly (as it sometimes does) you should be ready to react in a way that will at least give you a chance.

> ### PRACTICE DRILL
>
> This is a good drill for enhancing your awareness and observation skills. As you go about your business you must spot people who are wearing a certain item of clothing. So for instance, you may elect to notice only those people who are wearing a red item of clothing or a blue item of clothing. It doesn't really matter which. The idea is just to focus your attention on one particular group of people. By doing this, you are forcing yourself to become aware of everyone around you as you filter out the ones who aren't in your chosen group. You can do this drill while you wait outside a shop on your partner (as I often do!) or while you are sitting on a bus or wherever. Just be casual about it. You'll be surprised how much you end up observing just by doing this drill.

Threat Awareness

Threat awareness, or threat recognition, is having the ability to spot a threat to your person before it does you any kind of harm.

This can mean seeing a particular kind of threat from a distance, such as a gang hanging on a street corner, or picking up on threatening behavior from someone who is in your immediate vicinity.

If you are switched on enough you should be able to spot distant threats and avoid them. Another example of this would be if you are in a bar and someone was staring at you in a threatening manner from across the way. You would know to avoid that person then, or to keep a close eye on them, rather than not notice them at all and perhaps be blindsided by them later.

Awareness also comes into the equation when an aggressor is right in front of you. You need to be able to spot the signs that your aggressor is going to go from aggressive to violent. These signs are called pre-contact cues and include the following:

- "Grooming" -- fiddling with hair, face, ears, eyes, hat, etc., basically hands on the head/face area rubbing or smoothing, etc.
- The 3-6-9 glance, checking from side to side just before they attack
- The planted step, or setting their base just before they hit you
- Clenching of the teeth and setting of the jaw
- Verbal descends into monosyllables—"Yeah", "And", "So", "What"
- Closing of distance

Those are just some of the pre-contact cues to watch out for when facing off against an aggressor. Spot them early and you will have a better chance of acting before they do.

"Your new attitude should include an awareness of where you are and what's going on around you. It's like when you're driving: you check the rear-view mirror, watch for flashing brake lights up ahead, quickly rehearse the turns you'll be making... all at once."

Stanford Strong

4: IMPROVE YOUR COMMUNICATION SKILLS

"The single biggest problem in communication is the illusion that it has taken place."

George Bernard Shaw

When it comes to how we communicate with each other (especially in a self defense situation), the words we choose in our exchanges are less important than how we actually put those words across. Being an enlightened and educated reader, I'm sure you know this already.

I'm also sure that you are aware of the following:

Only a small percentage of communication involves actual words: 7%, to be exact. In fact, 55% of communication is visual (body language, eye contact) and 38% is vocal (pitch, speed, volume, tone of voice).

Given these statistics, when it comes to dealing with a potential threat or threats in conflict situation, we can see that it is our body language that will have the biggest bearing on whether or not the outcome of said situation will be in our favor.

Or to put it in simpler terms: How you present yourself to a potential threat will decide whether that threat sees you as predator or prey.

The Four Levels Of Communication
Broadly speaking, there are four levels of communication in self defense:

1. Non-Fight Communication

2. Pre-Fight Communication

3. In-Fight Communication

4. Post-Fight Communication

Let's look at each of these in turn.

Non-Fight Communication

Non-fight communication is basically how you put yourself across in your daily life, those times when you are not involved in any kind of violent conflict (which is almost all the time for most of us).

Thugs, street hustlers, predators, when they look for a victim, one of the first things they look for in a person is how they carry themselves.

Think about it. If you're a predator looking for prey, who do you go for? The person who carries themselves with confidence and moves with assured purpose, or the person who carries themselves meekly, who acts unsure of themselves and who gives out victim vibes?

There are other factors involved in choosing a victim, of course, but body language is a clear indicator of victim suitability.

Making yourself a hard target for those who wish to harm or take advantage, starts with how you put yourself across to the world around you.

What kind of person do you want to be? What kind of person do you need to be in order to make yourself a harder target for criminals?

This is fundamental. If you don't have confidence in yourself, if you are unsure of yourself, if you are meek in front of others, people will notice, because your body language (as well as your words and tone of voice) will communicate this.

In the case of criminals, they will hone in on the kind of vibe you are putting out. They don't see a person with issues, they see an easy target.

Street criminals want minimum fuss from their victims. They just want to do what they have to do and move safely on to the next victim. They try not to choose people who look like they would put up too much of a fuss, who will probably fight back and not take too kindly to being hassled in such a way.

You have to put out the same vibe; you have to communicate with your body language that you do not fit the normal victim profile.

Not fitting the victim profile will ensure you lead a relatively un-victimized life.

Despite our best efforts though, shit still happens sometimes. Some people just insist on trying it on anyway, and this is where the next level of communication comes in.

Pre-Fight Communication
The way in which you communicate in the early stages of a potentially violent conflict is vitally important.

If someone does decide to test you in a threatening manner, you still need to put yourself across with confidence and self-assurance. You have to look like you are not rattled by the situation, even though internally, you may well be.

When you fence a potential threat, you are not just controlling your personal space; you are communicating your intentions to the threat.

And your intentions are: to try to diffuse the situation non-violently, but if need be, you will use violence and do so without hesitation.

Put another way, you are drawing a line in the sand and letting it be known that the consequences of crossing that line will be severe.

The threat will pick up on this vibe, if only subconsciously. Many situations can be diffused straight away just by presenting yourself to the threat in front of you in such an assertive manner.

If the threat has misjudged you, that will become obvious to them in your demeanor and they will most likely retreat.

Sometimes, that's all it takes.

Other times, for whatever reason, violence becomes inevitable. Communication however, does not stop there.

In-Fight Communication
If you hit first and hit hard, you are sending a message, a very clear message to the person you just hit that they chose the wrong person. They'll get it when they wake up.

If you get into a fight, your every strike, your every movement, has to hammer home the same message:

YOU FUCKED WITH THE WRONG ONE!

Meaning you have to go in hard and fast to overwhelm the threat, to do the exact opposite of what they expected you to do.

You are not just attacking the body but the mind as well.

You're trying to break their will, beat down the bad intentions in them.

Put the fight out of them- literally and figuratively.

Even during the fight, you give verbal commands: "STAY DOWN! DON'T MOVE!"

If there are other threats around, this will communicate a message to them as well: Try anything and you'll get the same.

Post-Fight Communication
This is the final level of communication in self defense, the post-fight communication. The way in which you put yourself across here is most important, especially if you have to deal with the law and explain your actions in court.

All you have at this stage, no matter what happened previously, is your ability to communicate.

Many people fall foul of the law due to bad or ineffective communication skills. If you come across as arrogant or cocky to the police, or if you are unable to justify your actions in court, you will suffer the consequences, which could mean jail time.

If you don't want to get swallowed up whole by the judicial system you must know exactly what to say and exactly how you should put yourself across. You must learn good articulation skills, which means making the practice of such skills a part of your self defense training.

If you are unsure of how to communicate properly post-fight, then I suggest you read Facing Violence, by Rory Miller. In that book you will learn all about how to put yourself across to the law afterwards.

Learn To Communicate Effectively
Communication is fundamental in self defense.

Physical skills matter less than the ability to communicate effectively, and on all levels.

When you walk down the street, when you are faced by a potential threat, when you have to physically deal with a threat and when you have to explain your actions afterwards, you have to be vitally aware of what you are communicating at all times through your body language, your tone of voice and with your choice of words.

Self defense is not just about hitting someone.

Learning to communicate in the right way will save you a lot of trouble in the long run.

PRACTICE DRILL

Be conscious of how you present yourself in public. How are you coming across to other people? Do you carry yourself with confidence or are you unsure of yourself? For the next while, be aware of how you walk, how you stand and how you talk to people. Try to present yourself as being a confident and assertive type. I don't mean you have to be arrogant and in everybody's faces. You can be quietly confident as well. Just do what fits your personality, even if it feels like acting at first, eventually you will begin to feel more sure of yourself for real.

Another drill you can do is the Articulation Drill. Play out a self defence scenario and then afterwards, explain your actions like you are explaining them to the police after the incident. When you are finished a partner will play the role of the bad guy and put across his side of the story, or they will play the role of a cop and question your statement. The goal here is to work on your post-fight communication and practice justifying your actions in the eyes of the law.

5: KNOW YOURSELF

"One's own self is well hidden from one's own self; of all mines of treasure, one's own is the last to be dug up."

Friedrich Wilhelm Nietzsche

You must learn to control your own mind as much as possible if you want to have the bottle to fight when you need too.

Through working doors and training in Combatives, I have realized the importance of being in the right mindset when it comes to engaging in real violence.

But we hear that all the time, don't we, people talking about the right mindset? So how do we get that mindset?

Well first of all, I believe you have to square it with yourself that if you are left with no choice, that you absolutely will, without hesitation, go like fuck and put the other person down.

In the midst of a confrontation is not the time to be debating this. This will only cause indecision, which will lead to hesitation and most likely failure to act when you need too.

You must make a pact with yourself that you will act when you have to and also have the self-belief to carry that through. You must be steadfast in this decision.

At a certain point in a confrontation, when you believe that things are about to take a turn for the worse, you must have the ability to flick an internal switch that allows you to access cold aggression and a forward drive mentality, only hitting the off switch when the situation has been dealt with, which usually means your opponent lying on the ground and unable or unwilling to cause you any more aggro.

The fear of violence is very deep rooted and I'm not advocating that you try and eradicate it because it can't be done. That fear is there for a reason. But when your life is on the line, you need the ability to act despite that fear.

There are many reasons why some people don't act when they need to, so you need to go deep and find out what issues are surrounding your inability to act when you need to.

For me, I had concerns about seriously injuring someone, which quite often meant I didn't take action when I needed too. But over time, I worked on this issue and told myself that if I didn't take action then I may just end up being the person who is seriously injured. Once I realized this, I felt better able to hit when I had to.

Such issues are not easy to get rid of. To this day I will always try to use low force options to sort out a situation. However, if I feel the situation calls for it, I am fully prepared to use more damaging options.

If you happen to struggle with finding that willingness to act, it could also be because you don't get angry enough. I have found anger to be very good for displacing fear. You must say to yourself, *"Who does this person think they are, bullying me like this? What right do they have to treat me in this way?* WHO THE FUCK DOES THIS CUNT THINK HE IS? WELL FUCK HIM, I'M NOT STANDING FOR THIS SHIT!"

You get the idea? You're riling yourself up for action through the use of self-righteous anger and moral indignation. When you are angry, you are not afraid so you will find it much easier to go for it then.

So strengthening your bottle for real violence, finding that will to act, is about doing proper Combatives training that addresses all stages of a violent confrontation and doing so in a realistic way that makes you tougher, mentally and physically, and allows you to practice accessing a good combative mindset that will make it possible for you to act when you have to.

It is also about doing internal work, discovering what issues you have around the use of violence (morally and ethically) and also what kind of person you are. If you are too timid, what steps can you take to become more assertive? How can you practice being assertive? Do you value yourself enough to not let people push you around? If not, why not? These are the questions you must ask yourself.

Your Capacity For (Survival) Violence

Could you gouge someone's eye out if you had too?

There is a big difference between saying you could do something and actually doing it.

You may be fully capable of gouging out someone's eye, but you may not have the capacity to do so when needed to.

The truth be told, I don't know if I could gouge someone's eye completely out of its socket so that it is hanging there like some gruesome conker.

I'd like to think I could relieve someone of their sight in such a horrific way, if I really had to do so.

If someone where trying to kill me, for instance, I'd like to think I would dislodge that blob of jelly in a heartbeat if it meant I was going to stay alive a bit longer.

The truth is however, I will never really know until I am put in that situation.

I may freeze.

I don't know.

And that's one of the paradoxes about self defense training: *You will never really know if any of what you are training will work until you actually have to use the stuff for real.*

We can be *almost* sure of our training, yeah, based on other factors, like physics, combative principles, past experiences, the experiences of other people who have been there, but...

You yourself will never know for sure.

And there is nothing you can do about that except go out and test the stuff for real. That's a road I have been down. I got into bouncing, but obviously that isn't for everyone, so in a moment we will look at a different way to get that experience.

In the meantime, how can we narrow the gap between what we are capable of, and what we have the capacity to actually do (gaining experience aside, that is)?

Capability And Capacity (Or All Talk And No Action)
Before we answer that question though, let's look at the two concepts of capability and capacity in a bit more detail.

As Rory Miller puts it in *Facing Violence: Preparing for the Unexpected*, capability is a psychical skill. You do Combatives or martial arts, you can therefore hurt someone.

Not everyone is emotionally equipped to hurt another human being however. If the thought of doing so makes you uneasy, then it's safe to say you have a low capacity for inflicting violence.

And maybe no capacity for survival-violence—the kill or be killed type of violence that is intended to inflict maximum damage on the other person.

That can be fixed however—to an extent. The fact that you are aware of your capacity levels, and the fact that you are acknowledging them, is enough to increase those levels somewhat.

After that you have to scrutinize your capacity levels and decide if they are really true or not. You may automatically think you don't have the capacity for doing a certain thing—ripping of an ear, for instance—but on closer examination you find that the idea is not that repulsive to you, at least not enough to put you off from doing it if you really had to.

When put in a situation where you have to fight for your life, your capacity for survival-violence will increase. Your in-built survival mechanism will insist on it.

Most people have the capacity for brutal violence. You may think you don't, that your capacity for such things are non-existent, but believe me, it is there, buried deep within you, lying dormant and ready to be tapped under the right circumstances, or when stimulated in some way.

If this were not true, then we wouldn't have all those examples from history, where ordinary people have somehow found it in themselves to do horrible things to their fellow human beings, horrible things that include torture and cold-blooded murder. I live in a country where people maimed and killed each other for thirty years or more.

Human beings are capable of anything under the right circumstances.

You just have to look at your capacity for survival-violence and shed the light of reality on it—ask yourself, would I really be able to do these horrible things if my life (or the life of someone I loved) was on the line and I really had too?

For most people, the answer to that question would be a definite YES!

Some acts (of violence) can still be hard to imagine yourself doing however. Pay special attention to those acts because you are going to use them in the practice drill.

Before we proceed any further though, let's talk about something else that may prevent you from defending yourself to the fullest extent—social conditioning.

Social Conditioning
According to Wikipedia, social conditioning can be defined thus: "Social conditioning refers to the sociological process of training individuals in a society to respond in a manner generally approved by the society in general and peer groups within society. The concept ... [can also] determine their social actions and responses."

Social conditioning can have a profoundly powerful effect on a person, which is why it is utilized so much in our society. Good for maintaining the status quo, bad in many other ways, as we are about to find out.

You see, from a very early age we are taught to behave and react to things in a certain way. In the case of violence we are taught that it is wrong to hit another person and that there will be potentially severe consequences if we do.

This attitude is completely ingrained in us by the time we hit adulthood and it influences how we react to violence a great deal.

So when we need to use violence, even in self defense, our social conditioning reminds us of how wrong it is to hit a fellow human being and that the consequences for doing so could be grave.

(Interestingly, most criminals who seem to have no problem dishing out violence do so because they have a different social conditioning that makes it easy for them to "other" their victims so they can treat them like a resource or piece of meat instead of a real person, which makes it easier for them to do what they do. You want to be able inflict violence at the drop of a hat? Model the criminal mind.)

So no matter how good your training has been or how much faith you have in it, social conditioning can still kill your willingness to act, or at the very least, cause fatal indecision, and indecision is the last thing you want in a violent confrontation when a positive outcome depends wholly on being decisive and quick acting.

This is something I struggled with for a long time. I knew I had the physical skills to handle most of the situations I found myself in, but somewhere in my mind, something was causing me to hesitate or even not strike out at all.

This is very serious because it can cause great anxiety and further feelings of fear. It can also completely kill your confidence in such situations because you will inevitably beat yourself up (after your attacker has, of course) over the fact that you didn't act when you should have.

In short, you will feel like a failure and the next time you find yourself up against someone, your past experiences of perceived failure will come flooding back, along with a load more fear. It becomes like a vicious cycle.

Even when I was bouncing, this social conditioning was constantly reinforced by the management of the places in which I worked. It was made clear that hitting the punters was frowned upon and could end up in a loss of your job. Even if the punter attacked you first! You were forced into doing your job with one hand tied behind your back.

It is because of this very powerful social conditioning that many people are unable to act when they should in a violent confrontation, because some Nanny-like figure is in the back of their mind waving their finger at them to signal no, don't do it or else.

Well, I learned that you have to take that finger-waving bitch and shoot her in the head!

You are a grown up, a very intelligent person who is fully capable of making justifiable force decisions. You do not need the equivalent of the Nanny State inside your head telling you what to do when your life is potentially on the line.

Like most things, it comes down to just being aware that these hindrances to performance exist and after that acknowledging their presence before kindly telling them to fuck off out of it.

For me that was enough. The social conditioning was no longer subconscious and I could consciously over-ride it. I also worked on changing my beliefs about violence, challenging what I was taught about it.

I made sure I knew when it was justified–ethically, morally and lawfully– to hit someone. I developed certain boundaries that if crossed by someone else would result in a violent response from me.

I did all this head-work when I was bouncing so I was able to change myself very quickly, only because I was given many chances to do so through the job, many chances to put myself to the test and consciously over-ride the social conditioning we've been discussing here.

Survival-Violence Capacity Exercise

Before we begin with this, I should warn you that this exercise is pretty dark and it will take you to some horrible, disgusting places. It is necessary to go to these places however, if you want to increase your capacity for survival-violence (read, brutal violence).

And as awful as that sounds, we should remember that the kind of violence we are talking about here will only be used in life or death situations. We are not talking about social violence here, like a fight outside the "chippy" on a Saturday night. We are talking instead of asocial violence, predator violence; the kind of violence that may severely injure you or take your life.

Brutal violence must unfortunately be met with equally brutal violence–survival-violence. You are kidding yourself if you think it can be dealt with by anything less.

So let's proceed. Get yourself nice and comfortable, preferably doing a relaxation exercise first.

Once you are nice and relaxed, start to think of a situation where you would have to fight for your life. It could be a mugging gotten out of hand or some psycho trying to stab you to death for the pleasure of it, or even a rape scenario. Try to make the scenario as plausible as possible, like a situation you could actually find yourself in if you were having a really bad day and luck had abandoned you.

Okay, put yourself in the scene, engage as many of your

senses as possible, at least three of them. Now put yourself into the fight. Put yourself in a position where you have to do something horrible to your attacker in order to save yourself—preferably one of the violent acts that you struggled with imagining yourself doing earlier, one that really turns your stomach, like gouging out both his eyes, or ripping of his ear, or biting of his nose.

Vividly imagine how that would feel– the texture of his flesh, the coppery taste of his blood, the warmth of it spilling into your mouth. Yes it's disgusting. But your life is on the line here. If you don't act you will get killed. This is survival. You have to do what you have to do.

Feel the powerful force of righteous indignation coursing through you. Use it to fuel your actions.

See yourself causing damage to your attacker until you are able to completely stop the attack.

See yourself handling the situation.

Tell yourself that you can do anything you have to do to survive, without a second thought, you just do it.

You survive.

You're a survivor.

Believe that.

Okay, now, wipe the slate clean in your mind. Take yourself out of the previous scenario.

Now I want you to imagine a different scenario in which you will solve the situation without having to use violence. You will see yourself escaping or avoiding the threat altogether, or you will defuse the situation through dialogue.

This is important. Make sure you do this.

For every scenario you create in which you have to use violence, create another scenario where you don't use violence.

Vividly imagining violent scenes like the one above will have a negative impact on your psyche over time. It will alter your character and you will possibly end up in a lot of violent situations in real life.

The mind cannot really distinguish between fantasy and reality. You most likely know this already. Creating such vivid scenes can actually attract more of the same into your life (it works both ways: positive stuff can be attracted also).

So we balance the negative with the positive. Hence the non-violent scenario.

Repeated practice of this exercise will help to burn new neural pathways into your brain, just as if you actually did the things you imagined for real.

It's very powerful stuff, which is why you have to be so careful about balancing the positive and the negative.

This is the only way to increase your capacity for survival-violence without actually being brutally violent in reality.

6: LEARN TO MANAGE FEAR AND ADRENALINE

"There are times when fear is good. It must keep its watchful place at the heart's controls."

Aeschylus

This is by far the longest chapter in this book, and that's because fear and adrenaline play a massive part in the self defense equation, so I thought it worth it to spend a bit of time on the subjects. So let's get going.

Handled incorrectly, fear and adrenaline can really do a number on a person, turning them from normal to quivering wreck in a heartbeat.

The best plans, the best intentions, can be decimated in the wake of these two titans of mind-body control.

Despite the havoc they wreak on a person, these individual reactions are completely benign. They hold no more malevolence than a hurricane which passes through a town and leaves the town in splinters and its inhabitants desolate and traumatized, even dead.

You can't apply human constructs of morality against what is only natural in the world. A hurricane is a hurricane. It is what it is.

Likewise, fear is fear; adrenaline is adrenaline. Natural occurrences in a natural system.

The Human Bio-Computer
Or to put it another way, essential software in a finely programmed bio-computer.

They exist to help.

It's your fault if you can't control them properly. You can't blame the response. You must find the correct process to follow so you can control those responses.

That's on you as well.

You are the end user of the bio-computer in question. It is up to you to program that computer so that it runs right and does exactly what you want it to do.

If a program is not running the way you want it too then you must re-configure it until it does.

The hard part is figuring out just how to reconfigure the program.

If your own fear and adrenal responses are currently crippling your ability to act in a violent confrontation, it is because you have not developed a suitable control mechanism for them both.

Kind of like a temperature gauge that you can turn down if it starts to get too hot.

Or an over-ride switch that you can hit whenever you need too, something that allows you to act despite what you are feeling in your mind and body.

Unfortunately, we have yet to get to the stage where re-programming ourselves is as easy as re-programming a real computer.

So I suggest to you here that changing our behavior and our reactions to things is more of an art than a science. That's what I've found anyway. It's an on-going process. There is no magical switch to hit unfortunately.

In computer programming terms it's the equivalent of sitting down and coding and re-coding an entirely new program, and then perhaps doing the same with many of the other programs that relate to it. After that it's a never-ending process of checking and tweaking to make sure the programs are still running correctly, and also to make continual improvements, for we can always be better, can't we?

In the case of fear, and of adrenaline, we have to constantly work on managing our reactions to them. To do that we must turn our full attention on them and we must come to know them intimately.

You must totally familiarize yourself with every aspect of them, which means not running away from them, which can be hard in the case of fear and adrenaline. They are bogey-men, after all.

They are also inextricably linked. Both are part of our survival mechanism. That should give you a clue as to their importance. They help keep us alive in dangerous situations. We need fear and we need adrenaline, especially in extreme stress situations like in a violent confrontation with someone who is trying to kill us.

The key to handling both fear and adrenaline is realizing and accepting that they will always be present in high-stress situations like violent confrontations.

I could end this chapter right here. That one sentence contains everything you need to know about learning to handle your own fear and adrenal response. You just have to let the truth of it sink in.

The fear response and the adrenal response are very much different sides of the same coin. One almost always accompanies the other. However, it may help us if we consider them separate for a moment and look at each response in turn.

Fight Adrenaline

It really helps to know the physiological response to adrenaline, since like I've already said, you need to know a thing intimately in order to become truly comfortable with it, and also in order to control it.

For this book I am more interested in the psychology attached to adrenal response management, and the type of training we need to do in order to manage it effectively.

One of the main reasons why so many people handle adrenal dump so badly is because it is a completely alien (and thus terrifying) feeling to them.

Back in the day when we used to live like the Flintstones, danger in the form of huge beasts was always right around the corner. The adrenal response came in pretty handy back then when you had to try and outrun a ten ton hairy beast with massive teeth that would cut you in half with one bite.

Living in that kind of environment you soon got used to feeling adrenal dump. It was a completely natural feeling and one that was probably welcomed if it helped get you out of danger.

These days, hairy beasts with big teeth can usually only be found at amateur porn sites. They may be scary but I doubt they would bring on adrenal dump, unless one of them tried to sit on you...

My point (yes, there is a point!) is that we live pretty safe and secure life's now, despite what the news would have you believe. It's perfectly possible for some people to go a whole lifetime without ever experiencing the adrenal dump brought on by a violent confrontation.

Most people will experience it at some time or other, however, and when they do, their internal wiring tends to go a bit awry. Things stop working the way they are supposed to. *What's happening to me? they cry inside. Why do I feel like this? Am I dying? Oh God, oh Jesus…I'm fucking terrified!*

It can feel quite bad. Sickening.

Still, the more you experience it, the more comfortable you become with it, if comfortable is the right word. Maybe functional is a better word. Not quite so incapacitated.

Exposure therapy (incorporating proper training) and education. These two things will help you remain functional under the influence of fight adrenaline.

Study its effects. Get to know the biology of it, the psychology of it. Learn to view it as a completely normal and helpful response. Or like a superpower, whichever one floats your boat.

In any case, don't dread its onset. Learn to welcome it instead.

The enemy is in front of you. Not within you.

Adrenal Stress Training
Training will certainly help a great deal. Okay, so your experience of adrenaline in the gym will never match the real thing, but training still helps.

Train with real intensity. Bring your imagination into it. Keep it as close to the bone as possible without getting seriously injured.

Find a good instructor who can take you a little beyond your limits each time without actually breaking you. Your confidence will grow and you will become better equipped to handle the adrenal response in a real violent confrontation.

Put yourself in other situations where you may feel adrenaline. Do some public speaking. That never fails to bring on the adrenal response in me.

Learn to be present with the response. Don't try to pretend it isn't there. That doesn't work and will cause anxiety and even fear.

Instead, acknowledge that the adrenaline is there, acknowledge how it is making you feel and just sit in it.

Float in it. Just try to float in it and stay calm. Then do what you gotta do.

It will always be unpleasant. But I guess if it was pleasant we wouldn't feel as compelled to do something with it, like try to get rid of it through focused action (or fighting back).

Adrenaline is what it is. You can't change it. It is a perfect human response to danger. Completely pure.

And it works like a charm every single time.

Your reaction to it may leave a lot to be desired, but that reaction can be changed, through proper training– mental and physical conditioning, intellectual and dare I say it, philosophical study.

Managing fight adrenaline is only really a problem in the pre-fight phase of a confrontation. Once things kick off it's not really something to worry too much about. But as I've said before, handling the pre-fight phase correctly is essential to a positive outcome, so therefore handling fight adrenaline is essential to a positive outcome as well.

Changing your reaction to adrenal stress comes down to motivation: how much do you want to learn to perform well under adrenal stress conditions?

If you are motivated enough you will go to surprising lengths to achieve that end. I went as far as spending my weekends working as a bouncer in pubs and clubs for years, exposing myself to situations that brought on the kind of adrenal response we've been talking about here.

Did that help me? Yes, of course it did.

Am I completely comfortable with the feelings of adrenaline now? No, not at all. It still turns me sick and I hate how physically draining it can be.

But I have learned to perform reasonably well under the influence of adrenaline, because I was motivated to do so.

You may not choose to go as far as becoming a doorman. You may instead choose to pit yourself against a padded assailant on a regular basis, or indulge in full contact sparring. Whatever. It's all good training. Whatever you do, it's better than nothing.

Fear
Just like adrenaline, fear has to be managed or it will turn you into a useless quivering wreck.

I'm speaking from experience here.

I remember one of the first big incidents I had to face in my early days on the door. It was myself and two other doormen against six big farmer types who didn't take too kindly to their mate being turfed out on his ear earlier in the night. Arguments ensued and things quickly escalated. Plate glass windows were kicked in and shards of glass covered the whole floor of the foyer.

I was about twenty years of age at that time. I hadn't seen much action up till then and the fear I was feeling gripped me like a vice. The accompanying adrenaline drained every bit of color out of my face.

I just remember being in the midst of this totally chaotic situation and feeling oddly disconnected from the whole thing, like I was an observer in some parallel universe. I was too scared to even move at one point. It took one of the other doormen being ganged up on to force me into action again.

Things finally got sorted out after what seemed like an age. The manager came and ushered me and the other two doormen out the back door, since the guys we were fighting wouldn't calm down while we were there. The police were called and we left the rest to them.

I have never felt fear like I did then, before or since. It was an intense experience, not to mention a valuable lesson in how crippling fear can be if you let it.

What I learned that night was that you had to stay active, you had to keep facing the music, so to speak. Backing away only worsened the feelings of fear and made it harder to get going again.

Real Fear And Psychological Fear
Before we go any further we have to make a distinction between real fear and psychological fear.

Real fear is what you feel when you are in imminent danger. It's a part of your survival mechanism and as such is there to help you.

It is what you feel in most violent confrontations, for obvious reasons. Being in a violent confrontation means that you are in harm's way. Your brain will therefore send the fear signal to kick-start your adrenaline so you can run or fight.

Just like with the adrenal response, the fear response is completely natural and there isn't much you can do to get rid of it. It's there and that's all there is to it. You just have to deal with it.

Psychological fear is ego based and has nothing to do with your survival mechanism. It is all in your mind.

To use a familiar acronym, this type of fear is False Evidence Appearing Real.

When you feel psychological fear it is because your ego feels under threat. There is no real danger present, nothing there that would physically harm you in any way.

The danger, if you can call it that, is in the form of perceived humiliation, failure, wondering what others will say about you, or because you are stepping outside of your comfort zone.

This is a different type of fear and one that I won't be addressing in this article. In this article I want to look at real fear, the fear that comes from when someone is about to attack you.

You'll notice I said when someone is about to attack you. When you have been attacked and you are in fight mode, in my experience fear isn't usually a problem because you are so focused on surviving the encounter.

Fear is essentially a warning signal that danger is imminent. So when you are facing an aggressor intent on violence those warning signals will be firing of like crazy in order to get you to take some kind of action that will neutralize the danger. Hence fight or flight.

When you are in fight mode however, you don't have time to feel fear because you are so focused on the fight. In actuality, you tend to feel more calmness than fear. A tiny voice in the back of your mind may even be saying, *Hey, this isn't so bad actually, I'm dealing with this and this guy I'm fighting, he isn't really up to much. What was I so afraid off anyway?*

Once again it is the pre-fight stage that is the problem, the build-up of tension and fear before-hand. If you let fear get a grip on you at this stage, you won't take proactive action and instead you will be at the mercy of your aggressor.

Methods For Managing Fear

So what methods can we use to help manage our fear? We can't eliminate it, no more than adrenaline. It will always be there to some degree or another, depending on how much experience you have in dealing with violent confrontations.

As a doorman I ended up in quite a lot of violent confrontations. It was my job to sort them out, after all. Repeated exposure to such situations definitely helped to lessen the fear I was feeling, but it didn't eliminate it.

(Only sociopaths don't feel fear like the rest of us and unless your name is Patrick Bateman, it's doubtful you're a sociopath, and if you are, don't you have your next victim to stalk? Just saying.)

The way to tackle fear in a violent confrontation is to first mold yourself into someone who is able to handle it.

That's why we train, is it not? To reinforce our minds and bodies so they can withstand the effects of high stress.

So that's where we will start, with the training.

Combatives Training

Combatives training is the only kind of training that really counts when it comes to hammering the mind and body into shape in preparation for a violent confrontation.

Martial arts training takes way too long and still doesn't cut it in the end. Combat sports training, although probably better than martial arts training in terms of physical and mental conditioning, doesn't quite cut it either. The goals are different. The training methods are different.

Combatives' trains people to handle real violence from the start. There are no rules involved, no rituals to follow, no belt ladder to climb or trophies to hold high; no fluff of any kind. Combatives is all about what works in a fight.

It stands to reason then, that if you do this type of training on a regular basis, you will be much more confident about your chances should you end up involved in a violent confrontation.

Combatives training quite literally exploded my self-confidence. I also see it explode the confidence of my students and private clients, far more so than any martial arts student I've had in the past.

And this is because you are training to handle real violence, not fantasy violence. The stuff you learn in Combatives is as practical as it gets. And because it is all pressure tested on a regular basis you get to experience just how well it all works (within reason).

What I am getting at here is that you need to have faith in your training. Some of you reading this may have religious faith, faith that God will keep you safe in your life. Well, having faith in your training is the same thing.

You must choose to believe that your training will get you through whatever situation you find yourself in, be it against one attacker or many.

I have great faith in my training. When I was working doors I took a lot of strength from that faith. And guess what?

It helped me deal with whatever fear I was feeling. I knew–I knew– my training would carry me through and it always did. Not once did it let me down when I needed it.

You have all that power behind you; the power of faith, the power of your training and the whole arsenal of tools and tactics you have gleaned from it.

YOU CAN'T LOOSE!

How could you?

There is only one thing that may let you down in the end and that is social conditioning, which we have already discussed.

Supra States

A supra state is the wilful creation of a split in the personality to create a persona that can deal effectively with violent confrontation. The conspiracy theorists among you will recognize this principle technique as being the foundation for MK-ULTRA, the CIA mind control experiment started in the 1970's.

Supra states in the context we are talking about are not quite so sinister however. It basically involves you creating another persona for yourself, one which you will only go into when you have to really put someone down.

To quote Lee Morrison:

"This is like a shotgun under an overcoat that would only be called upon worst case scenario, outside of that it remains tightly covert and boxed away. The control of such a mindset will allow anyone to control their emotions during the full spectrum of a violent event."

If you think about it we all take on different personas when we are with different people and in different situations. What we are talking about here is the same thing, just having a separate persona in place for when we have to dish out violence.

The value of this technique is obvious. By assuming the guise of this one-dimensional persona (whose sole purpose is to inflict violence) we can bypass all the usual baggage and hang-ups we have normally, all the social conditioning we have been talking about.

If you are good at imagining and visualization then you should have little problem in creating this persona and installing it into your mind. You can then use an anchor to call upon this persona in times of need.

Tactical Arousal Control Techniques

Tactical Arousal Control Techniques (or TACT for short) are techniques that are used to keep you calm and focused in high stress situations.

The most common form of TACT is Tactical Breathing. There are few different variations on this, including combat breathing, four-count breathing and diaphragmatic breathing. Choose whichever one works best for you.

We also have what are called Centering Techniques, which derive from traditional martial arts. Centering involves taking a deep breath and on exhalation allowing all of your awareness to settle in your center of gravity, bringing about a sensation of inner calm. I've found this particular technique to be quite useful when under stress.

A more advanced form of centering involves the use of an image as you breathe out. On exhalation picture something light like a feather or a leaf, slowly, slowly drifting down in front of you, until it stops and hovers just at the height of your belly button. The purpose of the image is to enhance the relaxation effects of the breath. Try it, it works really well.

Practice the exercise with your eyes closed at first. Then when you get comfortable with it, do it with your eyes open. The goal is to be able to do it with eyes open while still maintaining situational awareness, which isn't as hard as you think. It just takes practice.

And just so you are not floating in some far away over-relaxed state after using this technique, you can add on a "command action", a one-word command to bring you into sharp focus and attention. Once you are in the relaxed state, say to yourself something like "focus" or even "scan" to bring yourself fully into the present situation will still maintaining your sense of inner calm and relaxation.

Muscle relaxation techniques are another option, but these must be practiced quite a bit before trying to use them in an actual situation. You must first make that mind-body connection, making it stronger with every practice. In the beginning it will take about fifteen minutes or so for you to get rid of muscular tension and get really relaxed. After a fair bit of practice you should be able to bring about this state instantly.

7: LEARN SITUATIONAL CONTROL SKILLS

"No situational control = you're going down."

Neal Martin

I don't care how good your punch is, or how many techniques you happen to know. The bottom line is that if you can't control the pre-fight you don't stand a chance of winning the fight overall.

I know this from bitter experience. Let me tell you a story from my early bouncing days.

I was on the door one night and I'd only been doing the job a couple of months. I was green. I knew jack shit about proper violence, except what I'd learned through martial arts training, which wasn't much.

I was ignorant to the concepts of situational control and pre-emptive striking and I was about to suffer the consequences of that ignorance.

So I was alone at the front door of the shit-hole pub I was working in and one of the regulars, who had been tossed out earlier in the night, approaches me and demands to speak to the head doorman. I politely told him he would have to wait to later on, that the head doorman was upstairs in the club and otherwise engaged.

The guy was persistent. He demanded to be let in. At this point he was right inside in my personal space. A few of his mates had also gathered outside as well. He continued to ask to be let in and was getting steadily more agitated.

I kept my cool, but I was allowing him to control the situation. I should have been more assertive and either told him to clear off or just shut the door in his face.

Violence was impending but I was too naive to see it coming.

I saw him look left, then right (a classic pre-contact cue) and then I felt his fist smash into my forehead and I reeled back into the hallway, instinctively grabbing on to the guy as I did so.

I ended up on the floor with him on top of me. For a few seconds I couldn't think what to do. Luckily neither could he. He threw a punch at my face which I managed to slap aside.

Years of martial arts training wasn't really helping me much here. I eventually slapped my hands over both his ears, but not hard enough to really impact him much.

At this point he got to his feet and grabbed my leg, and then he began to pull me across the floor. His mates stood outside in the street like a pack of hungry wolves, egging him on. They wanted me outside so they could go to work on me properly. I felt helpless.

Luckily, one of the other doormen came running down the stairs at this point and got the guy off me. I jumped to my feet, shaken, but otherwise fine. A few punches were thrown by me and the other doorman as we forced the guy outside to the street so we could finally close the door on him and his mates.

So that was a harsh lesson. I never let anyone get that close to me again.

Defining Situational Control
Situational control is the art of controlling the pre-fight stage of a violent confrontation. How you handle the pre-fight will determine the outcome of the fight over all--whether you win or

lose.

Mismanage the pre-fight and the consequences can be very serious, which is why it is so important to learn situational control tactics.

In its most basic form, situational control means just as it sounds: you maintain control of the situation from start to finish as best you can so as to affect a favorable outcome. The pre-fight stage is where you will be able to affect the most control. If it goes to fight stage it becomes difficult to exert any control except through the use of violence, but things tend to be very spontaneous and also very frantic, so maintaining control in that situation can be difficult. What happens happens.

Assert Yourself

As people go, I'm a pretty laid back sort of guy. My Dad always says that if I was any more laid back I'd be horizontal!

There is nothing wrong with being chilled and laid back. Being of that nature means I am a very tolerant and reasonable kind of guy. I don't fly of the handle easily with people, which means I am better able to listen to them and hopefully find a non-violent solution to whatever conflict is happening.

My laid back and diplomatic nature allows me to exhaust all possibilities before I even think about using violence on someone, which is after all, good practice as far as self protection goes. Violence should always be your last resort.

Don't feel bad if you are not the fighting type (an asshole in other wards). Sometimes your ego will chide you for allowing people to say certain things to you, and it will make you feel bad for not just lashing out in defense.

People may say bad things, even very hurtful things, but they are just words. To your ego it is fighting talk, but your ego doesn't know what it is talking about so don't feel bad for letting things go over your head. That's just good tactics that will save you from being involved in a violent incident.

Having said that, you need to know where to draw the line and you also have to be prepared to reprimand that person if they cross that line. If that means violence, then so be it. As Tim Larkin is fond of saying, "Violence is not the answer, but when it is, it's the only answer".

Only you will know where that line is. Only you will know how much you can take. How long are you going to allow this person to try and bully you into submission or build up to hitting you?

I will always give people a chance. I will allow them to talk and shout all day if they want to, but if they cross the line into physical bullying by putting their hands on me or trying to encroach upon my personal space, then I will immediately assert myself in some way and make it clear that their advances are not welcome. If they continue to push things then I will be left with no choice but to use physical violence.

The trick to being okay with using violence is to make sure that you exhaust all other possible avenues for resolving the situation. If the other person continues to push things, then it's on them, not you.

Just knowing your actions will be morally and lawfully justified can help spur you into action in the first place, but we will talk about that in a moment.

For now, know that in order to deal with violence and violent people, you must be confident enough to assert yourself when you have to. Just asserting yourself in a calm and reasonable manner can sometimes be enough to influence the other person into backing down.

Self-assertion is a skill like any other, and therefore needs to be practiced. You can do so in the gym by doing drills.

Have a partner play the part of an aggressor. His job is to try and bully and intimidate you through aggressive dialogue and body language. It is your job to not be intimidated by this, to assume a confident demeanor through body language and calm but assertive dialogue while also making sure to control your personal space well. The more you do these types of drills, the better you will get at asserting yourself and the more confident you will become in general.

Most importantly, you will find it easier to hold your bottle when you need to.

Non-Violent Postures
The most effective way to exert situational control over a situation is through the use of the fence, a concept most of you should be very familiar with by now.

For those who are not, the fence is fundamentally a way for you to control your personal space and prevent an aggressor from entering into that personal space. It is a difficult concept to explain with just words.

Essentially you are adopting and open-handed fighting stance, with the hands held high above those of your aggressor. This allows you to control your space. It also allows you to strike from a good position if need be and adopt a default position very quickly if caught off guard by your aggressor.

Physically speaking there are quite a few different variations on the fence position. The type of fence used depends on the person using it and the circumstances in which it is being used. In general though, whatever type of fence you use, it should be non-aggressive, since the object is to de-escalate rather escalate (unless escalation is your goal, which can work in some cases).

What I am most interested in for this article is the psychology behind the fence concept. By standing firm and not allowing the other guy to get close to you, you are communicating calm and confidence through your body language and tone of voice.

Think of it as drawing a line in the sand. By doing so you are telling the other guy that you will be reasonable with him but if he pushes things too far then you will, without hesitation, use violence to resolve the matter.

That should be your intention at this stage: to avoid using violence if possible, but if you have to use it you will do so, and do so very fucking scarily. Everything about you must give of that exact intention. This in itself is often enough to make the other guy back off.

Pattern Disruption
By asserting yourself in this way you are also disrupting the other guy's pattern. Let me explain that.

Most violent types tend to stick to the same patterns of behavior when victimizing someone. They will approach everyone in the same way, use the same words and phrases, and adopt the same body language, all of which goes to make up a pattern of attack that they know, from experience, works very well for them.

The success of that pattern of behavior is also dependent on the victim being drawn into the aggressor's reality, so that the victim ends up being controlled like a puppet, reacting in just the same predictable ways in which the aggressor wants them to, which usually means they become intimidated and scared, victims of their aggressor's will.

By exerting situational control from the get-go, you are effectively disrupting that well-worn pattern of behavior. Just by stepping back into some kind of fence position and saying to your aggressor, "Wow, hold on a minute mate. Don't come any closer. Stay there and I'll talk to you", you are throwing a spanner in the works and messing up your aggressor's plan of attack. They now have to re-think their strategy, which is often just too much trouble and they will go find someone else who maybe won't disrupt their plan as much.

Disrupt your aggressor's pattern as quickly as possible and don't allow yourself to get locked into his reality.

I teach people to use their peripheral vision when they are using the fence. I find if you look straight into your aggressor's eyes it is too easy to get locked into their reality. Intimidation sets in quickly and before you know it, you've lost your bottle and he's controlling you instead of the other way around.

So when fencing, get used to looking out of the corner of your eye, rather than directly at your aggressor. This will help you stay calm and detached. You will also pick up movement quicker since the brain interprets peripheral vision signals faster than focused vision signals. If you read my e-book, you will find drills in there to help you develop your peripheral vision.

So by taking control of the situation in the way that you have, you can much more effectively employ a verbal de-escalation strategy or a pre-emptive striking strategy, things you wouldn't be able to do if you were locked into your aggressor's reality and they had control of the situation.

8: GET FIT

"If you don't exercise, put the Twinkie down and get off your ass."

Kelly McCann

If Combatives is all about preparedness, it makes sense that that preparedness carries over into your physical or combative conditioning. But what is considered adequately fit in relation to defending yourself in a street fight? There are different opinions on this, so let's examine them now.

There are those who believe that physical fitness does not matter much when it comes to self defense because self defense techniques are supposed to incapacitate an attacker so quickly that fitness becomes irrelevant.

That may be true in an ideal world, but we don't live in an ideal world, so that viewpoint is a little naive and maybe even dangerous. In my experience, street fights don't usually go down the way you expect them too. Unexpected variables always come into play to mess up your perfect game plan and often times, the quick finish you were hoping for eludes you and you end up in a protracted brawl.

As Kelly McCann has said, you can't depend on technique, power and luck all aligning perfectly to create a guaranteed outcome. Remember what I said before: there are no guarantees in self defense, so you shouldn't expect them. Neglecting your combative conditioning completely is therefore folly and could get you in serious trouble.

Those who take the middle ground on this issue believe that physical fitness is a requirement of good self defense, and these people generally achieve this level of fitness in their own way, through running or weight training or through some kind of cross training program.

This level of fitness will get you through most self defense situations, which is why most Combatives practitioners tend to settle for this middle ground.

The ideal level of fitness to have would be higher again, putting you in peak physical condition. It takes a lot of training and dedication to get to this stage though, and not everyone will achieve that. It largely depends on your overall goals when it comes to self defense, how dedicated you are and how much time you can spur.

What is more important is doing the right kind of physical conditioning. You have to look at how most fights go down. They are generally short, brutal affairs as opposed to long drawn out brawls (although these can happen also), so it makes sense to tailor your conditioning and training to that.

There is also the fact that adrenaline during a fight can drain you of energy very quickly, so it makes sense to allow for this as well.

During an attack you will rely mostly on your fast-twitch muscle fibers for speed, power and explosiveness, so training that will develop these muscle fibers is required. Interval training that consists of short, intense activity is ideal for this. It also would make sense to develop your aerobic endurance to some extent as well, through running or such like.

The Combatives training itself will also help to develop your combative conditioning. Doing lots of pad work and plenty of intense training drills will by themselves, raise your level of conditioning.

It boils down to giving yourself the best chance in any given situation, so the better your combative conditioning, the greater chance you will have should you have to really go for it on the street.

9: TRAIN IN COMBATIVES

"Combatives is what works in a fight."

Dennis Martin

Combatives, and reality self defense training in general, has become quite a popular pursuit these days. There now exists a plethora of different schools and systems in the world teaching self defense, all with their own particular take on things (although usually, the difference is just in the marketing). For someone who is looking to gain instruction in Combatives, it can get quite confusing and overwhelming trying to find good information and instruction.

Here, I'm going to give you some advice on how to go about finding proper instruction in Combatives and what to look for in an instructor. I'm also going to explain to you how to stand on your own two feet and think for yourself when it comes to learning Combatives and self defense in general.

Firstly, you need to know what you are looking for. A good Combatives system should fulfil the following criteria:

• Basic strikes that will work pre-emptively or defensively

• Natural everyday positions as a starting point for situational control, and which are easy to strike from

• An emphasis on power striking, with heavy impact

• A head-hunting mentality--striking the head wherever possible

• Simple but effective counters to common street attacks

• An emphasis on mindset and the cultivation of ferocious resolve or the willingness to do what it takes to survive

• Brutal ground fighting techniques

• An emphasis on dirty fighting and tactics

• Skills that will work under high stress conditions

• Stress inoculation training to aid an understanding of stress and how to operate under it

Those are some of the main defining characteristics of a Combatives system. It's a very no nonsense approach to self defense and one you should seek if you want instruction in how to defend yourself.

Try to find an instructor who has some sort of real world experience behind them, such as security work or even military experience. Instructors who have experience in what they are teaching tend to be better instructors because they have been there and know from hard won experience what works and what doesn't in real violent altercations.

As well as this, an instructor should know their subject very deeply, they should understand every single aspect of it and this should be apparent in how they put the material they are teaching across. Avoid instructors who see everything in black and white terms, and who see themselves as being right all the time. A good instructor will change their mind often and re-evaluate things as new information comes along.

Combatives training should be a constant process of discovery, interplay between instructor and student(s). Classes should be fluid, wherein everyone involved is continually re-evaluating, questioning and re-thinking things.

It's a creative process from which everyone benefits. The student gets the best possible instruction and the instructor gains a clearer picture and deeper understanding of what to teach and how to teach it.

More importantly, it's more fun this way. Operating within a rigid, structured program (such as in traditional martial arts) where everything has to be done just so, is not conducive to having fun. And having more fun only aids in the learning process (as we shall see shortly).

Structure can still be present, but it must be loose, not constrictive to the point where it kills creativity or discovery.

That's the kind of class format you should be looking for.

Thinking for Yourself

There are often arguments in the Combatives/SD community, about who is right and who is wrong; about what techniques/concepts/principles/tactics/strategies etc. are right, and which ones are wrong.

The bottom line however, is that anything that leaves you standing and your attacker on the floor unconscious, is good.

Right and wrong do not matter.

How you put the other guy down doesn't matter.

It only matters that you did.

If you say a technique is wrong and someone else uses that same technique to survive a physical confrontation, is that technique (or tactic, strategy...whatever) still "wrong"?

Of course not. How can it be wrong when it was used

successfully? Even once.

Just because a technique or way of doing something does not fit your definition of what is right--or even what makes good self defense-- it does not mean that the technique in question is wrong or invalid.

That's just how you perceive things.

There are so many different approaches to self protection because there are so many different people teaching it. What an instructor teaches is just their learning of the subject.

We can put too much stock in instructors-- in what they say and teach. We never seem to look beyond the personality or system and realize that what is being taught is merely one person's experience of a very large and very complex subject.

You would do much better if you became your own instructor and figured out what your particular take on self defense is.

You have to own what you do. You must have your own approach-- not a bad carbon copy of someone else's.

That approach doesn't have to be ground-breaking or new, and can pull from many different sources, but it should fit you perfectly. It should feel natural and flow from you when needed.

To achieve this means taking full responsibility for your own training and not leaving it in the hands of an instructor (however good the instructor). It means thinking critically about everything and going with your gut on what feels right to you.

It means taking proof over opinion and conjecture.

It means testing stuff out until you are satisfied.

You may not become invincible with this approach, but you

will certainly increase your chances of survival if the shit hits the fan sometime.

Your self defense is the only self defense that works. In my experience, it's the only form of self defense that does the job. Not someone else's take on it.

There is no right or wrong in self defense, not really.

There is only what works for us as individuals, and what doesn't.

So by all means, gain as much instruction as you can (the right instruction, of course), but be aware that the final say rests with you.

The problem with following particular instructors is that you end up putting them on a pedestal and treating them like demi-gods, which can affect your objectivity. Look at what each instructor is teaching, evaluate it and take from them what you think is good and discard the rest (although only after thorough testing, of course).

I'm a big believer in teaching yourself; it's what I've always done. You will get a deeper understanding of the subject this way, rather than taking things at face value because another instructor says this or that is right or wrong.

Just like in martial arts, Combatives to me is about following your own path, it's a personal journey and the more you think and do for yourself, the more you will get out of it and the better you will be. This understanding, more than anything, has allowed me to make the most progress in my training, and if you follow this credo, so will you.

If you have no wish to go to any classes then your only other option is to do things for yourself. Get hold of some books or

DVD's and start to learn the techniques for yourself.

Here are some tips on solo training for self defense.

Solo Training

Don't try to do too much in one session. Pick just a few techniques or drills to work on throughout the session and stick to them. If you try to cover too much you will scatter your focus and end up learning nothing. Remember that good Combatives training is about repetition. To get good you have to train a select few techniques over and over until you master them. If you try to master too many techniques at one time you will end up mastering none.

Train with the street in mind. This means you do not train in a sporting manner. So no shadow boxing or long endurance workouts. Everything you do must be combative, not sporting. Warm up first, then practice your drills and techniques in short bursts. A real street fight is an explosive burst of energy that doesn't last very long. There are no rounds. Only periods of intense combat lasting only several seconds. Your training must reflect that. So basically, go like fuck for no more than ten seconds then stop and repeat.

Add emotional content to your training. Whatever you do, you must back it up with the correct mindset. If you hit the bag, do so with full intent and aggression. Really imagine that you are in a situation and you have to put this guy down. Anything less will not do. You are practicing accessing state as much as the physical techniques. Hit the switch, go like fuck and then knock the switch off again, making sure to check state every time. Training in this way, you are making sure the techniques will come out under pressure when you need them. This is the only way to train.

Resist the temptation to do long sessions. Long training sessions are for endurance athletes and sport fighters. You will benefit most from shorter sessions of about fifteen to twenty minutes, but train at full intensity during that time. If you feel one session isn't enough, train twice a day.

In the meantime, here are some suggested solo drills.

1. Fence And Strike Drill

What's good about this drill is that you don't need any equipment and it can be done anywhere.

Start from a square on stance, then move into a fence position with your arms out front as if controlling your space, then from there throw a pre-emptive strike.

Repeat a number of times.

To make the drill more useful, bring your imagination into play. Pretend there is someone in front of you, giving you grief. Control your space as they try to enter it and then, when you think the moment is right, strike with full intent and see yourself knocking the guy out. Remember, emotional content is what makes these techniques stick.

2. Fence, Strike, Blast And Finish

As above, only after you strike pre-emptively you continue to blast your opponent with multiple strikes, moving forward as you do so (forward drive) before finally finishing your opponent off with knees and elbows or some other technique of your choice.

3. Imaginary Brawl Drill

For this drill you are going to be playing out a whole attack scenario from start to finish. Think of a scenario first. You could be walking to your car in a dimly lit car park after a particularly tiring day at work or you could be standing outside the chippy on after having had a few drinks with friends. Whatever. Your imagination is the limit here.

Once you have a scenario in mind, really put yourself into it, mentally and emotionally. Begin to act it out the way a real actor would.

Let's take the car park example. You are walking to your car when you spot two dodgy looking guys loitering near your car. Your spidey sense starts to tingle and you can feel the adrenaline begin to bubble up inside you. Something isn't right (really feel this!). As you continue to walk to your car, one of the guys (dressed in jeans, black jacket and baseball cap) asks you for a light. You tell him you don't have one. No sooner have you answered him when the other guy (wearing track suit bottoms and a dark colored hoodie) suddenly rushes towards you, drawing his fist back in preparation to hit you. The fight is on.

That's the set up. What way this scenario goes is up to you. The important thing is that you mimic every move as it happens. If you strike one of the guys, then do so for real and really feel the impact. If you get hit or grabbed, react to that for real.

Fall to the floor and grapple. Enact the whole fight. Then when it's over, walk away.

Done right, with your imagination in full swing, this can end up feeling like a real fight. It's almost like visualization practice but you are physically acting out each movement instead of just picturing it in your head.

Try to be alone when doing this drill. If anyone sees you, they will think you've lost your mind as you throw yourself around and fight imaginary attackers!

10: LEARN TO HIT HARD

"If I had to give someone self defense advice it would be learn to hit fucking hard."

Geoff Thompson

One of the most fundamental skills to learn in Combatives is the ability to generate powerful strikes that will take an attacker down in the quickest time possible. You may still get away with having little power in your strikes–you may still prevail–but it will take you longer to do so, because you will have to hit your attacker more times in order to put them down.

Having to throw more strikes takes time, and that's time you are giving your attacker to possibly come back at you, or for someone else to join in. No one wants to get involved in protracted fights. Most just want it over and done with in the quickest time possible, and one of the best ways for that to happen is to hit your attacker as hard as you possibly can. This means you have to spend a lot of time on power generation.

Obviously this does not mean that you will drop attackers like flies every single time. It merely means that you have significantly increased your chances of dropping the other guy quickly.

That's reason enough to spend time on power generation, don't you think?

What Is Power?

When we talk about power generation we are really talking about force generation. However, a better way of looking at it would be in terms of momentum, which can be defined as being the product of accelerated mass.

The bigger picture of what you are doing when you strike is that you are accelerating your mass (your body) in the direction of your target (an attacker) in order to create an impact between you (specifically, your hand or fist) and the opposing force (your attackers head).

For this process to occur with maximum effect and efficiency, a number of biomechanical concepts and principles are brought into play.

The scale of impact of your strike is measured against how skillfully you are able to engage this momentum process to full capacity.

Power (momentum) is first generated in the core of your body, as well as with the hips, which will also cause the spine to twist. This is the beginning of a kinetic chain or kinetic link that ends with you throwing the strike. The faster you can engage all the links in the kinetic chain, the more acceleration you will produce and thus the more powerful (forceful) the strike will be.

When looking to generate momentum the larger body parts (hips, abdominals etc.) are the first to move in the sequence, quickly followed by the smaller body parts (arms, hands) that feed of this momentum to produce fast, dynamic movements. This is also known as force summation.

Power is not about pushing of from the ground as some people think. Pushing off from the ground will add weight to your strike, but it won't add velocity.

It is more important to maximize the velocity of the strike than the weight behind it. Weight is still important, but velocity is even more so.

Driving up from the ground will not add to the velocity of the strike because of the direction of the force vector. The force is travelling upwards instead of forwards.

Generating force from the hips/core ensures the velocity travels forward into the strike, which is where it is needed.

The twisting of the leg and foot therefore, is just a by-product of the force generated in the core and through the spine.

Keeping the rear leg weighted behind you, as is the case with the classic boxing mechanics, will not aid velocity. It is much better to allow the rear leg to travel forward with the hips to ensure max velocity and momentum.

Everything has to contribute to the forward momentum in other words. Nothing gets left trailing behind to hinder this process.

To aid balance, you post on the front leg.

The key to this summation of forces is timing. Each link in the kinetic chain must be activated at precisely the right time.

The Stretch Shortening Cycle

Another key factor in power generation is something called the Stretch Shortening Cycle (SSC). This occurs when you quickly stretch a muscle and then just as quickly contract that muscle. This will add a significant amount of elastic energy to your strike.

This is done by simply pulling back and loading the strike. The more distance the striking tool (the hand) has to travel, the more velocity it will gain and thus the more force/impact will be generated.

This obviously raises the issue of telegraphing, which really, is a non-issue, as I've already said in a previous article. At such close range, it matters little if you telegraph the strike for it only takes a split second to do so and it will make little difference in terms of your opponent seeing the strike coming. Loading up in this way however, will make a significant difference in the power of your strike.

The quicker you can stretch and then contract the muscles involved in loading, the more power you will generate.

And speaking of elastic energy…

Plastic And Elastic Energy

The kind of impact you cause with your strike will largely depend on which of these two kinds of energy you use.

Plastic energy is utilized by pushing through your target. Allowing your strike to carry on through your target until it fizzles out, having the effect of sending an attacker flying backwards, may seem like a good thing to do, but it actually isn't in terms of impact. By allowing your strike to carry on unchecked you are giving your attacker the chance to absorb the energy of the strike with 100% of their body mass. In effect, they will absorb what you give them and come right back at you again, since you haven't really done anything to hurt them or cause them any real trauma.

Elastic energy on the other hand, is utilized by allowing the striking hand to bounce back of the target naturally using the recoil generated by the impact. The effect will then be that your attacker will absorb all of the impact in a concentrated area of their body (the head), which will have a much greater traumatic effect on them because it will rattle their brain more inside their skull.

Care must be taken not to pull the strike too soon, as this will impede the energy transference of the strike. Follow through with the strike and allow the hand to bounce back naturally. It takes some practice to get this right, but the effect is well worth it.

The Serape Effect

We also have something called the Serape Effect. The Serape Effect is a band of muscle that criss-crosses the body from opposite shoulder to opposite hip on both sides. It is designed to aid rotational movements in the human body.

Logan and McKinney explain it this way in their book, The Serape Effect:

"The serape effect incorporates several major concepts which are vital to the understanding of movement. In ballistic actions such as throwing and kicking, the serape muscles add to the summation of internal forces. They also transfer internal force from a large body segment, the trunk, to relatively smaller body parts, the limbs. For example, the serape effect functions in throwing [striking] by summating, adding to, and transferring the internal forces generated in the lower limbs and pelvis to the throwing limb."

Speaking of a right-handed thrower (substitute "thrower" for "striker"–the movements are much the same), Logan and McKinney state:

"There is a definite interaction between the pelvic girdle on the left and the throwing limb on the right by way of concentric contraction of the left internal oblique, right external oblique, and serratus anterior on the right at the initiation of the throw. The pelvic girdle is rotating to the left and the rib cage is rotating to the right."

This means we should base our strikes around rotational movements, as opposed to linear ones.

So as you throw the strike you shouldn't just be thrusting directly forward, but down and across to match the pulling movements of the muscles connecting from the left hip to the right shoulder. As you do this, you will notice the left hip rotating to the left and the tension in the left ribcage as it pulls in and rotates to the right. These movements together will combine to aid in your explosive power generation.

So basically, as you throw the strike, you are angling downwards to match the natural movements involved in this Serape Effect. I hope this makes sense, because it is very important.

If you were to throw a right palm strike, you would not just be thrusting forward with it in a linear fashion, but rotating your whole body to the left and downwards slightly at the same time, posting on the left leg to aid balance and allowing the right leg to come forward to aid momentum.

Head movement also comes into play here as well. For a right handed strike, the head will fly forwards and to the left to allow the body to rotate forwards.

This does not mean that all you have to do is throw your head quickly forwards to do a powerful strike. The head movement is more of a by-product of all the other movements involved, just as the leg and foot twist is a by-product also.

Other Factors

In order for power to occur, we have established that you must move your mass as quickly as possible with maximum velocity to the target.

For this to be effective however, you must also present a solid structure to resist the recoil that will come from the impact. A weak structure will result in a weak transference of force and the energy you generated will end up going back into you again.

Strength is another factor effecting power. The use of strength should not be your initial concern when striking. Your initial concern should be correct body mechanics and transference of power. Once that is accomplished, you can then add in your strength to the equation, using it just at the end of the process to gain added force and impact.

You can also gain further momentum by stepping quickly forward with your lead leg, but this is obviously only possible when you have the space to do so.

There will also be times when you are unable to utilize the full kinetic chaining process, because you may be in an awkward position or completely lacking in space. In this case, you would then use your spine to generate power. It is possible to generate tremendous power with just the spine alone. When you see someone strike almost casually with little movement to affect a great impact, they are doing so by using the spine, twisting it very rapidly and forcefully.

(You can practice this by placing your open hand very close to a focus mitt so you can practice delivering impact at very short distances, without using your body much, except the spine. You'll be surprised by how much impact you can generate.)

Inner-power, generated by emotion, can also be helpful in hitting hard. Aggression, anger etc. will help fuel your physical movements. I talked about this in another article.

Finally, relaxation is also a key factor to power generation. Tension will decrease your potential velocity in two ways:

1. *You have to overcome the force of the muscles that are*

tense (this is how most beginners strike – they are very stiff).

2. You can't stretch the muscle to use the SSC, since it's impossible to stretch a contracted muscle.

You must therefore learn to fire of only the muscles needed to do the job, and relax the opposing muscles.

Explosiveness
Biomechanical technique is only half the story when it comes to hitting hard.

Technique is important, but what's even more important for a strike to reach its full potential, is explosiveness. You must be able to load up your strike with explosive energy, and reload it just as quick, repeating the process as many times as you have to, something that Steve Morris calls the "Uzi Effect", likening the process to the rapid and continuous firing of a submachine gun.

For a strike to be truly effective, you must also be able to engage this process at the drop of a hat, without any preparedness whatsoever. There is no time in fighting to ready yourself. There is no cocking of the gun before you shoot. You just shoot. That's it.

There is definitely an art to throwing a great strike, one that is effortless and devastating at the same time, and this aspect is often lost on those who try to reduce striking (or any other technique for that matter) to simple mechanics without any consideration for the deeper aspects that go into it.

It's almost ironic that the martial arts are called such, for they spend more time teaching people how to move like robots, how to perform in an unnatural manner, instead of stressing natural movement and unique personal input from the practitioner (the art). The same thing exists in self protection, where every technique is boiled down to simple mechanics, but with a bit more emphasis on mindset and "violent intent".

When technique is stressed above all else, you turn a person into a robot, one who can perform moves that are identical to the ones in the instruction manual. This kind of learning goes against the very personal nature of real learning. In real learning you do not simply copy what someone else is doing, but instead you express the specific movements in your own way. Learning a technique should therefore not just be a process of replication. It should also be about creating as much energy as possible from nothing, and efficiently and explosively directing that energy to a very precise area outside of yourself, which in this case would be your opponent. You can't learn to do that just by concentrating on technique alone. Or as athletics coach Vernon Gambetta puts it in an article from his excellent Functional Path Training Blog:

"The body is so efficient and remarkable in its ability to solve complex movement problems. It just never ceases to surprise me, in many ways it is predictably unpredictable in its ability to adapt. The body is not a machine constructed of interchangeable parts, it a kinetic chain consisting of interdependent links that work in harmony to reduce and produce force in reaction to gravity and the ground. In coaching to refine human motion we must stress connections, linkages, coordination and rhythm. This allows the body to work its magic, produce the poetry of motion that allows it to self-organize and solve complex movement problems. The human body has the remarkable ability to produce finely tuned movements that in the initial stages of learning appear uncoordinated and disjointed but through error detection and subsequent correction discard what does not work and refine and perfect what does work. So coaching is learning to guide, to direct and sometimes to stay out of the way and allow the wisdom of the body take over and be confident in our guidance."

There are also other factors that you must consider if you want to increase the explosiveness of your strikes. Let's look at those other factors now.

Internal And External Focus

Where you put your focus as you do a strike is important. If you over-obsess about your technique and your focus is largely on the mechanics of your strike, where you are concentrating on getting the moves right, then you are focusing internally, and your strike will not flow as it should, which also means it won't be very explosive either.

Another important point to bear in mind is that pausing to think about what you are about to do, and keeping your main focus on just your movements, you are giving your Golgi Tendon Organs time to perform their inhibitory function, which will result in less muscle contraction, which obviously will affect the explosiveness of your strike.

To overcome this you should switch to a more external focus with your strike. In other words, your focus should be on the effect you want your strike to have. If want to hit your opponent hard in the head, then that's what your concentration should be on– the target in front of you.

Having such an external focus takes your focus out of yourself and on to your opponent, allowing your movements to be much more fluid and natural. Your focus is only on hitting your opponent however hard, not on how you are going to do that.

You can test this approach yourself. Simply strike a focus pad or bag with your focus on the movements of what you are doing. You may find yourself almost locking up slightly, over controlling and pulling the strike. Your movements will feel unnatural and lacking in spontaneity. Now put your focus only on the pad and hitting it as hard as you can. Give no thought to your movements, on whether you are doing them right or wrong. Just do. You should find your strikes to be much more explosive and spontaneous. You may also be surprised at how much more impact you can generate with your strike.

It doesn't matter that your technique is not exactly as you've been taught it by someone else. It's the effect of a movement that is important, not the movement itself. Measure your techniques in terms of effectiveness, not in terms of some biomechanical or aesthetic ideal.

Rate Coding

Rate coding refers to the frequency that your brain sends messages telling a muscle to contract. The faster the frequency the greater the intensity of any given muscular contraction.

Rate coding appears to be highly related to the excitability of the central nervous system (CNS). A highly excited CNS can produce greater force at a faster rate due to the positive impact on rate coding.

This factor is also known as the *Psycho Factor* because it is inherently influenced by the psychological state. To have a positive impact on rate coding that will increase the explosiveness and power of your strike, you must be able to excite your CNS enough, which means you must be able to psych yourself up at a seconds notice, without any build up at all.

Adrenaline will obviously do the job of exciting your CNS and improving rate coding, which is why you are always faster, stronger and more powerful when adrenaline or nervous energy is in your system.

You can't really rely on an outside stimulus to trigger excitement in your nervous system however. You must be able to excite your own CNS at will, to generate explosive power and energy from nothing.

How naturally excitable your CNS is, is actually one of those intangible factors that separate why some people seem to be able to really fly and others struggle. The natural high flyers have a CNS that is simply more excitable and as such they are able to more readily turn on their muscles and generate power.

To improve rate coding you can practice an exercise called the Stimulation Method. Here you perform one exercise to really activate or excite the CNS. You then follow it up with an exercise to take advantage of the CNS excitability, which temporarily boosts rate coding. Gradually your body becomes more sensitive to the neural discharges from your CNS and learns to accept a new level of force as being normal for a particular movement. For striking purposes, you could therefore practice throwing a medicine ball or performing the striking movement with a dumbbell first of all, to excite the CNS, before training the strike without weight, taking advantage of the boost in rate coding.

Relaxation

Obviously relaxation is going to play a role here, as it does in most other aspects of training. It stands to reason that the more relaxed your muscles are before you fire them, the more explosive you are going to be.

Learning to stay relaxed will also aid in helping to reduce the reflex action of the Golgi Tendon Organ, which I mentioned earlier.

The same goes for your mind. Learn to stay mentally relaxed

as well.

Exercises To Improve Explosiveness

Plyometric exercises are good for building up power and explosive force in the body, with exercises like clapping push-ups or sit-ups while throwing a medicine ball.

You can also throw a medicine ball at the wall as hard as you can to develop power, making sure to keep the movements similar to when you are striking.

Also practice just exploding into your strike every time you do it, especially in an internal sense.

It's all about exciting the CNS, and to do that you need as much emotional content behind what you do as possible. Fill your strikes with hate, anger or whatever emotion or emotions most drive you. Every time you practice a strike you are not just practicing, you are engaging an opponent. Thinking in this way will help you explode into the strike more.

11: TAP YOUR AGGRESSION

"In a self protection context, learning to use your aggression is an essential key to success."

Neal Martin

In our society, aggression is not really prized as one of the more noble qualities in the human race, yet it exists and has existed since we started living and breathing on this planet. It has fuelled countless wars amongst us, both on a massive scale and also on a smaller, more interpersonal one. Most people don't like aggression in any of its forms, yet it is always there in all of us, ready to be used at any time.

Aggression is a form of energy, and like any energy, it is neither positive nor negative. All energy is neutral. Only our actions can be judged positive or negative. It is up to you to use the energy you have in the most responsible way you can.

So aggression is neither to be feared nor frowned upon. It is merely energy that you can use to help manifest your desires. If you decide to use that energy to unjustifiably hurt another human being, then that it is up to you. That's on you. You may have used aggression to help you hurt that person, but aggression did not create the desire to do so in the first place.

You cannot blame your aggression when you cross the line. The blame lies with you for not being able to control it.

Aggression can be used in a very positive sense, especially when it comes to self protection. In a physical altercation, aggression, properly used, is one the most powerful weapons you have at your disposal. It cannot be underestimated how powerful an energy source aggression can be. To put it mildly, it can really pull you out of hole.

What Is Aggression Exactly?
Wikipedia defines aggression in the following way:

"Aggression, in its broadest sense, is behavior, or a disposition, that is forceful, hostile or attacking. It may occur either in retaliation or without provocation. In narrower definitions that are used in social sciences and behavioral sciences, aggression is an intention to cause harm or an act intended to increase relative social dominance. Predatory or defensive behavior between members of different species may not be considered aggression in the same sense. Aggression can take a variety of forms and can be physical or be communicated verbally or non-verbally."

There can be a number of causes to this behavior. One theory suggests that aggression is biological, that it is built into us a species, similar to the hunger and sex drives. There may be truth in this, given how much aggressive drive and behavior has shaped human history, and how aggression seems to exist just as prevalently in the animal kingdom as it does in the human one.

The theory also suggests that this biological drive causes a build-up of energy in us that can only be released by "catharsis", or a release of emotional tension. Again, this release can result in either negative (hurting someone) or positive (channeled) action.

Other theories on aggression suggest that it is more of a learned response, more so than a biological one. We learn to be aggressive by watching others be aggressive, and if this aggressive behavior results in a reward of some kind, then we adopt it even more. This is part of our social conditioning to a large extent. If the environment we grow up in is a particularly aggressive one, then we will naturally learn to use aggression to your own ends, especially against those who are less familiar with aggression.

Another theory, called Negative Affect Theory, proposes that negative feelings and experiences are the main cause of anger and angry aggression. Sources of that behavior may include pain, frustration, crowding, sadness or depression. Thus we may walk around taking our aggression on other people, as a means of directing the bad feeling away from ourselves. It is also the cause of much of the violence in our society, as we displace our aggression on to one another.

The truth about aggression is wrapped up within all of these theories however. Aggression cannot be narrowed down to a single point of origin. It may be there on a biological level to begin with, but we also learn to use our aggression by watching others do it, and we also fall victim to feelings of angry aggression due to negative thought processes and negative behavior patterns.

Finding Your Aggression

In a self protection context, learning to use your aggression is an essential key to success. Most people can find the aggression within themselves quite easily, but a surprising number of people cannot. It always interests me when I first take a new student, to see how easily they can rouse the aggression within themselves. Some people really struggle with it.

Being able to tap into and use your aggression, turning it on and off at will, is a skill like any other, and like any skill, it takes a bit of time to master. It's just one of those things that are cultivated through the right training over a long period of time.

In a more immediate sense however, there are things you can do, physical and mental drills, that will help facilitate the longer term process.

In a mental sense, you can start by thinking of things that will naturally arouse your sense of aggression, things that may make you angry even. This kind of thinking will drag the raw aggression to the surface so you can start to work with it and get a feel for it. Notice how it makes you feel in every sense, and try to feel the energizing power of it. You can also take this a stage further by doing focused visualization drills.

Now you can do some physical drills, a good one being what I call simply the aggression drill, where you stand in front of a heavy bag or pad and a partner holds you around the waist. On the go signal you lay into the bag or pad with everything you've got while the person holding you around your waist adds resistance by puling you backwards, forcing you into really driving forward. The only way you will reach the bag or pad and hit with power is if you use aggression to fuel your actions.

Controlling And Using Aggression

Being able to tap into your aggression is all well and good, but if you don't know how to control and channel that energy it can feel a little like you're a trainee Ghostbuster who's just wielded a Proton Pack for the first time—it can be hard to control the stream!

To properly control and channel aggression you must become adept at switching it on and off at will so that you have complete control over it, no matter your physical or mental state.

Remember: aggression is just a form of energy. Certain mental and physical states are just ways to initially find your way to that source of energy. Once you can tap the source without the need for catalysts, you will gain instant access to it at any time. And like everything, the more you use this ability, the stronger and more powerful it gets.

Uncontrolled aggression is not really what you are after in a self protection context (nor indeed, in any fight context) simply because it will largely control you and dictate your behavior and actions, instead of the other easy around.

Many SP instructors can be heard telling their students to tap into their inner animal and go fucking nuts in a self defense situation, but to me, this is just too over-simplistic to be of any real use to you. Going apeshit in a fight may win you the fight, but it may also make you take things too far, to your detriment. Skill would also go out the window to a great extent, making you vulnerable to some who knows how to fight.

Fair enough if your back is really up against the wall and you need that added energy you get from getting really mad to get you out of trouble, but that's it. In the main, relinquishing control to your inner animal isn't a good idea in a lot of cases.

I've seen the red mist come down over a lot of people and it usually aint pretty to watch. It's also hard to come down from if rage or extreme anger is the driving force behind the aggression. It inevitably gets displaced everywhere.

Cold and controlled aggression is much easier to work with. In this case, the energy is tightly focused and contained, directed only at the threat before you and used in a fairly controlled manner (I say fairly because a lot of time you can't help losing your temper in a fight–you're being hit after all!).

Controlled aggression is a powerful force indeed, and it will make whatever strike you do very powerful also. The trick is channeling your aggression into your movements, something that will only come with deep practice over time.

You must get a deep kinesthetic sense of your aggression, of how it feels in your body and mind. It is that kinesthetic representation that you want to create before you strike. Through continued practice you are essentially anchoring that feeling and/or visual representation every time you draw upon your reserves of aggression. This anchor will then be used to trigger your explosive action each time.

The bigger the jolt of aggressive energy you can generate, the more explosive and the more powerful your strikes will be.

On top of this, you must also be conditioned enough, in a physical sense, to sustain this aggression over time. The more aggressive you are the more energy you will burn and the more lactic acid you will build up in your muscles. You must therefore work on increasing the threshold of your lactic acid system through continued physical conditioning exercises.

The energy of cold aggression will also affect your mindset. It will make you naturally more inclined to press forward and attack your attacker. Sustained, controlled aggression can help you overcome even the most difficult of opponents. It definitely won't make you unbeatable or any such nonsense, but it will make you a force to be reckoned with. Whether that force is enough to overcome your circumstances is another matter entirely, and will depend on your skill as a fighter, the extent of the danger you are facing and a large dose of luck as well.

Like I often say, there are no magical solutions in self defense and aggression is no magical solution either. It is just another tool to help stack the odds in your favor.

Beyond Self Protection

In a personal development sense, it doesn't hurt to learn to cultivate your aggression and channel it into the pursuit of your goals in life. I'm not saying you have to turn into some arrogant corporate go-getter, but to go after your goals with verve and aggressively follow up on whatever opportunities come your way.

When times get tough, as they inevitably will in the pursuit of anything worthwhile in life, and you are met with seemingly insurmountable obstacles, channeled aggression can really help you get fired up enough that you will be able to overcome whatever blocks to your advancement that come up.

Aggression is an energy source, and a powerful one at that. You would do well to learn to tap into that energy source and to further use it in any positive way you can, be it either in protecting yourself.

12: LEARN TO HIT FIRST WHEN IT'S NECESSARY

"Hit first. Hit hard."

A common remark I often hear from people who are interested in or train in some kind of self defense is that they just don't have it in them to hit first– to pre-emptively strike a would-be attacker.

This unwillingness to take pre-emptive action is very serious. Not only does it put you at a severe disadvantage--tactically speaking-- in a physical confrontation, but it also betrays the fact that you have underlying issues that need to be dealt with (such as fear and lack of confidence).

If you happen to be one of those people who "just doesn't have it in them to hit first", and if I was a more brutal type of guy, I'd just tell you straight, "Man the fuck up and just do what has to be done!"

I'm only brutal when you cross me, however. The rest of the time I'm a gentle soul, so I'm going to take a slightly more sensitive approach and do my best to help you clear this thing up once and for all.

Seriously though, you need to get over that shit quick. Your lack of assertiveness makes you look weak, especially in the eyes of the psychopathic thug who wants to rip your face off. A physical confrontation is no place to be a shrinking violet.

Shrinking violets get trampled by violence.

But Neal, you may be saying now. *It's not my fault, I can't help it…I just can't throw that first punch and I don't know why!*

If you don't know why, you obviously haven't done enough

searching for answers. If you haven't done enough searching and trying to get to the bottom of why you can't act pre-emptively, even knowing the full scale of the problem, then you are not serious about your personal safety. Neither are you serious about developing a combative mind, so to speak.

There is also another problem– the problem of credibility. If you are not prepared to do what it takes, what else are you not prepared to do? What is the point of training in self defense at all if you are not prepared to do what it takes?

I used to have the same problem, you know. Suffice to say I got over it. I did what I had to do to fix it. I was motivated to do so. I had no choice since I was working as a doorman at the time.

Don't go thinking now that just because you don't have the same motivation that I had, that you don't have to worry about it.

You *do* have to worry about it. It will leave you very vulnerable in a number of ways if you don't get it sorted.

So let's start by defining the problem here. The problem is that for some reason you can't pre-emptively strike another person, even if that person is about to strike you. That's the problem—you can't take the initiative and hit first

So what reasons do you have for this unwillingness or inability to act (besides the usual fear that accompanies any physical confrontation, and of course, social conditioning)?

Legal Concerns

Sorry, but no. That's not a reason. We should all be very clear on the fact that the law allows us to pre-emptively strike another person if we are acting on the belief that we are about to be attacked, and that if we have exhausted all other possibilities, hitting first is an acceptable course of action.

You should be clear on the law, you certainly shouldn't fear it, and not when it comes to defending yourself from harm. Read up on the law, know what you can and can't do and do your best to stay within the law, but not at the expense of your life.

Fear

This is the most used excuse for lack of action--fear. But fear of what exactly?

The fear of hurting the other guy? That's pretty astonishing, considering the other guy is about to hurt you. Yet I know this fear exists because I used to have it myself. I got rid of it by accepting the fact that it was me or them. That's pretty much all there is to that one.

The fear of making the other guy mad? Newsflash: He's already fucking mad! Would he be trying to launch an assault on you if he were not mad at you for something? No, he wouldn't! Will you make him even madder by hitting him? What does it matter? He's going to hit you no matter what anyway. At least if you get one good shot in before he does, you'll more than likely end the confrontation right there.

If you don't get that first shot in, you're going to be on the back foot and that's never really an ideal place to be in a brutal assault. You'll take damage, sometimes a lot of damage. You may even lose your life.

Oh, but I forgot, your defense is pretty good, right?

Good Defences

There is no such thing as good defense. It is never good to

defend in a fight. You should always be attacking in some way. Defending means you are losing, temporarily or not. You're still taking a risk that your defensive skills will work. Given how unpredictable an attacker can be, how surprising they can be in strength and aggression and sheer violent intent, it is asking quite a lot for you to deal with that and do so without taking any damage.

And do I need to remind you that action will always beat reaction? Why go against the math? It doesn't make sense.

Defense is still needed, but in the right circumstances, not because it is the only option you have.

This isn't Hollywood. Defending against a determined attacker is very difficult indeed. If you don't believe me then get some protective gear on and try to defend against some full contact attacks. You'll quickly see how difficult it is.

So those are the main reasons why you think you don't have it in you to hit first. You obviously must know by now that your self protection game-plan is not a sound one.

Let me remind you of a few things. Hitting first in a physical confrontation will give you the best chance of ending that confrontation, with no damage to you and possibly less damage to the other guy. If you'd gotten into a brawl, you could have ended up seriously injuring the guy, maybe even killing him. Not to mention the fact that third parties could have gotten involved while you were distracted and indisposed. The consequences are many.

More than that though, you're inability to hit first is creating a weakness in you that will detract from your confidence and leave you vulnerable. Knowing, or just believing, that you have the ability to hit first will greatly increase your confidence, which will positively affect the way in which you deal with confrontation.

You will feel calmer, more in control, to the point where you are better equipped to de-escalate the situation through a combination of assertiveness and the confidence that comes from knowing that you can end things at any time.

That's very empowering. It's a true combative mind.

Now let's look at the steps you have to take in order to banish this unwillingness once and for all. (And by the way, if you don't do all these steps to completion you might as well give up self defense training and go do something else instead, for you will just be kidding yourself. Despite what you think, you will not be fully equipped to handle a real physical confrontation. And if you think I'm being too blunt, you will have proved my point.)

Step One: Do Your Homework
The first thing you have to do is look at the evidence supporting the use of pre-emptive action. You must clearly see that wherever possible, hitting first is the wisest course of action there is. Find out for yourself why this is so. Think about it logically, do the math and you will see why pre-emption is the best strategy. Look at the anecdotal evidence as well. Talk to people who have used pre-emptive action and find out there experience of it.

Gather all the facts and look at them in the cold light of day, then let them back up your conviction that pre-emptive action is the best course of action in most cases.

Step Two: Make The Decision
Now you have to make a firm decision that you will adopt this strategy of pre-emption, that it will now be your first course of action should you find yourself facing a would-be attacker.

You have to commit yourself to this. You should have worked out in your head, after weighing up all the evidence in the first step, why you need to do this, why you must persist with this strategy

Commit yourself and tell yourself that there is no turning back now. Read the quote below from Goethe, it is one of my favorites and sums things up nicely:

"Until one is committed, there is hesitancy, the chance to draw back– Concerning all acts of initiative (and creation), there is one elementary truth that ignorance of which kills countless ideas and splendid plans: that the moment one definitely commits oneself, then Providence moves too. All sorts of things occur to help one that would never otherwise have occurred. A whole stream of events issues from the decision, raising in one's favor all manner of unforeseen incidents and meetings and material assistance, which no man could have dreamed would have come his way. Whatever you can do, or dream you can do, begin it. Boldness has genius, power, and magic in it. Begin it now."

Step Three: Train With The Goal In Mind
So you've done your research, you've made the decision to commit to pre-emptive action should the need arise; now you must focus your training around this strategy.

Basically, this means that you must practice being pre-emptive in your training. It means practicing your pre-emptive strikes over and over, to the point where you are completely comfortable using them. You must develop total confidence in each of your strikes.

Take two to three strikes at most and drill the hell out of them. Get each strike totally right. Work on the body mechanics so you get the most power behind each strike. You must be confident that your strikes will do the job—that they will knock a would-be attacker out cold.

You also have to practice scenarios where you strike first. There are plenty of pre-emptive striking drills in my free *Combatives Drills* e-book, the link for which is in the resources section of this book.

Start with a partner who is being verbally aggressive while holding up the focus pad. Practice striking at the right moment.

From there, move on to full pressure testing. Have a partner wear a helmet and have him go at you with full aggression so you can practice striking with (almost) full power. The more you do these types of drills the more comfortable you will get with pre-emptive striking.

Feel the confidence you get from these drills. Anchor it and let that confidence fuel your actions every time.

Step Four: Believe You Are That Person

Self-belief is important. Look at the kind of person you need to be in order to use pre-emptive action. What attributes do you need? What kind of mindset do you need?

You should discover most of this while you are doing the training drills. Take how you are doing the drills and believe that you can carry this through to real life if need be.

Think of all this as a journey of self-discovery, for that is exactly what it is. To get to the bottom of your problem you must know yourself, what fears you have, what holds you back, what really motivates you.

Combatives training is the best way to do this. You will not find what you are looking for by doing typical martial arts training. You must push yourself more than that allows.

Remember that no one has the right to attack you in any way, and that you have every right to stand up for yourself. Why would you let some twat get the better of you when it is within your power to put the guy in his place, to put him down, before he gets the chance to hurt you or your loved ones?

These people want to hurt you. Be clear on that. They wouldn't be accosting you if they didn't.

It's you or them. That's the bottom line, my friend.

When all is said and done there is no excuse for castrating yourself by taking your most effective self protection strategy out of play for flimsy reasons.

Grow a pair and stand up for yourself, and don't let fear undermine your personal safety.

13: SELF DEFENCE AND THE LAW

"Legitimate use of violence can only be that which is required in self defense."

Ron Paul

In this age of extreme political correctness and litigation, the law has essentially become the second enemy as far as self defense goes, and potentially it could inflict a lot more damage on you than any attacker on the street. The days of punching someone to the ground and walking away with no fear of the law getting involved are over. These days, everyone runs to the cops, or some other third party gets the law involved. This is just one more reason why you should do all you can to avoid violent conflict. The paperwork afterwards, even you were justified in your actions, is a nightmare.

This is why is pays to know the basic ins and outs of self defense law. The particulars will vary from country to country and from state to state, but the essentials remain the same, so let's take a quick look at those essentials now.

Force Justification
If you were involved in a violent incident where you had to use force then in the eyes of the law you must be able to articulate why you saw the person as a threat and how you knew it. "I had a feeling about the guy" just won't cut it in court. To be a valid Threat an individual must exhibit four things:

1. Intent:
The Threat must indicate that they want to harm you. How did you know? What was the Threat doing or how where they behaving to make you think they were going to attack you

(remember threat recognition and pre-contact cues?)?

2. Means:

The means to carry out intent. Basically, if a person has arms and legs then they have the means to carry out an attack.

3. Opportunity:

The Threat must be able to reach you with the means. If they are on the other side of a door then they don't have the opportunity to reach you.

4. Preclusion:

You must convince the court that you did not have any other viable option. You couldn't leave, couldn't talk your way out, you couldn't call for help. You must articulate why force was the one option that would safely work.

Scaling Force

A force incident may change quickly. If IMO are lost then you are no longer defending yourself and you are using excessive force. If you could safely leave and you don't then you have shattered your affirmative defense. For instance, if some guy in a bar tries to pick a fight with you and you had the opportunity to walk away, but instead bit back and got involved in a fight, in the eyes of the law, that's not self defense, that's just fighting.

If you happen to be ambushed then a high level of force is justified as you don't have time to gather enough information to gauge a proper response.

Articulation

We talked about articulation earlier in the book. You must be able to explain each element of your defense: Intent, Means, Opportunity and Preclusion. You must also do so in a clear and logical fashion.

In other wards you must adopt a professional attitude and keep the emotion out of it. "The bastard deserved what he got..." just won't do you any favors in front of a judge and jury.

My Own Views On Self Defence Law

A consensus has formed in the self protection industry and that consensus is this: The law matters more than your own personal safety. It is therefore prudent to think of the law before you think of your own personal safety, even if the law hampers your efforts to keep yourself safe from harm.

Or to put it another way: You just got your head handed to you on a plate by some psychopathic thug, but at least you didn't break any laws in the process.

You may think I'm being over simplistic here, but the fact is I'm not.

It's really very simple: *You cannot adequately defend yourself in a violent confrontation while thinking of the law at the same time. In a self defense situation, especially in a very serious one where you stand to get badly injured or killed unless you act with full violent capacity, you must do what you have to in order to survive.*

Even if that means acting outside the current self defense laws.

It's ridiculous that you tell someone they must take one for the team, so to speak. Why should anyone open themselves up for physical abuse or death just to stay in line with the rules of a corrupt system that doesn't give a shit about them at the end of the day?

Oh here we go, another macho rant from one of the "better to be judged by twelve than carried by six" brigade...

It's not like that at all. I'm not so irresponsible to be so blasé about the law. I'm also not so irresponsiblc to be so blasé about violence either, which is kind of the point of this article.

Yeah well, you may be saying now, *you won't be saying that when you're lying in a jail cell with a guy who has a chin like the Desperate Dan look-a-like in Tango and Cash.*

You'd be misunderstanding me if you said that however.

The law is the law. I know that. I have to try and abide by its rules like everyone else. And so do you.

The point is though, I don't need the law to tell me what is right from wrong, just like I don't need any religion to dictate my morals to me.

I, like most other decent people, have an in-built moral compass that works just fine.

I know right from wrong.

I can therefore make justified force decisions. I can trust myself enough to do that, and have done so many times in the past.

I am very aware of the law and what constitutes right and wrong in a situation.

But I will not put lawful considerations above my own personal safety. I will not allow them to hamper my ability to defend myself against someone who is trying to hurt me or my loved ones.

It is simply too risky to err on the side of caution when it comes to defending yourself against a valid physical threat. Such circumstances require no fucking about. Such circumstances require you to get in there and do what you have to do.

And you notice I said "valid" threat? That's because I am not going to use violence against someone unless they intend to use, or are using it, on me or someone I love.

I will satisfy the lawful requirements of intent, means, opportunity and preclusion. I will only use physical violence as a last resort.

And not just because that is the legally right thing to do, but also because it is the morally right thing to do.

When I think about all the legal considerations that go along with defending yourself, I quickly start to feel paralyzed by it all, like I'm caught in a web. I feel like I am giving my power away to the bad guy, handing myself to him on a plate.

That's not a good mindset to have in a self defense situation. That kind of mindset can get you killed.

And what effect will all this legal shit have on actual self defense training in the long run? Will it eventually render self defense training completely inadequate and not up to the job anymore? Will it make people afraid to train in a combatively sound way because they think using certain techniques will land them a prison sentence?

Without combatively sound principles to underpin our training, our training becomes useless and a waste of time. But hey, at least we're abiding by the law...the law that doesn't care about you anyway, just to remind you.

Look, it's like this: when faced with violence you use violence to get you through it, not the law.

When faced with the judicial system, you use the law to get you through it.

It's about keeping things in context.

Yes, the law is a consideration, but by no means the only one.

If you are a basically good, right thinking person, you will understand the concept of reasonable force and you will make right decisions. You don't need to clutter your mind with legalities. You can do that afterwards when you have to justify your actions.

The question of going too far in a violent confrontation is also a moot point to me. I train so I won't go too far. Training gives me self-control. If it didn't, what would be the point in training at all?

If you are not responsible enough to keep yourself from going too far in your use of violence, then you really shouldn't be training in self defense, for you can't handle the power the training gives you.

But don't criticize others who can handle the power that training gives them. Just because you think a technique or fighting method is dangerous, doesn't mean I'm going to kill somebody with it or even use it in an unlawful sense. It also doesn't mean I shouldn't be training it.

I train for every eventuality, and for extreme cases, I train extreme techniques. I am also very aware of the context in which such techniques should be used. I trust myself enough to apply the right response to whatever situation I'm facing, and in all the confrontations I've been in, that's exactly what I did.

You respond as best you can to the threat before you and hope for the best.

If you think you can respond like some mechanical robot,

always making just the right moves, then you are sadly mistaken. Violence doesn't work like that, I'm afraid. And if you think that it does, you are only showing your lack of experience in such matters.

Responsible people will always train responsibly. Irresponsible people will always end up in trouble no matter what they do.

The law may be important, but avoiding death or serious injury is even more important.

The law will not help you when you are six feet under or hooked up to a life support machine in a hospital.

Remember that the next time you are facing some slavering psychopath who intends to leave you in a bloody mess.

APPENDIX A: VIOLENT INTENT AND INSTILLING PANIC IN YOUR ATTACKER

"When I fight someone, I want to break his will. I want to take his manhood. I want to rip out his heart and show it to him."

Mike Tyson

There is a saying that I'm fond of: *"Amateurs fight bodies. Professionals fight minds."*

Effective self defense is not all about how much bodily damage you can inflict on an attacker. It is also about how much damage you can inflict on them psychologically.

Without the will to back it up, the body is useless. If you take away your attackers will to fight you will leave them with nothing but the sour taste of defeat.

Musashi was a master of this type of psychological beat-down. He employed many tricks to mess with an opponent's head before and during the fight. It was this psychological cunning, backed up with supreme physical skills that made Musashi one of the greatest fighters to ever live.

If you want to be more effective at self defense and be a more superior fighter, then you must find ways in which to instil a sense of panic into your attacker or would-be attacker.

You must find ways to break their will and take away their fighting spirit in order to defeat them.

It's a fact that most people do not like to fight. Physical violence is a scary proposition to most people.

Social violence is motivated by ego and peer pressure and as such, most of those who instigate social violence would much rather win in a confrontation without fighting. They will try to win by using bullying and intimidation tactics first, only turning to violence if that doesn't work for them.

Resource and process predators want something from you first of all. Violence is just a tool to get that something from you. If they can get it without using violence, all the better for them. Less hassle that way.

My point here is that you should be aware of most people's unwillingness to engage in violence, and that you should learn to take advantage of this unwillingness.

Most people will only fight because they think they have too for whatever reason. They don't really want to be doing it and they will look for a way to disengage as quickly as possible.

By using certain tactics before and during a fight you can take advantage of this inherent weakness in people and force them to confront the hard fact that they were not really up for violence in the first place.

Use the following tactics to break the will of your attacker and force them into disengaging from the fight.

Project Violent Intent

Without a doubt, this is the number one tactic for forcing a would-be attacker into capitulation.

At the pre-fight stage, when a would-be attacker is giving you the interview, you must be able to project enough violent intent that your have-a-go asshole picks up on it and decides that starting a fight with you may not be a good idea after all.

In effect, you must scare him into backing down.

But what exactly is violent intent?

Violent Intent in this context is the PURE will to do harm to another human being by any means necessary. It does not concern itself with the frontal lobe deliberations of how this is best done. It simply desires to cause damage.

Pure violence, in other words.

Or put another way:

Violent Intent only has one question and it isn't "how will I do violence?" but rather an impatient "*when* can I get to do it?"

If you have ever come across a truly psychopathic thug (and I've met a few in my time) you will know why this works. A person of this nature--someone with real violent intent, a truly violent psychopath--is very good at communicating that intent. Just by being in their presence you can pick up on the fact that this person will turn violent at the slightest provocation. They are live wires and unpredictable to boot.

A great example of this kind of personality (disorder) is Begbie in the movie *Trainspotting*, as played by the brilliant Robert Carlyle, who completely nails that role in every respect.

This is exactly how you want a would-be attacker to feel when they try it on with you. You want them to feel like they have perhaps bitten of more than they can chew.

In my early days on the door I didn't really project much in the way of violent intent. Consequently, a lot of people thought they could have a go with me or just refused to acknowledge my authority.

Eventually I realized that you had to adopt a certain attitude when dealing with troublesome punters. They had to believe you would turn on them if they didn't adhere to your instructions. Punters will look for weakness in a doorman when first confronted. If a punter sees any weakness at all they will play on it. You can't give them an inch.

Once I was able to project violent intent from the get go, I got a lot less trouble from punters. When they sensed I was willing to use violence if need be, they invariably backed down and did as they were told.

Here's the thing though: YOU CAN'T FAKE VIOLENT INTENT. YOU MUST MEAN IT.

In other words, you must really be willing to use violence if necessary.

In my experience, just by having the willingness to use violence, your confidence will increase, since you have already made your decision to act if you have too. This increased confidence will add to the potency of your violent intent and thus your would-be attacker will feel it much more keenly and will therefore be more likely to capitulate.

Remember, most people don't want to fight. Be aware of this and use it to manipulate the other person.

Use Overwhelm To Break Your Attackers Will

As I've just said, most people don't want to fight, even when they are fighting. It therefore doesn't take much to get them to capitulate and submit in most cases.

A very effective way to put the fight out of an attacker is to make them feel overwhelmed, physically and psychologically.

In a physical sense you do this by attacking hard and fast and just not letting up until the other guy is down.

Fuel your attack with violent intent and completely shock your attacker into giving up the fight.

A good way to do this is by hitting your attacker from all angles so that he doesn't know where the next strike is coming from. This tends to overwhelm their brain and force them into giving up.

An excellent technique for instilling panic in an attacker is the Shredder technique, as devised by Richard Dimitri. The idea behind the Shredder concept is to completely overwhelm an attacker physically and psychologically. It is a continuous attack on their senses that will very quickly cause the fight to go out of them.

When it comes to the crunch, it really doesn't matter what techniques you use, just as long as your actions are fuelled by violent intent, enough to shock your attacker into giving up.

Apply Forward Pressure
Putting your attacker on the back foot is one of the surest ways in which to instil panic in them.

Once you launch your attack, continue to move forward, railroading through your attacker and don't stop until they hit the ground.

Combined with the previous tactic, this will make your attacker feel even more overwhelmed as they frantically try to regain ground.

The important thing here is that you give them no space in

which to man oeuvre so that they find it impossible to regain their position.

Without positioning, they can't fight back.

There is a real sense of panic that comes when someone is constantly pressing forward on you like that and hitting you at the same time. The first instinct is to cover up, which makes fighting back impossible (you can't defend and attack at the same time). It almost feels like you are being pushed towards the edge of a cliff. You panic just as much.

Once again, pure aggression and violent intent should fuel your actions here. The harder and more aggressively you press your attacker back, the more panic you will instil in them and the quicker you will break their will to fight.

Employ Tactical Savagery

Using what Sammy Franco calls Tactical Savagery is another very effective way to instil panic in an attacker.

Tactical Savagery involves using biting, clawing and gouging techniques to make your attacker feel like they are being mauled by some kind of wild animal—which of course they are…you!

These techniques tend to be last resort tactics when you are in a tight spot. I certainly wouldn't recommend biting anyone unless you absolutely had to due to the amount of blood-borne pathogens and diseases present today.

A lot of the time it is enough that your attacker *feels* like they are being bitten. You don't have to break the skin to do this. You just make a show of biting them without actually doing so.

APPENDIX B: CULTIVATING A PRESENCE OF MIND TO COUNTER-BALANCE FEAR

As human beings we draw a distinction between ourselves and our furry friends in the animal kingdom, thinking of ourselves as rational creatures that, unlike our cuddly cousins, have the ability to think and reason. This is what separates us from other creatures.

Whilst that is true, what really separates us from other creatures on this planet is our ability to feel emotion: to laugh, to cry, to take the piss out of each other when we do stupid things (which is all too often!).

The illusion that we are calm and rationale creatures is maintained throughout our daily lives as we appear to exert control over things.

The reality is however, that we are never far from falling apart at the seams. Place any one of us in an adverse situation and our apparent rationality and self-control goes out the window.

We react to pressure by growing fearful, impatient and confused, whilst our apparently irrational furry friends look on in bemusement, seemingly unfazed by anything (except dogs when the vacuum cleaner is turned on, who proceed to lose all their marbles and go nuts chasing the damn thing around the house until you hit the off switch).

This is none more true than when we are faced with violent confrontation. Our emotions take over and we react to circumstances with fear, self-doubt, insecurity, or on the opposite end of the spectrum, uncontrollable anger and rage.

Your emotions will kill your presence of mind, and thus your ability to react rationally and calmly in a conflict situation.

The more you can maintain your presence of mind in the face of conflict and turmoil, the easier it will be to affect a more favorable outcome to the situation.

As Robert Greene puts it in his must read book, *The 33 Strategies Of War*:

"Understand: your mind is weaker than your emotions. But you become aware of this weakness only in moments of adversity-- precisely the time when you need strength. What best equips you to cope with the heat of battle is neither more knowledge nor more intellect. What makes your mind stronger, and more able to control your emotions, is internal discipline and toughness. No one can teach you this skill; you cannot learn it by reading about it. Like any discipline, it can only come through practice, experience, even a little suffering."

What you need in order to cultivate your presence of mind are exercises of a sort that will provide a counter-balance to the overpowering pull of your emotions.

Presence of mind is needed in all adverse situations, not just in physical conflicts, so when you read the following counter-balance exercises, think about how you can apply these methods to your life as a whole.

Expose Yourself To Conflict

Fear is the most destructive emotion for presence of mind. Given free reign it will decimate whatever presence of mind you have. It thrives on the unknown, which lets our imaginations run wild. It is therefore better to confront your fears and let them come to the surface, rather than ignore them or try to tamp them down.

If you have a major fear of physical conflict then the best way to dampen that fear is to expose yourself to it. No one likes to hear this however, because it means exposing yourself to the very thing that causes you fear.

But expose yourself you must, especially if you want to overcome said fear. Most people have a fear of violence and conflict in general. I did as well, but after so many years of working doors and being exposed to conflicts of one kind or another on a weekly basis, I eventually grew used to it, to the point where I am now able to maintain good presence of mind in such situations. In the beginning I was a total wreck. My presence of mind was often shattered when I had to deal with conflicts or get physical. I thought I would never be as calm and collected as some of the other bouncers I was working with. But eventually I got to that point where I was able to keep my emotions in check, which made it easier for me to deal with situations as they arose.

Exposure therapy is a process. Trust in it and you will eventually get to that place where you want to be.

The sensation of overcoming a deep-rooted fear will in itself give you confidence and presence of mind.

Public speaking was (and still is to an extent) another great fear of mine. As an introvert I found it difficult to speak with confidence to groups of people. Over the years however, I have made a point of putting myself into situations where I have to speak publicly, mostly through instructing classes, and lately to a camera (which is just the same as speaking to a group). My public speaking skills still need work but I'm getting there. Each time I do it, my confidence grows. I have faith in the process.

The more conflicts and difficult situations you put yourself through, the more battle-tested your mind will be.

Start small and go just beyond your comfort zone each time. That's all you have to do. Over time you will make progress and each success will build upon the next.

"There was a fox that had never seen a lion. But one day he happened to meet one of these beasts face to face. On this first occasion he was so terrified that he felt he would die of fear. He encountered him again and this time he was also frightened, but not so much as the first time. But on the third occasion when he saw him, he actually plucked up the courage to approach him and began to chat."

A fable that shows that familiarity soothes our fears.

Be Self-Reliant

There is not much worse than feeling dependent on other people. Dependency will make you vulnerable to all kinds of negative emotions like betrayal, disappointment and frustration, all of which can play havoc with your presence of mind.

When it comes to your personal safety, self-reliance is even more important. You can't depend on anyone to save you or come to your rescue. You must have the confidence and ability to deal with whatever circumstances you find yourself in.

Going back to my bouncing days, in the beginning I relied quite heavily on the other guys I was working with. If anything happened, I needed their support to deal with things, which didn't really increase my confidence much because I just felt dependent and unable to deal with things by myself. As I became more experienced and my confidence grew however, I learned to stand on my own two feet, and this increased confidence helped me deal with conflicts easier.

Being self-reliant is critical. You need to make yourself less dependent on others, and especially on so-called experts. You can't rely on any instructor or sensei to help you with your personal safety. Placing yourself completely in their hands (as many do) is not the way to go.

Take responsibility and work on expanding your repertoire of skills by yourself. To do this you need to feel more confident in your own judgment.

To quote Robert Greene again:

"Understand: we tend to overestimate other peoples abilities and we tend to underestimate our own. You must compensate for this by trusting yourself more and others less."

Unintimidate Yourself

Feelings of intimidation will always threaten your presence of mind, and it can be a difficult thing to combat. It's kinda hard not to feel intimidated when there is some angry, aggressive individual standing right in front of you who is giving of so much bad intention that you just wish you were somewhere else at that point, far away from the violence that is about to ensue.

Most of these feelings of intimidation are originated by your imagination however. The would-be attacker in front of you may look the part, but that doesn't mean he can act the part as well. Our imaginations give the other guy traits and abilities that they most likely don't even have. You have no way of knowing either way, so why upset your mental balance by thinking about it?

One of the keys to combating intimidation is to see the other guy as just a mere mortal, an ordinary Joe who is about to overstep the mark for whatever reason. See the person, not the myth your mind has probably already created.

Cutting the other guy down to size in this manner will help you to keep your mental balance and presence of mind.

Develop Your Intuition

Presence of mind depends not only on your minds ability to come to your aid in difficult situations, but also on the speed with which this happens.

Speed in this case refers to your ability to respond to circumstances with rapidity and making lightning-quick decisions. This kind of power is often read as a kind of intuition.

In terms of increasing that ability to respond faster to circumstances, there are things you can do to bring out that intuitive feel that all animals possess.

You should first of all have a deep knowledge of the terrain, so to speak. You must understand the nature of the situation you are in and what you have to do. The more you train, the better you get. The more experience you have, the deeper your knowledge of the terrain is going to be.

It will also help to have a good feel for people and a good level of social intelligence. You must know people and their general behaviors, the rituals, the social conventions etc. This will help you predict people's behavior to a good extent; it will help you understand these kinds of altercations, and it will allow you to spot such situations early, before they develop out of hand.

All of this will give you an intuitive feel for people and

situations that will help you in making faster decisions and maintaining your mental balance.

Maintaining Presence Of Mind In Every Day Life

Presence of mind is not just useful in times of adversity. It is not something which you should just switch on and off as you need it. It should be something that you actively try to maintain throughout your daily life. Cultivate it as a daily condition. Work on controlling your emotions and strengthening your internal discipline. Try to maintain a calm and level state of mind throughout your day.

Maintaining presence of mind can prove to be quite difficult at times of course, especially in the face of daily stresses and mental anguish of all kinds. If you find yourself losing your presence of mind, just try to check yourself and bring your mind back around again. It's no

big deal. You aren't going to die if you lose your presence of mind so don't beat yourself up about it. Just keep pulling it back into focus when focus is lost.

The better you get at maintaining this mental balance, the more you're focused and calm state of mind will do for you in your daily life. When a crisis does come, your mind will already be calm and prepared.

Once presence of mind becomes a habit, it will always remain with you.

APPENDIX C: SOME THINGS YOU SHOULD KNOW ABOUT REAL FIGHTING

1. In a real fight you lose power

Yes, that's right, you lose power.

You know when you hit the heavy bag in the gym, and you're just laying these hard and heavy shots into the leather and it seems like the bag is about to break free from its chains because you're hitting it with so much power?

Well that doesn't happen much in real combat.

Largely due to the cocktail of stress hormones coursing through your body, you end up losing quite a bit of power.

It makes sense. Turbo charges like that take a lot of energy to produce. A lot of the energy that you normally put into your strikes in practice goes into producing that adrenaline rush. After the initial burst you begin to feel weakened by it.

I've felt this effect and it can come as a bit of a shock when you throw a strike and it feels like you're hitting with a feather. You can't understand why you didn't strike the way you did thousands of times before in training.

That's why. Adrenaline. It has both positive and negative effects. The real key to maximum performance under its influence is knowing what to expect.

So you have to learn about it and you have to experience it first-hand a few times.

When you learn to cope better with the stress reaction, you will also learn to strike more powerfully when in that condition.

A good start to learning to cope would be doing pressure tests and scenario work in the gym. Exposure therapy. What you feel in the gym will not be what you will feel in a real situation exactly, but it'll be enough to get you started. You'll just know to expect more of it.

2. You scrabble in real fights

I know what you're thinking. In a real fight you get an uncontrollable urge to play board games. Something to do with the adrenaline, right?

Not exactly. Although suggesting a game of Scrabble to someone who is about to rip your head off and stare down your neck might be a good ploy to set up a pre-emptive strike, that is not what I mean by scrabble.

Here's the dictionary definition of scrabble:

To scrape or grope about frenetically with the hands.

Yes, that's right. Real violence doesn't tend to play out the way it does in *Hard To Kill*. Unlike Segal in the movie, you tend not to be that graceful or fluid in a real fight.

Physical confrontations are so hyped up and frantic that it is almost impossible to be graceful, at least not in the way you normally would be when doing techniques in the gym. The adrenaline messes up your co-ordination and fine motor skills a bit.

Hence, you scrabble. You just want to get it over with. You don't have time to be graceful.

That's why real fights always look so scruffy.

Scrabbling.

2. Your ego will often get in the way

You know your ego. It's that asshole who loves himself and is always rudely demanding things; the one who always thinks he's right; the one who can't walk away from a fight, who refuses to turn the other cheek in case they appear weak in the eyes of others.

Think back. In all the times you have had a physical confrontation with someone, how many of those times were at least in part caused by you? How many times could you have easily walked away without recourse to violence?

We've all been in a few bad incidents of our own making, times when we pushed things too far, when we said things out of pride, times when we should have left well alone and walked away.

It was your ego that made you stay when you should have walked, reacted when you shouldn't have, said things you shouldn't have said.

The ego is a powerful force. It has a massively tight grip on most people and its needs are hard to ignore.

It also has a habit of taking over in times of stress.

If you wish to lead a peaceful life then learn to guard against and control your own ego. In a conflict situation it will get you in trouble every time.

It will strive to make you feel bad about doing the right thing. The safest thing.

If some drunk says something rude to your wife your ego will immediately want to reprimand that person. You'll feel like you have to confront the guy, maybe even hit him.

From a self defense point of view that would be the wrong thing to do. Just whatever, the guys a dick, walk away. But your ego will pop up and shout "NO! Hit this dick-now! He insulted your woman!"

I don't need to tell you why that shouldn't happen. Your ego will keep telling you why it should however.

And it's like that in every situation. Unless you have a handle on your sneaky bastard ego it will continue to take over and cause more trouble.

So get a handle on it

Combatives Instruction

INTRODUCTION

I decided to write this book so I could lay down some guidelines on teaching self defense, or more specifically, "combatives". I wanted to lay down an underlying philosophy and some best practices that instructor's and would-be instructors of self defense would hopefully find informative and useful. Students of self defense who have no plans to become teachers will still get a lot out of this book though, for it will provide a means to grade your current training against. It will also offer ideas on how to improve the quality of your self defense training by showing you what you should be aiming to achieve through the training.

The main focus of this book is on combatives, i.e. the physical side of self defense. I have chosen not to concern myself with matters of law, morals, ethics, awareness or any of the other soft skills and theoretical concepts that make up the non-physical side of self defense. There are plenty of other books out there that go into great detail on these matters, so I didn't see the point of rehashing it all here.

The fact is there are many books out there that concern themselves with the physical side of self defense, but most of the ones that do are way of track when it comes to the matter of what should be taught as self defense and how it should be taught. This is why I wanted to focus on the physical aspects in this book.

This book will not give you all the answers, nor should it. Even though I have created a fairly detailed blueprint here for teaching combatives, you will still have to put the work in and build upon that blueprint.

I have spent years training and gathering information on self defense, not to mention purposely going out and getting real world experience in these matters. Such dedication to the cause has enabled me to become an instructor that gets results. I say that not to blow my own trumpet, but so as you understand that you will have to put the work in yourself if you also want to be a self defense instructor who gets results. Expecting a book or a DVD or another instructor to do all the work for you is not the way to go. Sure you can gather information from these sources, learn what you can from them, but you have to put all that information together in your own way.

Being a great self defense instructor is not about being a clone of someone else or being some other instructor's tribute act (nor indeed is it about blatantly ripping off other peoples work). In the same way that you have to make self defense techniques your own in order to use them most effectively, you must also make what you teach your own as well. This means having a thoroughly deep understanding of everything you teach, and avoiding the trap of superficially teaching other people's stuff. If you are going to teach what others do then at least know what you are talking about before you do it. That means having a very deep understanding of the material first, a step that many instructors fail to take, choosing instead to take the easier path of merely regurgitating what others do and say.

If you are serious about being the best self defense instructor you can be then you must begin a quest to be as unique as possible, not only in what you teach but in how you teach it. Of course it can prove difficult to find things that have not already been done. In terms of physical techniques, there is not much more to add. But that doesn't mean there are not different ways of doing things, or different ways of explaining things. You should at least strive for originality in what you are doing, rather than just blatantly copying what others are doing (if you are going to use other people's material, then at least acknowledge that you are doing so).

Unfortunately though, this is exactly what most people do. They look around to see what everyone else is doing first and then they play it safe by sticking to the same well-worn paths; the same ideas and the same ways of doing things. I'm not trying to say it is easy to be original or innovative, but that doesn't mean we shouldn't try. There is always more out there to be discovered.

Of course we all have to start somewhere. We all have to learn from someone. But at least try to add your own little twists to things whenever you can, or come up with different ways to train certain things. Taking the attitude that there is nothing new to be discovered, or that everything has already been done, is not the way to go if you want to really stand out as an instructor.

The good news is if you go deep into the subject of self defense/combatives and train the hell out of it, you will discover little things that few already know about. Sometimes, just in the way that you teach is enough to make what you do original or unique.

Of course you don't have to give a damn about any of that originality stuff. And that's fine. Not everyone is willing to push the boundaries. Some people just want to teach bog standard self defense. I have a deep passion for this stuff, so the standards I set for myself are quite high. I *want* to go beyond the norm, as do others that I know. I know plenty of other self defense and combatives instructors who have created completely original material and who have come up with quite a few different innovations that they can call their own. It *can* be done.

Wherever you stand though, you will still get plenty from this book. What I've laid down in these pages is a template for teaching self defense in a way that will produce results for those who are being taught. If you base your teaching around only what is included here and nothing more you will still be miles ahead of many others out there teaching self defense. It is my hope however, that you use this book as a starting point for your own development as an instructor, or if you are already an instructor, as a resource to further your current development.

Before we begin however, we should try to define a little what we mean when we talk about getting results in self defense. The goal of training is to achieve certain results. If you're an MMA fighter or a boxer then the results you aim for are wins in competition. Secondary to that you are judged on how effective a fighter you are overall.

But what about self defense? If you follow the same logic, the effectiveness of your training (at least the physical side) should be measured by how many street fights you've "won". Secondary to that you should also be judged on how good you are in a physical confrontation, generally speaking.

But how do you measure these results when you rarely if ever get the chance to put your training to any use? In the absence of real world altercations, "false altercations" are created in the gym. Your success is measured by how well you do in these false altercations. You are also measured on how well you know and execute the system you are training in.

In effect, what most self defense systems do (and most martial arts as well) is measure the effectiveness of a student by how well they operate within the confines of the system. That is not how it should be, of course, but unfortunately where most self defense training is concerned, that is the only option open to people. The other option, of actively testing yourself for real, is just too unsafe and irresponsible to even consider, unless it is done in some semi-justified way through security work or military service or whatever. Most people choose not to go down that path however.

So results in self defense are almost exclusively "internally" based, in that "external" real world experience or testing plays little or no part in the training. If it did then results would be a lot harder to argue with. Results that are internally based within the confines of a system are always open to argument by those who train in rival systems. The best thing you can do in self defense training is to make sure that everything you do is based on very sound principles and whatever real world experience is there to draw upon.

The point of this book is to highlight the combative principles that need to be present in a good self defense system. Although the whole idea of measuring results in this context is somewhat intangible to say the least, it is still possible to gauge how well a student is doing by testing their competence in various live drill scenarios, and also how good their fundamental technique is in terms of power, speed, accuracy etc.

As an instructor you should be able to instinctively gauge a student's progress just by watching them and working with them. If you understand just what you are trying to achieve with the training you are providing then you should be able to easily see how much progress your students are making and how capable they are under pressure.

To conclude this introduction then, if you have a thorough grasp of the material you are teaching and the problems you are trying to solve, you should be able to see whether or not your students are capable of solving those problems with the solutions you provide them with, and also with the solutions they have worked out for themselves, solutions which by the way, should be thoroughly tested by whatever means possible.

SECTION 1| THE QUESTION OF EXPERIENCE

In this first section of the book I want address an issue that often comes up in self defense circles: How much experience does an instructor need to have in order to teach self defense? It's a question that can plague you and if you are not careful, it can damage your confidence as well. This is why I thought it important to try and put this issue to rest first of all. This way you can get on with being an instructor and learning from the rest of this book.

CHAPTER 1: EXPERIENCE

One of the questions that often comes up in regards to teaching self defense is the question of experience. Just how much experience does an instructor need to have in order to teach self defense effectively? In this chapter I will answer that question and hopefully put it to rest so we can get on with the business of how to actually teach self defense. But first, a little background.

I grew up learning martial arts. For the longest time I felt the training would be enough to get me through if violence ever crossed my path. I had a few fights as a teenager and did okay. Instinct and some natural fighting ability got me through. When I became an adult and began to encounter a more brutal level of violence on the street and through working the doors, I quickly realized that all the training I was doing was woefully inadequate and mentally especially, I was ill-equipped to handle it.

I was still doing traditional martial arts back then, and some kickboxing. Later in my training career I started to get into the RBSD scene and I changed my training methods. I began to work on gross motor skills rather than the fineries of the traditional stuff I had been doing. I brought verbal de-escalation into my training, higher levels of aggression and also scenario work. I began working doors again. The new training methods made me much better equipped to handle violence, but it still wasn't enough. Invariably, the real thing turned out to be a much different experience, no matter how hard I worked in the gym to bring a new level of reality to my training.

I stayed on the doors and inevitably ended up being exposed to more violent altercations, both as a participant and as a spectator. I've gotten a lot better at dealing with real violence, partly because I'm older and wiser, and partly because I have exposed myself to quite a bit of it now. I'm not saying I can easily handle any kind of violent situation, nor am I saying that I'm even entirely comfortable being in those types of high stress situations (who is?). I'm just saying I've gotten better at dealing with them.

Without the experiences I have had, my self defense skills would be less than they are now. As an instructor, I'd be on a lower level than I am now. My experiences have informed my skills and my ability to teach people how to handle real world violence (that's violence that happens fast, brutally and by surprise). I wouldn't feel authentic as an instructor in self defense if I didn't have those experiences.

I purposely sought out bouncing work, not for the money (please...) but for the experiences it can provide. Bouncing gave me an opportunity to get involved in real violent incidents without starting anything myself and going to jail, and to test out what I was training in. Some things you are totally convinced will work for real--until experience tells you they actually don't.

So why go to all this trouble? Why put myself at risk like that?

Because I knew I couldn't dabble in self defense; that I had to live it for real, at least for a while. Long enough to get some much needed experience.

And that's what I'm saying: If you really want to know about self defense, as opposed to just learning about it, then you have to go out there and get to know it. There is no alternative. I used to think training was the alternative, but it isn't. It certainly helps a great deal, but it doesn't quite get you to the place you need to be in your head in order to effectively handle real violence. Simulated violence in the gym and real world violence outside the gym are two different animals. The real one has teeth and claws and isn't afraid to use them.

Now don't get me wrong here. I'm not trying to put myself across as this massively experienced guy. I'm not. I'm just someone who has been training in martial arts for a long time and who has gotten a certain amount of experience through bouncing and other personal experiences I've had with violence. I don't have a knock-out record as long as your arm, as some instructors claim to have. I've never faced an attacker with a knife (and I hope I never will).

What I have done is expose myself to enough violence that I now have a good understanding of it and its dynamics; I have a firm grasp of how to combat violence, both the hard and the soft way; and I also am able to effectively teach other people about what I know on the subject, well enough to give them a fighting chance if they ever encounter violence themselves (some of my students, past and present, have successfully used the skills I have taught them).

I'm saying here that if you want to take your knowledge off and skill in self defense to higher levels, then you must seek out experiences that are going to help you do that. Experiences that happen in the real world, not in the gym. Whether or not you want to do that is up to you. It is certainly not a prerequisite for becoming a teacher of self defense (as I'll explain in the next chapter), but it most definitely helps.

CHAPTER 2: HOW MUCH BLOOD IS ENOUGH?

At one point in my early teaching career I had what you would call a crisis of confidence. I didn't feel totally genuine as an instructor in self defense, mainly because I didn't think I had enough real world experiences of handling violence and using the skills that I was teaching people.

I was having doubts about myself. We all have those. We all doubt ourselves in some capacity at some point.

My doubts were holding up my progress as an instructor though, and I couldn't have that.

If I'm going to teach people self defense then I am going to do it to the best of my ability.

Nothing less will do.

I take the responsibility very seriously. So I knew I had to get past those doubts in order to keep growing as a teacher.

I think most instructors in the martial arts and self defense have the same feelings of doubt at some time or other. They will ask themselves, *"Am I really qualified to be teaching this stuff? What experiences do I have to back up what I'm teaching?"*

Someone who teaches pure traditional martial arts will not be too bothered by these questions, and that's not to offend any martial arts instructors reading this. In martial arts, you teach the techniques that have been handed down to you, and you carry on the traditions of your particular style. Yours isn't really to question why. So you concentrate on the art. That way, you don't have to prove that anything works. You're just doing it for the art. That's fine. I did it myself for years in Jujitsu. I still occasionally teach Jujitsu as an art. I enjoy just doing the movements for the sake of doing them. There's a lot to be gained from that, many fringe benefits.

In self defense it's different though.

You're supposed to be teaching stuff that works in the real world. You therefore incur the responsibility of making sure what you teach is practical and won't get people killed when they go to use it.

Experience then becomes much more important. You need to have credibility as an instructor. And I believe that you can't really teach self defense properly if you don't have at least some working knowledge of the things you are teaching.

It's like that oft-used comparison: You wouldn't learn to fly a plane from someone who has never flown a plane; likewise you would never learn self defense from someone who had never been in a fight before.

And that's the question that often plagued me: *How many fights was enough? How much blood had to be spilt before enough was enough?* I decided to seek advice on the matter from people who could likely answer that question—other instructors.

One instructor friend of mine had this to say:

"Would you feel less "fraudulent" with 400 KO's under your belt? I doubt it. I've travelled a lot and done the door in different countries and I must say I seriously, seriously doubt anyone who claims to have KO'D "hundreds" of people. To have gone on the cobbles with hundreds of equally weighted, equally skilled opponents and knocked them all out? Well they are a fool if they still worked the door, when there are millions to be made in the

ring if they are so skilled. To have knocked out hundreds of drunk kids who couldn't box eggs? Well they are a bully and if they got away with hundreds they are bloody lucky they never ended up in jail or shot. It's a silly claim. And no it wouldn't make your training of your students any more relevant. The training is itself I'm afraid, in its typical format, doomed to irrelevancy."

So basically no amount of experience is going to make up for irrelevant material.

Does it matter that you have knocked out a hundred different people when you are teaching your students stuff that either won't work, or stuff that will get them in more trouble if they use it?

So you're teaching people how to break jaws left, right and center when what they really need to be taught are social skills and self-assertiveness, things that will keep them out of trouble in the first place.

You could argue that it's not the job of a self defense instructor to teach those things. It's a self defense class, so you learn how to fight, right? That might be a fair point, if it weren't for the fact that these things are inextricably linked with proper self defense.

Self defense can't always be about the physical. Not these days. It would be irresponsible not to at least touch upon the softer skills when teaching people.

That would be like giving someone a loaded gun and not showing them how to use it properly, not explaining the safety rules to them. That could end badly.

So could showing someone how to do real damage to another person, without also showing them how to avoid doing so in the first place, or at least showing them justifiable contexts in which these skills can be used.

So in that sense, experience counts for very little if you don't use it responsibly. (And yes I am aware that this book will teach people only how to fight. However, if you want all that other stuff, check out the books in the resources section.)

My question still hadn't been answered to my satisfaction however. So I spoke with another high profile instructor and asked him the same question:

Here's his reply:

"I ask you this: if you've had one real experience that seriously tested you physically and emotionally, I mean one where you really had to give it everything you had to prevail! Example: three guys follow you in to the toilet, one has a broken glass and the other two bar the door. When one goes they all go yet somehow you hit the fucking switch and motor, you get out relatively unscathed and they end up fucked up not wanting any more of you. Such a single experience would, trust me, teach you a lot about yourself. How many such experiences would you need to know that you will stand or not? How many people do you need to clinically KO pre-emptively to know that if you go first with enough juice and intent to wipe their fucking blood line clean and end the situation before it becomes a fight, to know the concept of being first works? 400? 40? Or 4? When you know you can do it then you know. There is no substitute for experience, although you can learn from others and test to a fair degree with good simulation and still be a good instructor."

So this instructor is saying, it's not the number of experiences that you have, but the *quality* of those experiences that count. How much did you learn from them? What did you learn that might be useful to other people? Do those experiences make you better at what you teach?

What you are teaching matters just as much, as I've already said. If you're teaching shit to people then it doesn't matter who you are and what you've done. Shit is shit and no amount of experience is going to change that.

Your qualifications for teaching cannot also just hinge upon the fact that you did a certain job in the past either, as combatives instructor Mick Coup explains:

"Here's the thing as I see it - such background experience can be extremely valuable, but it tends to be incidental, therefore selling it as being the definitive qualification is simply ridiculous. If every single person who did 'that' job, or wore 'that' badge, etc, is not a consummate subject matter expert, then why did 'that' job, or 'that' badge, make you into one?

It didn't - if you are an expert, then this was down to you most likely, not your job - so hinging your credibility solely upon wearing a particular cap-badge, or standing on a club door once-upon-a-time is pretty lame...it should rest upon you...and not then, but now...

I feel that this can be a problem for some, when all that they seem to offer is the same old regurgitation of fairly pedestrian and often downright clichéd material that is ostensibly nothing original or innovative, so they need some other kind of unique selling point to make up for this - since the 'product' itself doesn't really stand out..."

It's clear then that what you are teaching and how you are teaching it matters a good deal more than how many fights you have had in the past. For myself, I only mention my bouncing experience in passing, to add to my overall credibility as an instructor. Most of my credibility (and this goes for all good instructors out there) comes from the fact that I have put a great deal of study and practice into what I do, and I am also able to put across what I know to other people in a clear and articulate manner.

To be honest, if an instructor is stammering their way through a presentation or demonstration then I would start to get concerned, no matter how much real world experience they supposedly had under their belt, for this would mean that they don't know their subject too deeply and have only a shallow understanding of the principles and concepts involved.

I'd be more inclined to give credence to someone who is able to clearly explain the aforementioned principles and concepts in a way that those listening can completely understand and have no trouble putting them into practice. Really, what good is experience if you can't put it across to people in a way that is going to help them with their own problems?

So to conclude this chapter, yes experience definitely helps when it comes to teaching self defense, but you also have to realize that this experience is often completely subjective (not to mention vastly over-stated and often exaggerated) and not necessarily of any use to anyone else. Being a bouncer, or a police man or a soldier does not immediately qualify you to teach self defense, far from it. There is a lot more to it than that.

And anyway, these kinds of jobs are often very restrictive in terms of what you can actually do and get away with doing. Most of these jobs are all about controlling and restraining, not all fighting. The most experienced fighters that I know have gotten most of their experience from the street in some context, not through one of these professions.

Quality self defense instruction hinges upon quality material being taught, it's as simple as that. The material must be able to stand on its own, without the need for instructors throwing their experiences (limited or otherwise) into the mix.

Experience can certainly add an extra dimension to your teaching, but it isn't an essential component. So yes, you can do without it. You can teach self defense to people without having much experience just as long as what you are teaching has real merit.

SECTION 2| THE COMBATIVES SYLLABUS OVERVIEW

Now we are going to look at what exactly should be included in a combatives syllabus. What constitutes a good combatives syllabus and what kind of material should you be teaching in order for your instruction to be credible?

As is obvious from the vast amount of different so called "real combat systems" and reality fighting systems out there, there exists a difference of opinion amongst many on what self defense training should be all about. For my liking there are far too many people out there teaching bloated systems that are full of pointless techniques, systems that are bogged down with far too much pseudo-scientific theory of one type or another or endless amounts of "combative psychology".

The people who advance these fluffed up systems are really missing the point about combatives training. Combatives should be simple and uncomplicated. That isn't to say it shouldn't have depth or that the concepts and principles it is based on should be over-simplistic. When I say simple and uncomplicated I just mean that it should be relatively easy to learn and implement under highly stressful conditions. Anything that doesn't follow those criteria will by default not be high percentage enough and simply won't work under real conditions.

When it comes to combatives, less is most definitely more. If you intend to start teaching people combatives, then please keep that maxim in mind, for you won't be doing yourself or your students any favors by needlessly complicating matters for them. If you already teach self defense, then carefully evaluate the system you are teaching and ask yourself this question: *Do I really need everything that is in here?* Quite often you will find that you don't need much of what is in your syllabus. The fluff can slip in between the cracks over time without you even realizing it sometimes, so make a point of regularly checking your syllabus and applying a cull every now and again.

A good combatives system should be streamlined and practical in the extreme, which means leaving out most of the low percentage stuff and putting the emphasis on high percentage techniques and strategies.

CHAPTER 3: CHARACTERISTICS OF AN EFFECTIVE COMBATIVES SYSTEM

What I teach is termed "combatives", which is just a collective term for the kind of things which have been proven to work in a fight. That's a very basic definition of Combatives.

Here are some of the criteria of a good combatives system, taken from my previous book, *Self Defense Tips Everyone Should Know*:

• Basic strikes that will work pre-emptively or defensively

• Natural everyday positions as a starting point for situational control, and which are easy to strike from

• An emphasis on power striking, with heavy impact

• A head-hunting mentality--striking the head wherever possible

• Simple but effective counters to common street attacks

• An emphasis on mindset and the cultivation of ferocious resolve or the willingness to do what it takes to survive

• Brutal ground fighting techniques

• An emphasis on dirty fighting and tactics

• Skills that will work under high stress conditions

• Stress inoculation training to aid an understanding of stress and how to operate under it

The above criteria should serve as a basic starting point when you are deciding what to teach in your self defense class. Or it may serve as a check list you can use to compare against your current system or syllabus. An effective and comprehensive (without being bloated) combatives system should contain all of the above elements to some degree or another.

Now let's look in more detail at some of these essential concepts and when they should be introduced.

Primary Strategies

Primary strategies and techniques should be introduced to combatives students first. When I take on a new student one of the first things I work with them on is showing them what to do when the shit hits the fan, so to speak. *Forget about everything else*, I tell them. *You're suddenly in a fight and you have to do something right away to defend yourself. What are you going to do?*

The answer to that is that they are going to hit back and they are going to hit hard!

If you suddenly find yourself under attack you won't have time to think or do anything complicated. The best and quickest thing you can do is to hit back with the intention of dropping your attacker as quickly as possible.

And what's the best way to drop an attacker?

Knock them out!

That's right, you have to try and knock them out or at least distract them long enough that you can escape the mess you're in. Knocking an attacker out means targeting their head area (the "central governor" or the "off switch") and the best way to do that is by striking their head repeatedly until they go down.

Using punching techniques is not necessarily the best way to do that, so we use an open hand technique, a palm strike.

So with new students, you teach them that palm strike and you teach them how to hit hard with it. This will at least give them a chance to get themselves out of trouble right away.

So already we are introducing the head-hunting mentality and the reasoning behind it. Now we have to show them exactly how to hit hard enough for maximum effect, and this means introducing the concept of power generation and all the underlying concepts that go with that, like using the hips to generate torque and making full use of the entire body to add momentum to the strike. I'll not go into detail here about how to train this kind of thing, as I'll be discussing it later in the chapter on training practices.

The purpose of this chapter is to provide you with a general overview of the kind of things you should be showing to your students. How to hit hard is one of those essential concepts that should be introduced right away, since this is what most fights in the real world boil down to, and nothing much more complicated than that.

From here you can go on to teach new students other high and low line high percentage techniques, like hammer fist strikes, elbow strikes, knee strikes and leg kicks. Nothing more complicated than that for a while, with the emphasis on lots of drilling and repeated practice of those techniques.

Alongside all of these techniques you can introduce other essential concepts such as explosiveness, using aggression and applying forward pressure.

The key here is teaching them the stuff that they are most likely going to need and use should they find themselves in a physical altercation. Most people who seek out self defense training have no intention of training at it for the rest of their lives, which is why it is important to introduce them to the primary stuff first. This is even more important if you are running short courses. Focus on the stuff that is going to get them out of the shit first.

Secondary Strategies

Once you have spent some time with students on the important primary techniques and concepts you can then move them on to some of the other concepts and techniques of Combatives. The goal should always be to put down the bedrock of primary strategies so you can build upon them from there, expanding out and adding things in as you progress with your trainees.

Defensive strategies would be high on the list here, or what to do when you are being hit (aside from hitting back, of course). This would be the time to begin teaching simple cover techniques to protect the head and give the trainee a chance to counter-attack. I'll go into some of these defensive techniques in the section on detailed training practices.

Another essential concept to be covered here would be the concept of controlling personal space via the fence technique, or the guard or whatever you want to call it. Once you show this concept in action allow the student to work on it and personalize it as much as possible while still adhering to the basic principles of the technique (an approach that should be used when training any technique).

I am assuming that you are already familiar with the techniques and concepts I'm describing here. If you teach self defense already then you should know about this stuff. If you are planning on becoming a self defense instructor and you are not familiar with this stuff then I strongly suggest that you get familiar with it before trying to teach. The whole point of being a teacher is after all, to know more than your students, and to know it deeply enough that you can adequately communicate the principals involved to your students.

Taking a two day instructor course does not qualify you to teach anything. You must have at least a few years' experience in just training self defense yourself before you go on to teach it. To do the job right, you must know your subject inside out. This is partly why there is so much nonsense being taught as self defense, because the instructors are neither qualified nor learned enough to be teaching the subject. As an instructor you have to have integrity and credibility or you won't be worth a damn to those you teach.

Lastly, it is a good idea to also include some kind of sparring practice at this point. Obviously the contexts of street and sport are completely different, and that should be clearly explained, but there are many benefits to be gained from sparring that are very pertinent to self defense. Many people who begin this kind of training have never hit anyone before, for instance, so allowing them to box with gloves on (even just doing chest shots instead of head shots) will give them a feel for what it is like to hit another person. Likewise, they will also learn to take a few hits in the process, which is also an essential thing to learn.

I wouldn't spend a vast amount of time on sparring. The occasional bout will do, just enough to allow the students to get comfortable doing it. Most of your time should be spent training the techniques and concepts we have so far been talking about.

Introducing The Softer Skills

As you teach people the hard physical skills of self defense, so should you be teaching them the softer skills as you go also. This would require you to put across the concepts of, and principles behind, pre-contact management such as controlling space (as we just mentioned) and verbal de-escalation. Get your trainees used to aggression, get them used to someone verbally assaulting them and show them how to handle that kind of behavior by staying calm and using non-violent postures. Also show them the kind of pre-contact cues that they should be looking out for as well. All of this can be mixed in along with the hard physical skills, which should always provide the backbone of their training and which they should spend the most time on.

Things like awareness and self defense law should also be touched upon. Some instructors feel the need to present this kind of information in the form of a lecture or power-point presentation. I personally feel that this kind of teaching method is not very effective and often has more to do with the ego of the instructor than anything else. People have a tendency to zone out during this kind of presentation and the information they are given is quite often forgotten after the presentation is over.

A better way to put this information across is to simply thread it in with the regular training. For instance you may be discussing the use of pre-emptive strikes. Now would be a good time to talk about the law for a bit. Drop the information in as you see fit and try to keep it pertinent to what you are teaching at the time. If you can put the theory type stuff in context as you teach, students will understand it better. It is better to discuss awareness when you are teaching ambush attacks than it is to dryly present that same information in a lecture. At least the students will grasp the context and importance of awareness if you teach it alongside other relevant concepts and techniques.

Having said all that, I am not completely against the use of presentations in self defense training. Presentations have their uses, I'm not denying that. They are good for getting over the bare bones of a topic, or an over-view of how things are structured, helping to put the eventual physical training into context somewhat. Some instructor's do use them as a crutch however, and it can also be difficult to really engage your audience enough to have the proper impact. It also depends on what kind of person you are and whether your particular way of doing things lends itself to that kind of teaching. Some people like to put things across very organically, letting information come as and when it is needed throughout training. It's really down to the instructor as to how effective either of these two teaching styles is.

Specialist Techniques

Once the basics have been learned and practiced often, you can also bring in other relevant stuff, such as ground defense and weapon defense. Many instructors teach these two things like they are separate from the basic stand up stuff when they are not. The goals and principles are still the same; you still have to hit your attacker hard in the head whenever possible, no matter if he is on the ground with you or has a knife or some other weapon in his hand. Also avoid anything complicated here and continue to keep things simple.

There are also obviously pressure drills and scenarios that can be used in training. Again, these should be introduced early on and continued from there on in. I won't go into detail on these as we will look at them in the next section instead.

For now, I hope you can see the merit and importance in starting with the fundamentals of self defense, the techniques that are going to get a student out of trouble when they find themselves in it. All else is secondary to that. Most of your training time with students should be spent on learning, drilling and perfecting these fundamentals.

Sure there is lots of cool stuff that you can do in self defense training and lots of interesting concepts and theory that you can teach, but none of that stuff is going to do a student any good if they don't know how to defend themselves at a very basic level.

These days, there is a heavy emphasis on avoidance techniques, conflict communication and the law as it pertains to self defense, and it has become very fashionable for instructors to jump on these subjects and preach them to death, often valuing them more than the fundamental combatives techniques we have been talking about in this chapter. That's all well and good. Avoidance and conflict communication are obviously important, as is knowing the law (especially these days), but never forget that most students who attend a self defense class or course do so because they want to learn physical self defense skills. They will come to you because they want to learn how to put somebody down. They will not go to you to be lectured at or be made to feel like they are attending a college course on self defense.

Never forget that! This is your responsibility to your students.

Of course mention those other skills, but do so as you are teaching the fundamental physical skills and mix things up a bit for your students. They will benefit more from this approach and will ultimately thank you for it.

SECTION 3| DETAILED TRAINING PRACTICES

In this section I'm going to outline a bare bones combatives syllabus that you can work from if wish to do so. It will not include everything that I teach personally but it will represent a good starting point for anyone who hasn't yet compiled their own syllabus. What you include in your syllabus and classes will be down to you. Your training background, level of experience and personal preferences and biases will influence exactly what you teach at the end of the day.

All I want to do in this section is provide a rough syllabus that contains what I consider to be essential techniques and concepts that need to be included in any combatives syllabus worth its salt. As well as the actual techniques I will also be providing notes on how to teach them and sample drills where applicable.

CHAPTER 4: THE SYLLABUS IN DETAIL

Primary Striking Techniques: palm strikes, hammer fists, elbow strikes, power slaps, short range punches.

Secondary Striking Techniques: knee strikes, groin kick, leg kicks

Extreme Close Quarters Techniques: gouging, head-butting, standing grappling techniques, chokes/strangles.

Ground Fighting: techniques for getting back to feet, positional techniques.

Defense: covering techniques, counter attacking techniques.

Situational Control Techniques: the fence/guard positions.

Multiple Attacker Defenses

Weapon Defenses

Okay so that's a barebones syllabus to work off. If you were expecting more in terms of techniques, you've been doing martial arts for too long. The point of combatives is to pare things down and keep the techniques to a minimum. Remember that focus should be on a small handful of tools that can be used effectively in any situation. That's how we're rolling here.

The above syllabus is deceptive in its apparent brevity however. When you really dig into what is there you will find a great deal of material to work with; all manner of drills and applications that will add the meat to the bones of this syllabus.

One of the main criticisms that is often levelled at combatives systems is that there is not much to them in terms of techniques or material. For those who wish to practice and study combatives indefinitely there is not enough material to sustain such a commitment. Well this is blatant nonsense. Anyone who throws this kind of flippant criticism around is only showing their lack of experience and even lesser understanding of what combatives is all about. Yes, on the surface, it would appear that the average combatives syllabus is a bit thin on the ground, especially compared to your average martial arts syllabus, which usually contains hundreds if not thousands of different techniques.

Take a look below the surface however, and you will see that there is still a lot going in a combatives syllabus, especially when you factor in the amount of different drills that you can do to practice each of the different techniques and tactics involved. The way combatives is trained is only limited by your imagination. Yes you can take a shallow approach and only basically train a few techniques until you are competent in them, but to me that's not what combatives is all about.

Combatives is about mastery, as far as I'm concerned. It is about taking a select handful of fundamental, generic and flexible techniques and tactics and completely mastering them through a process of continuous training, drilling and study. The deeper you go into these techniques the more you will discover about them and the better you will get at executing them in varying circumstances.

Some people see this kind of training as boring, but really, the only thing that is boring is the end result once you are able to execute a technique and get the same result every single time. The process of getting to that stage is far from boring however, and there is always more to learn, *if* you take an in-depth approach to the training.

There isn't much to be gained from taking a shallow approach to your training, but everything to be gained by taking a path that will lead to mastery, not only of your techniques, but also of yourself along the way.

Now you tell me, how is that not enough?

So let's now take a look at the combatives syllabus in detail so we can add some flesh to them bones. We'll take each part of the syllabus in turn, looking at what's involved in it in terms of training. We'll also look at examples of specific techniques and training practices, the stuff that is going to provide the results you are looking for.

CHAPTER 5: PRIMARY STRIKING TECHNIQUES

You may be wondering why I split the striking techniques into primary and secondary categories. Well, I did that because not all strikes are created equally. Some are more useful than others. The most useful strikes, the primary strikes, deserve a bit more attention given to them since they will likely be the most used. Remember we talked about the headhunting mentality? Well the primary strikes are designed precisely for that purpose.

Of course it is desirable to be competent and proficient in all the striking techniques. You never know when you might have to use any of them. But experience tells us that we are more likely to need techniques that allow us to deliver headshots. When it comes to fighting, the low line techniques are not used as much (low line techniques tend to be used when high line targets such as the head are unavailable). You need to train for the most likely situations. Of course you need to train for *all* situations, but devote most of your time and energy to the stuff you will use the most.

Palm Strike

The palm strike should probably be the first strike you teach a new student. It's always the first one that I teach for the simple reason that it is the most useful and it allows me as a teacher to impart important principles that will underscore everything else in the syllabus. The palm strike represents a basic formula that can be used to work out all the other strikes in terms of power generation and body mechanics, along with concepts like forward pressure, use of aggression, indexing (see Appendix F), targeting etc. It also introduces the student to basic training practices like the use of repetitive drilling, application of technique through dynamic pad drills and also live drills with resisting opponents. It in effect offers a blueprint for the training to come.

So the goal of teaching the palm strike is to teach the student to hit hard with accuracy (and good technique) under varying circumstances. Don't be tempted to rush this part of the training because essentially you are building a base on which to build the rest of the students training. The more solid that base is the better it will be for the student (and for you as the teacher because you won't have to keep going back to fix things that should have been learned already).

With the palm strike you should be going for maximum impact to your opponents head area. Targeting the skull is better than targeting the face, for the simple reason that it is easier to knock someone out by hitting them on the head. It shakes the brain more. The strike itself should not be done with an exaggerated follow through as many teach it, but with a bounce effect. In other words, the strike should be allowed to bounce of the target. The recoil of the strike will allow you to do this, although it will take a while for most new students to get the proper feel for this so they don't pull back too soon and lose the impact of the strike.

In the drills section of this book I will provide you with sample drills to train this strike, along with all the other techniques in the syllabus.

Hammer Fist

The hammer fist strikes should be self-explanatory. Use them for off-line striking and downward striking when an opponent is bent over (such as when they go for a leg tackle). Again, proper body mechanics and power generation should be emphasized, along with suitable pad drills.

Many people don't emphasis correct technique when doing the hammer fist strike. For the side hammer fist for instance, many practitioners simply swing the arm like a baseball bat in the direction of the target. A better and more efficient way of doing this strike off-line is to do so in a snapping motion, utilizing full body motion. So rather than swing the whole arm, you allow the forearm to extend out at the end of the motion, snapping the fist into the target, which will give a greater impact and allow for more control.

The downward hammer fist is very similar. The hips are used to create a whipping motion with the body which culminates with the downward strike. So it's not just a matter using the arm like a club. You are also bringing your whole body into play, creating energy for the strike. The initial movement is very similar to the double-hip concept if you are familiar with that. You throw the hip out first before quickly whipping it round again, which causes the rest of the body, including the striking arm, to come back around with it. This is where the power comes from.

All these strikes require correct body mechanics to be done properly. These mechanics must be thoroughly explained and demonstrated to students first, before allowing them to run through the motions at a slow pace first, before finally quickening up and adding in explosiveness.

Another thing to add here is the positioning of the thumb on the striking hand. The thumb is rested on top of the fingers rather than wrapped over the fingers in the traditional fist position. This allows for a better and safer striking surface. With the thumb in this position there is less chance of damaging the little finger, which tends take a lot of impact when the hand is kept in a normal fist position. With thumb on top, the flesh of the hand takes most of the impact.

Elbow Strikes

Elbow strikes are one of my favorite strikes because they are so versatile and powerful. Done right they can inflict a lot of damage on an attacker. In the main I teach them as close-in techniques, either for striking when in close or for striking to create space in which to follow up on. The mechanics are the same as the other strikes, with the hips creating momentum for a full body strike (that is, with your full body weight behind the strike).

In close the elbows can be used in a downward slashing manner. I always tell people to pretend they have a razor blade on their elbow and they are trying to slash their opponents face with it. Not nice, but the imagery helps get the movement right. Also keep the hand open when doing this kind of elbow strike. Keeping the hand open instead of closed produces less tension in the arm, allowing for a faster strike.

The straight elbow is used to create space when an aggressor has closed in on you and can be aimed at either the head or chest. Proper body mechanics are vital here, since you won't have the space to move forward. The only way to get enough power into the strike is to use good body mechanics. The strike is used to drive the opponent back, creating space for follow up palm strikes, or even escape.

Elbows are also very useful for striking anyone who happens to be at your back. One way to do this is to thrust your striking arm straight out in front of you and then snap it back so the elbow connects with your opponents head. Another way is to simply swing the elbow around to connect with your opponent. The latter motion is better for targeting the body, especially if you have been grabbed or been put in a choke. I teach women to go nuts with these elbows when they have been grabbed from behind, to just keep hitting until their attacker lets go.

The elbow strike can be utilized in a number of ways. Once a student gets familiar with it they should be able to adapt it to whatever situation they are in.

Powerslaps

Powerslaps are almost exclusively used for pre-emptive striking. They are not much good for in-fight situations when your attacker is hyped and adrenalized. Powerslaps need to be used before your aggressor gets to that adrenalized stage. They mostly rely on the element of surprise, so you need to introduce your students to the concept of pre-emptive striking before you teach these strikes, as well as the legal and moral aspects of hitting someone first.

Physically speaking the powerslap can be done from a neutral position with arms down or from a fence position with arms up. I suggest practicing the strike from both positions. The same body mechanics apply here, whipping the hips around for maximum effect.

I have created a video tutorial that goes into great detail on these powerslaps, as well as a number of other open hand strikes. If you sign up at my Combative Mind blog you can get this hour long video tutorial for free. In it I cover the mechanics of the strikes, how to set them up and what drills to do to practice them.

Short Range Punching

I have included short range punching in this syllabus as well. Even though most self defense/combatives syllabi emphasize the use of open hand strikes (less damage to hands etc.) some people still like to use punches. Also, despite your best intentions to use open hand strikes, when under pressure, many people naturally revert to punching, so it isn't a bad idea to teach punching methods alongside the open hand stuff.

In the main, these short range punches are used for pre-emptive striking from some kind of fence position, but they can also be used for follow-up striking. The type of punching I teach is done in a cycling manner, chopping down on the target. Think of using a claw hammer to hit someone with repeatedly. It's that kind of motion.

As an aside, it can be a good idea to get new students to punch the pads for a while with bare knuckles. Invariably they will end up with sore hands. This is a good way to show them how the hands can be damaged through punching, especially if they are striking something as hard as the human head. Doing this will reinforce in their minds the advantages of using open hand strikes instead of closed fists.

CHAPTER 6: SECONDARY STRIKING TECHNIQUES

As I've already said, some strikes tend to be more useful than others. The secondary strikes that follow here are only classed as such, not because they are not effective if done correctly and used at the right time (they are), but because they are slightly less reliable than the primary strikes. They are also a bit harder to pull off correctly. They can still be useful though, as you are about to find out.

Knee Strikes

Knee strikes are a bit over-rated when it comes to using them for self defense, mainly because they are hard to land well enough to cause any real pain or damage. What usually happens is the target area (groin for instance) is missed altogether and some other less vulnerable part of the body is hit. Or the target is hit but with the top of the thigh instead of the hard bone of the kneecap. The higher up you try to strike the more this tends to happen. So it is best to keep knee strikes for low-down targets, such as the attacker's head when they are down on the ground in an upright position. Striking at such a low level will insure the kneecap hits first and not the thigh. So knee strikes are more of a finishing move.

Having said that I know people who use the knee strike as one of their primary weapons, and who like to clinch an opponent before firing in multiple knee strikes to the body and the head if available as well. It's down to the individual at the end of the day. If a person can make something work for them, all well and good. No one can say they are doing wrong if it works for them.

This may be a good time to point out that everyone will have their own particular thing that they do that only seems to work for them and no one else. We are all human after all, and therefore all different in our skills and abilities. There are people out there who can get away with using high kicks in a street fight. Others who can quickly throw someone to the ground before they even realize what's happening. These are individual abilities that we each have and this must be allowed for when teaching students. If a student is able to make a normally less than ideal technique work, then let them do so. But only if they *do* make it work, mind.

Kicks

I'm sure you've heard it said that you shouldn't use kicks in a street fight, or more specifically, you must never kick above the waist in a street fight. This is basically good advice. You need to be fast to pull off a head kick. And even if you are fast enough to do it, it's still a risky move for obvious reasons.

That isn't to say high kicks don't work. They do. Of course they do. It's just that very few people could pull them off successfully without losing balance, losing their footing or recover quickly enough to follow up if need be. This makes kicking to the head in a street fight a risky proposition.

So the consensus seems to be that kicks should be kept below the waist, to avoid the pitfalls mentioned above, and in most cases, this usually means kicking to the legs of your attacker.

Low kicks are less risky to do so you have a greater chance of pulling them of successfully. This isn't to say you can't kick to the body. You can of course, and I've done so in the past a few times, but they have never been finishing moves.

I tend to use kicks to the body as warning shots only.

Attacking the torso in a fight is not really recommended anyway. The torso is quite padded on most people and can take a lot of impact, unlike the head. In a fight, when an attacker is adrenalized, it would be hard to kick the body to any real effect because your attacker probably wouldn't feel it enough to stop them. This is reason enough not to target the body.

Kicks to the body should be considered warning shots only. I used to use front kicks to the body quite a lot when I was bouncing. A good push kick to the gut of your aggressor can often be enough to make them think twice about attacking you. More often than not they will develop "sticky feet" as they are unable to press forward due to the adrenaline rush your kick just gave them. Back this up with a bit of verbal and you have a useful way of keeping someone at a distance or persuading them not to take things any further.

I've always been fond of kicking to the groin as well. When in close I have often used a very quick front snap kick to my attacker's groin. It's not a finishing move, but it gets enough of a reaction that you can press forward with shots to the head.

A more powerful groin kick is to go right up the middle, so to speak. You kick right in between your opponents legs using your instep or ankle to deliver a full power kick. It's very possible to end a fight using this technique, but it's also possible that your attacker will carry right on attacking as if they hadn't been hit. Groin kicks don't always work. But then nothing works all of the time. That isn't a reason not to practice this kick with your students. It can still prove very useful.

Kicks to an attacker's legs will obviously have a greater effect than a kick to the body. It is easier to cause hurt and damage to the legs, not to mention upsetting the balance. This makes them a better proposition as far as targeting goes. They are also effective when upper body targets are unavailable because you can then "chop" at the legs until another target opens up. That's if the leg kicks don't finish things first.

The obvious leg kick is the Thai kick to the outside of the thigh. This is the kick that is taught in most classes. It's an effective kick if landed properly and you get enough power behind it, especially if you catch the other person of guard.

I know of one instance where a guy got his leg broke from one of these kicks. I also know of other instances where the kick has had little effect. Like any other technique, it depends on who is doing it and on the person receiving it.

For maximum power you can slide across your opponent's center line, winding yourself up before releasing the kick. If you connect in this way, there is a high chance it will drop your opponent, especially if you connect with the shin. But that's only if you have the space to take such a step.

Throwing the kick from a static position without any step will generate less power but may still be enough to off balance an attacker long enough to make an escape.

To me, that's how leg kicks can be most useful, to distract the other person long enough so you can escape the situation. And obviously, if you really do need to follow up on it, the opportunity has now been created to do so.

Also bear in mind that this kick will not have the same effect on everyone. Say you're up against someone who trains in MMA (a likely scenario these days). This person would be well conditioned against such kicks and it's doubtful it would drop them.

If you are close in (as you often would be in a confrontation) it can be near impossible to pull of the thigh kick due to a lack of space. In this case, a lead leg kick to the inside of the thigh is an option, but it's doubtful such a kick would have much impact and it would need to be followed up immediately with something a bit more substantial, like a palm strike to the head.

A better option at this distance would be to target even lower down, namely the inside of the shin. This is done with the rear leg and is highly effective, mainly because it can completely break your opponents balance. Like every other technique, good body mechanic must still be emphasized when teaching this.

CHAPTER 7: FURTHER POINTS ON STRIKING

It should go without saying that you should find ways to drill these striking techniques from every angle possible, and to find as many applications for them as possible also. When you are having your students drilling your striking techniques make sure to have them work as efficiently and as effectively as possible. Always have them keep in mind the context in which the techniques are designed to be used. This will keep your students focused and stop them from straying into La La land and doing silly drills that have nothing to do with anything.

You also have the option here of adding in your own techniques. The ones I included in the syllabus represent the bare minimum that a person would need to defend themselves under most circumstances. There are other strikes that you can work on if you wish, like axe-hands, chops to the neck and throat etc. But in my experience these techniques are quite dubious in their usefulness. They are quite low percentage and would be fairly difficult if not impossible to pull off against a moving target. You can use any strike you want against an attacker if they are standing still with their arms by their sides, but moving? That's a different story and could likely end in disaster as you realize that lethal chop to the neck you've been practicing for so long isn't quite as useful as you first thought.

So my advice here is to stick to basic strikes with lots and lots of repeated practice and drilling. What you want in a syllabus are fundamental techniques that are easy to learn and flexible enough to adapt to any circumstances.

An important point to put across to students also is the need to use a full range of movement when they are doing the techniques, even if that movement seems somewhat exaggerated at first. The reason this is so important is because in a real situation something called stress compression occurs, where movements become shortened under pressure. If a student is already doing short movements in training then those same movements will become even shorter under stress, which will make the technique a lot less powerful and nowhere near as effective as it should be. To allow for this stress compression a student's movements must be kept at the full range of motion. This means drawing right back to full stretch when doing a palm strike, for instance.

Once your students get a good handle on the techniques you can then start to combine certain strikes together. This is not done in the usual sense of putting together combinations. There is no point in doing these set combination techniques because you won't be able to pull them off in that exact sequence. It is better to teach people to be able to transition from one strike to another at will and have the target dictate the strike to be used. You do this by holding the pads in a certain way. The angle and position of the pad will dictate the strike to be used. So if the pad is held at head height a student would use a palm strike. If the pad is lower and angled up then the student would use a downward palm strike. If the pad is turned over completely then a hammer-fist would be used. Any lower and kicks and knees come into play. The student should keep striking with whatever technique until the pad holder changes the angle of the pad, and then a different strike would be used. This is a much more natural and better way of practicing combinations and transitioning from one strike to another.

The whole time that these techniques are being practiced you should be constantly emphasizing the need for focused aggression, making sure that students give one hundred percent all the time. What they do in training will be carried over into real life. If they only give fifty percent in training they will end up giving the same or less in a real situation, so the need for one hundred percent commitment must be underscored at all times.

CHAPTER 8: EXTREME CLOSE QUARTERS TECHNIQUES

When we talk about extreme close quarters (ECQ) we are really talking about grappling/clinching distance. In other words, your attacker is right in on you, able to grab you, bite you or claw you. Working at this range your first priority should be to create space by driving your attacker back in some way, giving you room to strike.

Remember that the general philosophy here is still one of hunting your attackers head. The best and cleanest way to put someone down is to knock them out, and the best way to do that is to hit them on the head to affect a ballistic knockout (one achieved through striking). At such close range, getting a good range of motion to affect a good strike can be difficult, which is why you must first set the strike up or make room for it. There are a few good techniques that you can use to achieve this.

The first technique is the elbow strike. When an attacker is in so close you will most likely have your hands up in front of you as you try to keep them back. It's a natural instinct to do this, so the elbow strike at this distance should be taught from this high guard position. There is no room to move forward, since your attacker has closed in all the space, so body mechanics must be relied upon to get a decent amount of power into the shot.

Have the student stand in front of the pad (focus or Thai pad, or even a kick shield if you are working chest shots) then get them to place their hands on the pad to simulate having the hands on their attacker. Then have them do the strike from there. Because they can't move forward they will struggle at first to get any power into the shot. To get power they must generate torque with the hips, using the whole body to generate enough energy for the shot.

Like I say, this can be difficult at first, but with a little practice it gets easier. Eventually most students should be able to get power into the shot, which can either be aimed at the head or the chest, depending on the size of the attacker and the preference of the student doing the technique.

Once a student has become competent in using this ECQ elbow strike they can then begin to transition into palm strikes as a follow up, having now created the space to enable them to do so.

Another way to create space is through gouging and/or head-butting. These techniques are fairly self-explanatory. For gouging simply use the thumbs to gouge an attacker's eyes, pushing their head back to create space before switching to palm strikes. Same with head butts. Keep head-butting until the attacker steps back and then switch to palm striking.

Gouging is particularly useful for women. If you happen to be teaching a women's self defense class then lots of gouging is recommended, followed up with palm striking. This is easier and more natural for most women than using the elbow strike.

Chokes and spinal manipulation techniques can also be quite useful at this distance which is why I like to teach these as well. With the chokes you have to teach students how to transition into them, which usually means getting a chest to back position. This can be achieved by simply spinning the attacker around a bit whilst moving to their back, then applying the choke (the sleeper hold is most effective here). Pushing on the attackers elbow will enable you to spin your attacker around. Make sure you show students how this leverage works before teaching the choke.

The spinal manipulation comes into play in much the same manner, but instead of applying a choke as you move chest to back, you apply pressure to the attacker's lower spine, with the other hand preferably over their face, pushing back on the septum to force the head back. It is very easy to take someone down to the floor in this way.

Of course there are lots of different takedown techniques that you can do from here, but few if any are much good in real situations. With throws, they can be difficult to get, and if you do manage to get them, what will happen is, your attacker will hold on to you as they fall, pulling you down to the floor with them, which isn't really where you want to be. You want to be on your feet, not on the floor, where things get messy and much more difficult to manage. So I wouldn't really recommend you teach throws and take downs. They aren't really worth your time, especially for students who just want to know basic techniques to help them out in a scrape. Most of them won't have the time to learn complicated throws and take downs. If you have an on-going class, then you could maybe bring such techniques into the class once in a while, but that is up to you. Just remember fundamentals first, specialist stuff later.

Here's an article I wrote on my blog about the pitfalls of closing distance with an attacker. I suggest you read it for further insight.

CHAPTER 9: GROUND FIGHTING TECHNIQUES

Learning to defend from the ground should be another key component of any good combatives syllabus. It is okay to say that the ground is the last place you want to end up in a fight, but the fact is sometimes you do end up on the ground, and when that happens you need to know what to do. So once your students have gotten a good grasp of the stand-up elements of the syllabus, you can move them on to learning to fight on and from the ground.

One of the first things I like to teach is how to defend from the ground when you've been put there by your attacker or attackers. That is to say that you are on the ground and your attacker is on his feet still. If you don't do something to defend yourself you are going to get stomped.

There are a few different techniques that I have seen that are designed to fend off an attacker from the ground position, but the one I find the most useful consists of basically kicking out like crazy with the legs to prevent your attacker closing in on you. If they are close enough you can round kick their leg just before you try to get up. I suggest practicing these kicks from the ground on a pad, making sure to really turn the hips and body into the kick.

Get back to your feet facing your attacker. Never turn your back to them as you get up. You might also want to guard the head as you get up in case you are attacked again. From there you can go forward into your attacker or you can back away. You can do this drill with one student on the floor and one or more attacking.

The next scenario is when an attacker is actually on top of you in some way. If the attacker is in your guard then most of the time you can simply kick them of off you, creating distance so you can get back to your feet.

Another technique I teach for this scenario is the head wrench technique. If an attacker is raining blows on you then you must first guard your head from the blows. From there, reach up and pull your attacker down towards you, closing down their space and preventing them from hitting you any further. From this position you can hold the head and elbow strike or you can go straight into the technique I just mentioned. Keep one hand on the back of the head and with your other hand grab your attackers chin and twist their head away from you, while at the same time rolling them of you, using your whole body as you roll. You should end up on top of your attacker or in a side mount position where you can finish them from and get back to your feet.

I don't suggest you teach conventional grappling techniques, for the simple reason that most of them are based around submission techniques. You can teach some basic positional techniques, but forget about arm-bars and the like. Your main priority should be to show students how to get back to their feet as quickly as possible. Further down the line, if you want to teach grappling, then that's up to you, but just be sure to put it in context. When on the ground you are susceptible to third party attacks, as well as biting, gouging, knives and everything else that isn't allowed in UFC and grappling competitions. So make sure to explain the risks that exist when you are on the ground.

CHAPTER 10: STANDING DEFENSIVE STRATEGIES

Another thing you will want to roll out pretty quickly in a student's training is how to defend against attacks. One of the first things I always teach in this regard is how to defend against a barrage of blows to the head. There is no exact science to this and no one technique that works best. Under the kind of pressure that exists when an attacker suddenly launches themselves at you, it can be hard to know how you will react until come the time. However there are some basic strategies that will apply to most of these situations.

The main tactic that is usually taught in these situations is to cover the head and then lunge forward into your attacker with your own counter attack, be that striking back or simply closing down the space by grabbing on to your attacker in a clinching fashion.

The only problem I have encountered when it comes to this strategy is that once you cover your head to guard against the attack it can be difficult to take action after that. There is a tendency to just want to cover up and leave it at that, almost like a turtle that doesn't want to come out of its shell to face the danger. The problem is if you don't your attacker will continue unabated until you are down.

A slightly more proactive method to defend against such attacks is to simply keep the arms out in front of you in a "fend" position rather than covering up. From a mental point of view this makes you feel like you have more control over what is happening, instead of being at the mercy of your attacker. With your arms out, head tucked and shoulders hunched you will be a harder target to hit. From there you can go forward into the attack, striking back as you go. I've found this strategy to work quite well.

Once the arms go up to fend against the attack, a good strategy is to lunge forward so your hands end up in your attackers face, temporarily blinding him and also pushing him off balance, giving you enough time to switch to striking. A good tip here is to not focus on the type of attack that is coming. If you know the guy is about hit you, forget about what kind of punch he is going to use. Straight punch or hook punch, it doesn't matter. Your response will be the same.

This is where many people go wrong when it comes to defending against frontal attacks. By focusing on the kind of attack that is coming you are putting yourself one step behind your attacker because you will be reacting to his punch, rather than focusing on your own counter attack. So if you know your aggressor is about to go for it, just be ready to launch forward into him, using your arms to disrupt the attack and your hands to cover his face and push back his head.

Expect these kinds of situations to be messy as well. Things are never going to go smoothly when you are being attacked. As long as you manage to get in a good counter attack somehow, it doesn't matter. You may even take a shot or two in the way in. Suck it up. It's better than getting hit repeatedly until you are unconscious. Make sure to emphasis all this to your students.

In the case of genuine ambush attack, where you don't see it coming, then assuming you are still standing, you can use the full cover initially until you get your bearings back. After that you revert back to the tactics we just discussed.

As an instructor you should go through all available options, testing along with your students what works and what doesn't. It is important to allow the students to experience for themselves the different ways of handling these situations. Don't just tell them something doesn't work, let them experience for themselves why something doesn't work. Engage them in the learning process.

In training these defensive tactics, have the attacker wear boxing gloves so they can attack with a fair bit of contact. Get the students used to getting hit and let them repeatedly experience how it feels to be attacked. If you want to up the contact a bit more (and why wouldn't you?) wear protective helmets.

Another important point to emphasis here is that, as I just mentioned, you are likely to get hit when under attack like that. Tell the students not to worry too much if a punch or two gets through before they can counter-attack. This is normal. You can't expect to be attacked by someone and not get hit. If you are fighting you are going to get hit. Drive that fact home to your students so they can mentally prepare themselves for it.

CHAPTER 11: SITUATIONAL CONTROL TECHNIQUES

Learning to control your personal space is another vitally important skill for students of self defense to learn. I usually make references to this right from the beginning, but because I first teach the stuff that is going to get them out of trouble when the shit hits the fan, situational control is often left for a while, until students get a handle on basic strikes and defenses first.

I'm not going to go into the finer details of situational control here. As an instructor you should already be familiar with situational control, fence/guard positions etc. If you need more detail on this then read the appropriate chapter in my other book, *Self Defense Tips Everyone Should Know*.

The thing that I try to stress with fence/guard positions is that they should be as natural as possible for the person doing them, while still maintaining a good semblance of control. There are different ways to control your space, so allow students to find the one that suits them the best.

Suffice to say, controlling your space is as much about bringing out your confidence and asserting yourself as it is about physically controlling someone. I always like to make students aware of this as they practice situational control. To a large degree this is where most students draw their increased sense of confidence from, by knowing they have the power to take control of a situation if they have too.

To drill these positions, I simply have one person play the role of aggressor and have them try to encroach upon the space of another student, the defender. The defender must keep their aggressor back and prevent them from getting too close. For added realism the aggressor can raise their voice and use lots of bad language to simulate a real encounter. This has the added benefit of getting the student defender used to such aggressive behavior.

You can also have students learn to strike from these guard positions. I'll go over a couple of drills in the drills section later.

CHAPTER 12: MULTIPLE ATTACKER DEFENSES

With multiple attacker scenarios I usually start off with defenses against two attackers first, building up from there. There are different ways to approach these drills, depending on what you want to focus on with your students. If your focus is on pre-emptive striking then you simply have two pad holders stand in front of a student so that student can practice striking the pads. You can also have one or both pad holders use verbal for added realism. Also vary the positions of the pad holders.

If your focus is on situational control then you would have one of the pad holders try to get to the defenders flank while his mate does all the talking. The focus of the drill would be on maintaining situational control and not allowing the flanker to get into a position where they can strike you from the side.

If your focus is on defense then you would simply have one or both pad holders attack the defender, at different times or at the same time.

You can play around with these drills and come up with different scenarios and different aspects to focus on.

With a whole crowd of attackers things change a bit. The focus then becomes about the defender covering and moving and then escaping as soon as possible. Again, there are a number of drills you can do to practice against multiple attackers. I'll cover them in the relevant section of the book.

CHAPTER 13: WEAPON DEFENSES

Personally, I don't devote too much time to weapon defenses, but that's just me. I feel it is more important to devote time to the stuff we have just went over in the syllabus than to endless knife and gun defenses. Most of the principles and techniques we've already discussed will apply to weapon defense anyway. Contrary to what many people say about defending against weapons, it isn't much different than defending against an unarmed attacker. The focus is still on headhunting and taking out the central governor.

Before you begin with any of the physical stuff you should broach the subject of awareness when it comes to weapons, which can prove to be more important than any physical defense technique. At the end of the day, if you are not aware of the possibility of a weapon in a situation, or if you are not trained enough to look for one, no defense will do you much good, for you won't even see it coming. See Appendix G for more on knife awareness.

When it comes to actual defenses against weapons, the simpler they are the better. For blunt weapons focus on closing distance to prevent the weapon being swung, then the usual rules apply from there.

For edged weapons, it isn't much different. If you have to defend against a knife then focus on controlling the knife arm and also attacking the head. Again, the same rules apply. Not much changes just because your attacker has a knife. You still have to try and take them out. It's just a lot more dangerous when there is a knife involved.

Try to refrain from doing any of those martial arts type techniques. They are too complicated and will undoubtedly get most people killed who try to use them. Simple is best. Experiment with different things with your students and make sure they know just what they are up against when knifes are involved.

As I said, your focus should be on training awareness first and wherever possible engaging an assailant on first sight of the knife. Too much knife defense is focused on defending once the knife is out and in action. It is better to focus on taking the other guy out before he has even had a chance to brandish his weapon. It's all about getting in as early as possible. I'll cover some drills for this later.

So that's a basic combatives syllabus that you can work off if you wish. Any syllabus worth its salt should cover what has been listed here. As an instructor, you should know every single detail of your syllabus inside out. You should know every nuance of the techniques and principals involved and you should have the ability to teach it all in the simplest terms possible. Bring your own experience into the mix as well. If you've had experience in certain aspects of self defense then use that experience to add detail and credibility to what you are teaching.

You should always be working to improve what you do. Keep looking for different ways of doing things. Find new drills to do. Find a different way to explain something. Keep progressing. Keep moving forward. You want to provide the best possible level of training to your students. Do that and you will build a good reputation for yourself and people will want to train with you.

SECTION 4| TRAINING PRACTICES AND GUIDELINES

In this section we are going to be looking at some general training practices and guidelines that will help you maintain the integrity of what you do and also help you to provide the best possible experience for your students. These practices will insure your students get the most out of their training and of course, that they get those all-important results.

CHAPTER 14: THE ISSUE OF FITNESS

Fitness is certainly important in self defense, and the more you have of it the bigger advantage you are going to have over a less fit opponent. Fitness and conditioning however are things that should really be done in your own time. When students come to me I don't put them through grueling fitness routines before we start with the self defense stuff. To me that's a waste of time and it's not what the student is usually paying you for. They are paying you to show them how to protect themselves, not to win the next Crossfit games.

As a self defense instructor, your efforts should be put entirely into helping students get better at self defense. This means only a perfunctory and light warm-up before the training starts. I typically spend no more than five minutes on this. Just some light exercises and dynamic stretching to warm the muscles and get the blood circulating.

I believe it is important also that students get used to going from cold. You shouldn't need to be warmed up in order to fight. You won't get the chance to warm up outside, so why do so in training?

Having said all that, if you really want to focus more on "combative conditioning" as it is known, then what kind of training should you be focusing on?

Endurance type training should be mostly avoided, for the simple reason that fighting (real fighting, not sport fighting) isn't really about endurance, nor fighting for long periods of time. That's okay if you are fighting in the cage or in the ring, where endurance is obviously important, but not on the street. In the main, most street fights are over and done with very quickly, usually in a matter of seconds. It would make sense then to train for that kind of time frame. This means you would have to do short and intensive bouts of exercise, also known as interval training.

These bouts can last up to about thirty seconds at most, but in that thirty seconds you must give it your all, no holding back. As an instructor you could have your students attack the heavy bag for short bursts, repeating the bouts several times with only a very short break in between. This way you would be working on the anaerobic fitness as well working on aggression and power striking. To make the drill harder, have someone hold the student back so they really have to work to even hit the bag. This will drain them even more.

That's just a one example of the type of fitness training you should be doing for self defense purposes. If you look around online you can find many other drills that will work your anaerobic fitness and general conditioning. I'm not going to waste space by detailing them all here. Do your own research.

Like I said, you shouldn't really be concerning yourself with fitness training if you are a self defense instructor. If you want to do that stuff then put on a separate class.

And with that out of the way, let's move on to the real meat of self defense training...

CHAPTER 15: TECHNICAL LOCK

Robert Greene, in his excellent and must read book, *Mastery* talks about the concept of "technical lock" in the following paragraph:

"In many fields we can see and diagnose the same mental disease, which we shall call technical lock. What this means is the following: in order to learn a subject or skill, particularly one that is complex, we must immerse ourselves in many details, techniques, and procedures that are standard for solving problems. If we are not careful, however, we become locked into seeing every problem in the same way, using the same techniques and strategies that became so imprinted in us. It is always simpler to follow such a route. In the process we lose sight of the bigger picture, the purpose of what we are doing, how each problem we face is different and requires a different approach. We adopt a kind of tunnel vision."

This concept of technical lock obviously applies very strongly to self defense training, and I'll explain why.

Training For Results

Self defense and combatives training is, or should be, predicated on the notion of extreme practicality. It's the type of training that is meant for the real world and real physical altercations. The training has to therefore be as realistic as possible, while still retaining an element of safety for its practitioners.

Your approach to combatives training should be ruthless in

nature, training only what is practical, efficient and effective; and forgetting about anything that is impractical, too complicated to pull off under pressure or anything that is just plain silly and unworkable in a street context.

In short, combatives training needs to be about *results,* as we have already said. Yes, there are many side benefits to training, but the biggest reason for doing it should be to affect real results which are reflected in your improved ability to manage violent confrontation.

To be even more concise: what you do must work, or at least have a high chance of working (remember...no guarantees).

So when it comes to combatives training, your overall goal-- your main focus--should be on doing stuff that works, stuff that produces real measurable or observable results. That should be your driving force, your raison d'être, and it should be at the forefront of your mind at all times.

Trouble is though, sometimes we forget that this is our main purpose, that this is all that matters or otherwise what's the point of training at all. We lose sight of the bigger picture and our focus becomes myopic. We begin to concentrate too much on the little details and the finer points, sometimes to the point of obsession.

Or we turn into collectors, collecting techniques and entire styles and systems in order to satisfy some urge that we have, an urge that makes us want more and more, that makes us feel like there is always something better somewhere else, that what we have isn't enough, or what we have is inferior or lacking in some imaginary way.

You can see this type of behavior on display throughout the traditional martial arts. It's rife with technique collectors. I used to be one myself until I wised up. You just don't need ten different shoulder throws for self defense. Spending your time collecting one technique after another makes you a collector. It doesn't make you someone who trains for self defense.

Obsessing over the finer points of a technique is also very common practice, often in SD circles as much as in martial arts. It's human nature to get lost in the minutiae of things. It's one of the gifts we have as human beings, but like all such gifts it can have its downside as well.

I'm not saying that the details of a particular technique should be overlooked. On the contrary, I believe it's important to know a technique inside out, and to look at it from all angles over time.

But, if you are going to zoom in on things, make sure you remember to zoom out again.

Everything you do has to be set in context first. Putting a technique into proper context first will save you a lot of time down the road. There is no point in obsessing over the details of a technique that isn't going to bloody work anyway! Yet I see people doing this all the time. Why spend your time on something that isn't going to work under pressure?

I'll give you an example: wrist locks. These techniques are still widely practiced by traditional and non-traditional practitioners alike. I myself have spent countless hours over the years in Jujitsu practice, practicing and debating the finer points of wristlocks like they really mattered, which they don't in self defense terms.

And yes you could possibly make one of these techniques work in the right circumstances. Hell, you can make anything work in the right circumstances. But when are the circumstances ever right?! It makes no sense to spend time on such low percentage techniques, never mind debate their finer points.

Yet people do though. And why? Because they have lost sight of the reason why they are training. Fair enough, if that is what you want to do-- if self defense is not your main goal. But if self defense is your main goal, then there is no excuse for entertaining these kinds of techniques.

Getting Lost In The Details

Even if you have been careful to put everything in context, and you've made sure the overall technique has a high chance of working under pressure, and that it makes sense in terms of efficiency and tactical application, you can still manage to get lost in the minutiae again.

When your focus is so narrow, you end up spending inordinate amounts of time on small details, details that maybe don't matter as much as you think in the grand scheme of things. Like I say, look closely and examine the details, but remember to pull back and see the bigger picture again.

Whatever kind of details you are looking at, they should always be put in context to see how they fit into the bigger picture. Certain details can sometimes seem monumentally important when you look at them, but add a bit of distance and put those same details into perspective and they tend not to seem that important after all.

Becoming mired in details can also make your training seem stale and unsatisfying. It's like you are stuck inside a bubble with nowhere to go, nothing to do but wallow in the minutiae that floats all around you like plankton in the sea. Wallowing in anything for too long can make it stale (just ask the dead baby in my bathtub...starting to smell up there). The only solution is to burst the bubble and take a good look around you again. Take in some fresh air and bask in the glory of the bigger picture for a while before subjecting yourself to that bubble again.

Having a bigger picture outlook will help keep you on track in your training. It's the results that matter, not how you get those results.

So what if you don't move a certain way when you strike. Are you getting good results from your strike? Would spending so much time trying to move a slightly different way really give you better results? Is it worth your time? These are questions you should ask yourself when you find yourself getting caught up in the details. Asking such questions will help you see the bigger picture again and help you put things into their proper perspective.

Despite the hard man image of most martial arts and self protection practitioners, most of us are just geeks who love to obsess over and discuss every little tiny detail. Having a passion for something can do that to you. It's nice to be a geek sometimes, but other times you have to lock the geek in the cupboard (because he's a geek and he deserves it) and allow the cold, hard realist to take a look at things for a while, just to make sure the geek hasn't transformed the landscape into a complete fantasy land.

Just be aware of technical lock. If you zoom in, zoom back out again. Give yourself a reality check and remember why you are training. This you must communicate to your students if you intend to teach.

CHAPTER 16: TECHNIQUE DEVELOPMENT

As I've already stated, when teaching self defense you want to start of teaching basic strikes that will get a student out of trouble quickly should they find themselves under attack in some way. Techniques need to be simple and based upon, for the most part, gross motor skills. They should also be based around the Time/Space/Effect principle. For a technique such as a strike to be completely effective it must adhere to this three-part principle:

Time: The technique must be able to be performed in the quickest time possible by someone of average ability. This means that techniques which contain many different components and movements are definitely out. A technique like a palm strike is simple, easy to do and can be executed very quickly with no time to prepare. You just shoot it out and that's it. The more complicated the technique the more time you will need to execute it, and that is time you are giving to your attacker. Most fights are so fast paced that you just won't get the chance to pull off anything fancy or complicated anyway.

Space: You must go on the premise that you have very little space in which to man oeuvre. Techniques which require a lot of space to do are not suitable here. Likewise if you have to step forward to make the technique work. You should be able to go from exactly where you are, without having to step or wind up first. Again, a simple strike like a palm strike can be done in the minimum of space.

Effect: How effective is the technique you are teaching? Will it have the desired outcome of knocking out or knocking down an attacker? Why teach something that isn't going to have that effect? Any technique taught for use in these deep-shit situations should be geared towards inflicting maximum impact on an attacker.

Anything less is pointless and could prove dangerous to the defender.

When you apply this particular principle to a technique you will find that quite a lot of the techniques which are taught as self defense simply don't stand up to scrutiny in this way. The clipping hammer fist, for instance, which is a downward hammer fist to the face. This is a technique which is often taught in self defense classes (even though I've never seen nor heard of anyone using to it to any great effect) and one which seems to adhere to the first two principles of time and space, but which fails pretty miserably on the third principle of effect. It's just not powerful enough nor effective enough to be using when you could be using something much more effective like a palm strike or even an elbow strike.

You'd do well to bear these principles in mind when you are deciding what to teach students, especially in the beginning phase of their training when what they need is straight to the point, effective techniques that are going to put someone down.

When you first begin to teach a technique, explain it fully and put it into context first of all. Demonstrate the technique several times at full power so students can get a good idea of what they are supposed to be doing. Then they can unconsciously form a mental template of the movements as they are supposed to be done. Then tell your students to hit the pads as hard they can and let them drill the technique until they begin to get used to the movements.

A lot of instructors insist upon slow movements in these beginning stages, which is fine to an extent. It *does* help to go slow for the first while, just to get the fundamental movements down, but it must also be remembered that these are explosive techniques that are being trained. Explosive movements must be trained explosively. There is no evidence to suggest that training such movements slowly helps in the learning process. There is plenty of evidence however, to suggest that fast movements are better and that training at full speed and power from the get go is more beneficial in the long run.

So by all means allow students to go slowly at first, but make sure they start doing the movements explosively pretty soon after getting a feel for them.

There is no point in getting overly technical at this stage either, for most of what you say will probably go over their heads. The student's need context first, they need to get a feel for the overall movements first before you go into detail on the finer points with them.

What you want to do is explain the kind of results they should be aiming for when doing the technique, such as hitting with full power and explosiveness. Give them a few pointers and explain to them the use of the hips, how to generate torque and how to put their whole body into the strike. After that, just let them work things out for themselves as you provide them with a bit of course correction now and again.

The body has its own inherent wisdom; the wisdom of the body that will take over and get you from A to B in the most efficient way possible if you let it. Guidance from an instructor is of course still needed, but it is vital to understand that each person has their own particular movement patterns. No two people will move in exactly the same way and you shouldn't try to get students to move like you, or in some other particular way. Let them move in a way that is natural to *them*. As long they end up achieving the same result, which is efficiently hitting with power and accuracy, then that's fine. This isn't like martial arts, where everyone has to move exactly like their instructor. Self defense is about results, not process. How you do a movement matters less than the effect you create with that movement.

Over time, with enough drilling and practice, most people get the hang of the movements and find their own way to make them effective, by generating power and explosiveness each time. Simply be there to guide them and help them become more efficient in their movements.

Don't stalk around your students like a dictator either. Help them stay relaxed. The more relaxed they are the better they will perform and the more fun they will have in what they are doing. Fun is important because it will help people learn quicker, so create a relaxed atmosphere and encourage students to have a laugh now and again. Just because something is deemed serious doesn't mean you can't have fun doing it (see Appendix B).

CHAPTER 17: DRILLING TECHNIQUES

It usually doesn't take very long for students to get the hang of the basic movements involved in the primary techniques of combatives, but learning the movements is only the beginning of the process. Movement by itself is useless. Technique by itself has no purpose. Everything must be put into its proper context, so the next logical step here is to start introducing the students to tactical applications, or how to use their techniques in action. How long you wait to do this is up to you. Personally I like to add this in to a student's very first lesson, so they have an immediate understanding of the context in which they are learning to operate within. A beginner may struggle with this or they may take to it easily. I find the latter to be the case with most people.

So what do we mean exactly when we talk about tactical application? Well there is nothing complicated about this. Applying a technique tactically simply means to use it within the kind of context it was meant for.

The problem with hitting pads is that it can turn into a kind of game, where the object is purely to hit the pad as hard as you can. In one sense this is fine, if you are just working on technique and power development, but at some point you have to step out of that context and into a slightly more realistic and most importantly, dynamic one.

In practice this means making your drills a bit more layered so they become more alive and less static. Once your students have gotten the feel for the fundamental techniques, you then need to allow them to feel what it is like to execute those techniques under different circumstances and in different ways. To do this you need to apply the concepts of layering and drilling down.

Drilling Down

Drilling down is an information technology term, and it basically means to focus in on something, to go beyond the superficial and explore the deeper aspects and applications.

Let's take the palm strike as an example of how to really delve into a technique and reveal its many layers and applications.

In a very basic sense we have a palm strike to the head. This is what most people see, just a very simple and basic strike that would not take too long to learn and get competent in. A person may learn the basics of this strike very quickly before proclaiming that they "know it" (as many do) and they will move on to something else, perhaps practicing the palm strike only occasionally or even not at all.

Having such a superficial grasp of a technique is like having a piece of steel before it is forged into a sword. Yes, that piece of steel could be used as a weapon, but it would have limited use, and it would be blunt and unwieldy. But as you begin to fold the steel, adding new layers to it, the original piece of steel starts to resemble something more like a sword. By the time the last layer of steel is folded in and the sword is polished and sharpened, that once lumpy piece of steel which was of limited use has now become a very deadly weapon that can be used to inflict surgical damage in any hand to hand situation.

Layering

You have to look at mastering a technique in the same way. You start with the basics and you get a good feel for the technique and how it should be used, then you begin to add in the layers, just like the sword smith folds in layers to the sword.

(Another way of looking at it is in painting terms. You start with a few broad strokes, gradually adding in details and layers as you go until finally you have a complete picture.)

Those layers will take the form of different drills that will work individual aspects of the technique, or they will help you practice some sort of tactical application, such as firing of the technique under different circumstances, like when you're back is against a wall, or when your hands are engaged doing something else, or when you are surprised or ambushed, or even when you are on the ground and your attacker is above you.

Pad drills are obviously the most effective means for students to practice these kinds of tactical applications. Pad drills will allow students to practice striking from positions that they will likely encounter in a real altercation, such as an aggressor trying to force his way into their space, or trying to grab them in some way. A student would then engage their hands in trying to control the pad holder, who would then flash the pad when ready, which would be the trainee's cue to immediately strike. That's just one example. There are many more.

Mick Coup does a lot of this kind of "layering" in his Core Combatives system, and he does it because he knows that this kind of deliberate practice will lead to true competence and mastery of a technique, more so than the set-piece padded assailant drills and pressure drills that many instructors rely on to get results (these kind of drills, although useful for exposing one to stress and raw aggression, are not very useful for developing technique or even tactical application of a technique. I'll expand on this shortly).

Layering in different drills and practice methods for students in this way, and then engaging them in continuous practice over a period of years (if possible), will insure they have the best chance of mastering a particular technique. And you would do this with all the techniques you teach, over time working your way through the system.

CHAPTER 18: PRESSURE DRILLS AND SCENARIOS

Pressure drills and scenario training are all the rage in reality self defense training. The padded suit was invented so trainees could practice fighting back full contact against a resisting opponent. While there are some benefits to doing these drills, they are not, as some proclaim, the be all and end all of self defense training.

Pressure drills and scenarios are just one aspect of self defense training as a whole. They shouldn't be afforded any more importance than any other part of your training. In fact, I'd say they are less important than pad work. You'll get better results with a student if you focus more on installing correct technique and application through pad drills than you will if you subject your students to endless pressure drills. After all, if a student can't hit properly, or doesn't know how to apply a particular technique, then why would putting them up against someone in a padded suit, or subjecting them to fatigue and stress drills, make them any better?

Know this: when you are under pressure your technique will degrade. Your movements will become shorter and your general technique will likely get quite sloppy. This phenomenon is known as stress compression. And it doesn't even take a huge amount of pressure for this to happen. A quick shot of adrenaline into the system of some students is enough to make them move like broken dolls.

It is for this reason that installing correct technique is so very important when teaching combatives. If you don't do this correctly your students will be useless and you won't be able to give them the results they desire and which they are paying you to get them.

The other thing about these pressure drills is that they rarely represent what they are supposed to represent, which is a real fight. Instead of two or more people trying to really hurt each other in the most vicious of ways, what you usually get is one guy in a padded suit doing a very sloppy attack that is lacking in many important respects (speed, power, technique) and another person (the student) throwing still fairly sloppy shots at the padded man's head while the padded man helpfully retreats from the counter-attack. I don't know about you, but that doesn't sound representative of a real fight to me. That's just a staged, low force encounter with a predictable outcome. Not the epitome of reality fighting that many proclaim these drills to be.

It may seem like I am completely denigrating the use of pressure drills. I'm not. Pressure drills of the type we are talking about here can be very useful if properly thought out and executed correctly. What I like about these drills is that they are a good way to see how someone *responds* under pressure. They also allow you to see just how well techniques have been installed into a student. If a student does a drill and completely messes up their strikes then you know it is time to go back to the pads and repetitive drilling of technique for that student. In that sense, pressure drills can be a useful test.

What they also test is a student's mettle, their resolve and will to overcome quite difficult, stressful and exhausting circumstances. You have to be careful here, of course. You are not setting out to break the trainee. You want to push them to their limits yes, but no further. If you push them further and they fail to act because things are too much for them to handle, then they will quickly lose confidence and feel like failures. That's not the kind of experience you are trying to install here. As much as possible you want to provide a positive experience for your students. This isn't to say you should make things easy for them. That would just negate the whole idea of a pressure test. Just make things hard enough and no more. Take them to the edge of their abilities so they can prevail if they give it their all.

As I've already said, you have to tread carefully with these drills. For one thing the danger of installing bad technique exists. There is a great tendency to pull strikes in these drills, mainly because of safety issues. No one wants to end up in a hospital, so strikes are often pulled, even with body armor on. This is why it is important that pad drills play a larger role in a student's training, because they can practice hitting with full power, without pulling any of their strikes. This should be the conditioned response. Too many pressure drills and not enough pad drills will inevitably result in a trainee being conditioned to pull strikes.

The other thing you have to be careful of as an instructor is not to instill a false sense of security in students. I'll talk about this in the next section of the book. For now, just know that if students get used to fighting padded men who barely fight back and who allow the student to prevail most of the time, then students can start to feel like they are better than they are, or that they are somehow invincible. I've seen this happen. You have to keep your students in check to prevent this from happening.

Example Pressure Drills

With pressure drills you would generally take whatever techniques you have been working on during a particular session and then formulate a drill around those techniques. So let's say you have been working on palm strikes. You might tire the student out first by putting them through a series of exercises, raising the heart rate and adrenaline levels to try to simulate how they would feel at the start of a real situation. Once fatigued, the student would then be surrounded by pad holders and the student would have to strike the pads using the palm strike they have been working on. Pad holders would be constantly moving around in all directions, forcing the student to track each target before striking. They would do this for a minute or so. To add more layers to this drill, you could have someone occasionally grab the student to hold them back, forcing them to break free before striking again, or you could hit them now and again with a pad or such like, just to distract them from their main goal of striking the pads.

One pressure drill I like to use is called the pad slap drill. The student will have a focus pad on each hand. They will also be fatigued beforehand. On the go signal someone will attack the student (attacker wears boxing gloves), forcing them to defend and strike back until the attacker has been subdued. Because the student is wearing focus pads, they can palm strike without doing any real harm to the attacking partner. Once the first attacker has been subdued, another attacker will take the student down to the ground, mounting them and striking them from this position. The student has to roll the attacker of and strike to finish before getting back to their feet. Once up they are attacked again in the same manner as the first attack. Once they have subdued this attacker they run to a prearranged point to simulate escaping and the drill is over.

If you have the proper gear then you can also enact force on force drills, where you put two students together and have them just go for it, all out fighting. I'll talk a little about these kinds of drills in the next chapter.

With scenarios you can set up certain situations, like being approached in a bar by an aggressor. The student must try to talk down the aggressor or escape the scene. If the aggressor persists then the student must strike pre-emptively or defend against whatever attack comes their way.

Use your imagination with these drills. Try to come up with scenarios that students will likely find themselves in for real. If you are teaching a student or students who work in a particular environment such as a hospital, then gear your scenarios and pressure drills towards this particular environment. Ask the student what kind of situations they have faced before (if any) and work from there, perhaps simulating past experiences to try to find better solutions to the problems that arose from them.

CHAPTER 19: SPARRING

Regular sparring is not something you will see practiced much in most self defense classes, mainly because most instructors don't see the point in it, as sparring is geared towards combat sport and not self defense. This is mainly true, but it doesn't mean sparring doesn't have its uses. I for one will always include it in my classes (on going classes and private lessons anyway, not so much in short courses or one off seminars).

There is an obvious difference between gym sparring and a real fight, the main one being that gym sparring is symmetrical in nature, i.e. there is a back and forth exchange of techniques. Real fights tend to be a lot more asymmetrical, in that they usually involve one person or persons beating on the other without much come-back. Your response in a real fight should be asymmetrical; it should be one sided for that is how you will prevail.

All this is not to say that sparring doesn't have its uses however. One of the main benefits of sparring is that it teaches people how to take a hit and also give a hit, something which many people struggle with. In sparring you will experience what it feels like to hit another person, to wrestle them and grapple with them on the floor. You will also experience what it feels like to be hit and to be tossed around. These are things that are very important for students of self defense to experience and it is difficult to experience these things through pad drills and scenario/pressure drills.

Students who engage in live sparring will also get the chance to work on different attributes that are very useful to have in any situation, such as speed, timing, distance control and co-ordination. Sparring is excellent for developing all of these things.

I also find sparring to be very good for building a student's confidence levels, especially in students who have never really engaged in any kind of fighting before, in or out of the gym.

So what kind of sparring should you do? I always start off with boxing first, before gradually building up to kickboxing and MMA type sparring, where takedowns and grappling are allowed. You should break students into this gradually. Forcing them into full contact bouts is not the way to go, not if you don't want to completely kill their confidence. They will walk and you will never see them again. As far as contact goes, start with little or no contact until the student gets a good feel for the sparring itself and what they have to do. As the student gets more used to it and their skill levels increase then you can up the contact.

Full contact is obviously the pinnacle of this kind of sparring but very few people are willing to take things that far. If two students agree to go full contact then by all means allow it, but be very mindful of safety and be ready for someone getting knocked out.

In my experience, you don't need to go full contact. You can go in hard without trying to knock your opponent out and still learn a great deal.

Again, you can mix things up for the students by having them spar multiple opponents at once or by having them spar in very low light conditions, or even have them spar outside the gym. This keeps things interesting for them and also teaches them to operate under varying conditions.

If you are after a more realistic type of sparring then you have a couple of options at hand. The first is the blitz drill, where two people face each other and on the go signal immediately begin to attack each other for a duration of 3-5 seconds. Obviously boxing gloves should be worn here. Head guards are also an option if you are worried about safety.

Another great drill is one called the Live Drill, which was created by Mick Coup. With this drill you would put protective gear (helmets especially) on two students, but no gloves as they will be palm striking only. Both students are told to lie on the floor face down and away from each other. A partner will kneel over each student and you as the instructor will be on hand to give the go signal. Once the go signal is given both students will immediately get to their feet and run at each other where they will begin to palm strike each other to the head. After just three seconds they will be pulled apart by their partners and forced down to the floor once again. You can repeat two or three times.

The point of the drill is to introduce the shock and awe element of a real confrontation, without all the build-up and feeling out of each other that is present in normal sparring. Fights begin and end very suddenly and this drill is meant to reflect that with the very short time duration and the getting pulled away at the end.

SECTION 5| STUDENT DEVELOPMENT

As should be obvious to anyone that knows anything about self defense, it is not enough just to know the physical techniques. You also have to be able to put those techniques to good use. To do that requires certain attributes be in place, attributes that are not so much directly taught as developed over time.

The mental attributes that I am referring to are as follows: confidence, thinking for oneself, critical thinking and an overall "combative mindset", or a state of mind that will allow you to act and do what you have to do in a physical confrontation.

Like I say, these attributes are not directly taught the way most physical techniques are. These qualities are developed over time, through various forms of training. How well they are developed will depend not only on the quality of the training being given, but also on the students themselves. If you have a student who is severely lacking in confidence then that will obviously take longer to bring out and develop.

So let's take a look at some of these attributes in turn.

CHAPTER 20: CONFIDENCE

It should go without saying that confidence is one of the major keys to success in any endeavor, and that includes learning self defense. It doesn't matter how many techniques you know, or how good you are at doing them in training. If you don't have the confidence to use those techniques when you need too outside the gym in a real situation, then they aren't much good to you.

In part, confidence will develop naturally in students over time. The training itself can be very empowering for people. I have taught many students who when they first started, had very low levels of confidence. But after just a few weeks or months of training and doing the drills, their confidence levels would invariably rise, sometimes quite dramatically. If a student notices this rise in confidence, and if you as their teacher helpfully point it out to them from time to time, then this will bolster their confidence even more. Success will build on success.

What it will take to build this confidence will vary from student to student. If you have a woman for instance, who has never even hit a pad before, then just showing them a basic palm strike and having them hit the pad with it can be enough to trigger that rise in confidence.

With most of the male students I've taught, it is usually the more dynamic pad drills or live fight drills that trigger this rise in confidence. Most guys can hit a pad quite easily, so it's no big deal to them. It is only when they are able to apply their newly learned techniques in the context of a dynamic pad drill or against a live and resisting opponent that you really begin to see a dramatic increase in confidence. Students have often told me after doing live drills a number of times that they are really beginning to feel like they could handle themselves in a real confrontation.

Such self-belief is critical to success in self defense training. At some point a student must begin to feel like they can use their training under real circumstances. They must develop that confidence in their abilities.

As an instructor you should insure that this is a gradual process. Throwing a new student straight into a live drill against an opponent who is trying to batter their head in is not a good idea. You will only damage their confidence in this way. If the student fails and takes a beating during the drill they will walk away feeling inadequate and like they just can't handle the pressure of a real fight. If you want to retain students, make sure they do not feel this way, at least not until they are ready to deal with failure.

You need to break students in slowly to these drills, gradually upping the pressure the more competent the student becomes. Doing it this way will insure a steady increase in confidence in the student.

On the flip side, it is equally important to prevent a student's success spilling over into over-confidence. If this happens you have to reign them in for their own good.

I've witnessed some students who after a year or more of training begin to think they can take on anybody and win. This can be a dangerous state of mind, so you need to keep this arrogance in check. I'll cover this in more detail when we get to the chapter on knowing your limitations.

First I'd like to highlight three ways in which overconfidence can rear its ugly head. The following will not just apply to your students, but also to you as an instructor as well.

1. Overestimating your accuracy and depth of knowledge about a situation. There have been many studies done that have involved experts from across many fields and every study has found that these people tend to put great trust in their opinions and overestimate their expertise. Sound familiar? The martial arts/self protection worlds are full of people who over-value their own opinions and overstate the extent of their "expertise". Even if you don't teach, as a student of self defense/martial arts, you can still fall into the same trap.

A recent study of anesthesiologists found that one of the most frequent cognitive errors was premature closure of the initial diagnosis. Once the physician made a diagnosis, they did not revisit it. This led to errors.

The same thing can be observed in people who practice or teach self defense. They make up their mind about something initially (the effectiveness of a particular technique, for instance) and they stick to that initial evaluation/judgment. Their minds are made up and they stay that way, even in the face of evidence to the contrary.

We all make snap judgments about things all the time and invariably, we like to stick to those judgments because backtracking is too much hassle usually. You may get away with this most of the time, but what if you make a snap judgment in a self defense situation that turns out to be completely off the mark? Your initial judgment could land you in deep trouble.

It can be very difficult to keep an open mind. Snap judgments are reflexive by nature and they can save us time when we have act fast, but just be aware that they aren't always right.

In making critical decisions, you should always question your assumptions, biases, and knowledge. Everyone perceives a situation differently, and your interpretation can be wrong. Seek out a diversity of perspectives, find opinions different from your own, collect additional information, and use that information systematically.

2. Ignoring or not seeking disconfirming information. In the same study of physicians it was found that a second common bias was the failure to pay attention to or actively seek information to challenge the initial diagnosis.

People tend to overuse information and data that support their current beliefs. Again, sound familiar?

Those involved in self defense training will often use lots of information and data to support what they are currently teaching or training in, conveniently forgetting the mass of information and data that contradicts what they think they know.

Use critical thinking to question what is being taught and what you are doing in training, and do not let over-confidence get in the way of evaluating things thoroughly.

3. Over-assurance from past success. A good example of this would be an instructor who swears by a certain technique because they used it once in a fight and through luck or some other factor, had some measure of success with it. They then go on to preach the benefits of this technique despite the overwhelming evidence that says the technique is pretty much worthless and unworkable in a real fight.

Many of these assertions are based on the fact that the person's opponent was standing still with their arms by their sides when the technique was used. I once witnessed a guy on a social media site trying to argue that a boxing jab was a valid self defense technique, despite the fact that all the evidence points to the contrary. A jab against a moving opponent in a street fight? Really? Good luck with that. That's as low percentage as it gets. Yet the guy who was preaching the merits of this technique could not be swayed from his judgment and was obviously ignoring disconfirming information on this technique.

Over-confidence created by success can lead to poor decision making. It also breeds complacency and can blind one to important factors.

Overcoming Over-Confidence

So those are some of the dangers involved in being over-confident when it comes to self defense. Now let's look at some ways to control that over-confidence so you can get the best from your training:

1. Be honest with yourself. Carefully consider your abilities and begin to recognize your limits. I'll discuss this further in a later chapter.

2. Do not compare yourself with others. Over-confidence is a way of depreciating other people's talents, skills, and abilities. Just because someone knows their stuff doesn't mean you do as well. That person has likely paid their dues with years of serious practice. Give credit where credit is due and keep your arrogance and ego in check.

3. Test yourself cautiously. Don't try to get ahead of yourself in training. Get a thorough understanding of the basics before moving on to the more "cooler stuff", whatever that may be. Take one step at a time instead of trying to lunge forward at every opportunity.

4. Listen to criticism, especially constructive criticism from people you trust. This may be one of the most important steps in abating your overconfidence. This is not necessarily to say critics are always right, far from it. There is a possibility they are right, and because they see you from a different perspective, you should hear them out. Your instructor, if they are doing their job, should fulfil the role of critic.

5. Take time to look at your failures, or incidences when you did not achieve your own personal goals. Not only will this help you to shape a realistic measure of your ability, it will help you to focus on skills, strengths, or other qualities that you need to work on.

6. Keep fantasies separate from realities. What you see being done in the movies does not necessarily translate into real life. You will never be as good as Jason Bourne or any other movie character. Similarly, some people can do amazing things, but that doesn't mean you can as well. Be realistic.

Don't Kill Your Confidence Either

Over-confidence can obviously get you in trouble if you are not careful, but overcoming over-confidence can also result in a loss of confidence as well. So be aware that killing your confidence is not the key to overcoming over-confidence. Be modest, humble and open-minded; take nothing for granted and you should be fine.

CHAPTER 21: AUTONOMOUS THINKING

As an instructor, you do not want to turn your students into a bunch of automatons who do only as you say and try to copy your every single movement. The martial arts world is full of such people, slavishly following their "masters" and afraid to do anything on their own. Such sheep-like behavior is not conducive to good self defense skills. As much as possible, you want your students to use their head and think for themselves. If you are serious about developing good students then you must find ways to emphasis this point during the course of training.

One of the first ways this can be done is when students are first learning the fundamental techniques. When it comes to strikes for instance, the end result matters more than the actual process of getting there. So you may demonstrate a certain technique and you may show students the body mechanics involved and the correct way to make their movements as efficient as possible. You will also demonstrate the kind of results you expect them to achieve, which is usually striking with power and accuracy.

It is important for you to realize that everyone moves in their own way. We all do not move the same because we are all individuals. It would be a mistake to try and get everyone to move in the exact same way. So you explain and show the type of results you after when doing a particular technique, but you also explain that it is up to the individual student how they achieve those results. You would give the students a basic framework, a template to work from and then you let the student adapt that framework to suit them. As long as the student is clear on the results they are aiming for, the "wisdom of the body" will take care of the rest. This is one way to help a student think for themselves.

You can also help matters by introducing an element of

playfulness and discovery into the training. When doing defense work for instance, have students play around with different responses to common attacks. Show them the high percentage responses of course, but also allow the students to experiment with their own. By doing it this way, rather than dictating to students what they have to do, you are allowing them to see why something works and something else clearly doesn't. They are seeing for themselves instead of you just telling them and them taking your word for it.

Students should also be encouraged to ask questions at every stage. You as the instructor must create a training environment where such questions are encouraged, which means you being open to answering them, no matter how silly a question may seem to you. We learn by asking questions. Asking questions is also a good way for students to get things clear in their minds. Also from an instructor's perspective, such questions may get you to think in a different way about something or open up a different perspective on things.

When it comes to doing live drills against resisting opponents there is also scope for students to make their own decisions about what they should do and how they should respond to the drills. So give them the scope to make their own decisions and respond in whatever way they choose. Afterwards you can evaluate those decisions and responses and ask students why they chose them and could they have perhaps chosen different responses?

Another way to help students think for themselves is to ask them to create their own drills for certain techniques. You may get them to create a drill that will allow them to practice a certain strike, but with different variables of the students choosing added in. Or you may ask them to come up with a scenario that will allow them to practice their soft skills in some way.

The point here is that training should be an interactive process instead of a one way street. Encourage students to get involved in this process at all times. Have discussions, work things out between everyone. Come up with ideas as a group.

In the end, you want a student to feel like they are helping to create their own form of self defense training; training that is specifically geared towards their own needs and wants, and not just a bunch of techniques being read of a syllabus.

Good self defense skills rely not just on rote training and repetition of good technique, but also on the fact that a student has really come to *own* those same techniques. They have internalized them completely to the point where the techniques are now a part of them. This can only really be done if the student has really thought things through and come to their own deep understanding and conclusions about things, which in turn can only be done through autonomous thinking.

There are enough "sheeple" in the world. Try not to add more to the flock.

CHAPTER 22: CRITICAL THINKING

First and foremost, one of the major benefits of getting students to apply critical thinking to their training is that it forces them to engage with what they are doing. Too many people show up for training and run through a load of prescribed movements without even thinking about the validity of those movements. The techniques may be shit or they may not be. Either way, a student won't know until they properly evaluate those techniques-- unless they are happy to take the word of others as gospel, which if they are, is something you should try to get them away from.

So encourage students to look at the techniques from a skeptical standpoint instead of having them just accept that the techniques work. Have them run each technique through their critical thinking faculties and force the techniques to prove their worth. Break everything down for them and get them to ask lots of questions. Have them identify the component parts and identify also the principles on which they are based.

This is about accepting nothing as fact until you can prove it to be so.

Of course, even after you have judged a technique to be technically sound, that doesn't mean it is going to work in the context of a real violent altercation, so students need to pressure test the technique as much as they can.

Some techniques can seem so practical and useful on the training floor, but when pressure tested or used against a live, resisting opponent, fall flat and turn out to be worthless. Students need to be made aware of this fact.

Make them aware of the physics and combative principles involved in the techniques you are teaching and you will be giving them a formula which they can use to critically evaluate what they are doing. Either something works or it doesn't.

Always ask why. *Why does this work? Why doesn't this work? Why this way and not that way?*

Asking why will get you to the heart of the matter. It is your job to make your students aware of this.

CHAPTER 23: OVERTHINK—THE PROGRESS KILLER

One of the biggest barriers I often see students create for themselves in training is falling into the trap of *overthink*, or overthinking things too much. Overthinking it leads to analysis-paralysis, which can be an awkward thing to observe in someone. You just want to scream at them to stop thinking and get on with it because you know they will benefit more from action than from chronic inaction.

Ironically enough I fell into the same trap before I wrote this chapter, debating endlessly with myself on how I should write it, to the point where all I was doing was thinking and not writing. Overthinking is an easy trap to fall into and it can manifest itself in many situations.

Imagine you find yourself in a physical confrontation, for instance, with someone who wants a piece of you for whatever reason. You do your best to walk away or de-escalate the situation but the other guy is insistent, he's not backing down. Very quickly it becomes clear that you are being backed into a corner. Violence of some sort is imminent. Your gut is telling you it's time for action, but your mind is still debating the situation, scrabbling for another solution that instinctively you know just isn't there. Yet your mind persists, throwing up a boat load of what if's and then…the other guy's fist impacts your face and you go staggering back…and still your mind persists with the overthinking, causing you to freeze again…

I could go on, but you get the idea. Sometimes the only thing that is required in a situation is for you to take action, to just *do*.

There is a time for thinking and there is a time for action. The trouble starts when your thinking time takes over your action time.

And this doesn't just happen in physical altercations. It can happen in training as well. In fact, with some people, overthinking can become a major barrier to their progress. For some, the ability to just do and let things happen is squashed by their seemingly greater ability to think themselves into near paralysis. In extreme cases, physical movement becomes hampered to the point where the person can hardly move, and when they do manage to get going they are so stiff and awkward that the only thing their movements achieve is to push them further into their own thoughts because they "just can't get it right". It becomes a vicious cycle of overthinking, lack of action, followed by more overthinking and on and on. It's frustrating just to watch this process, never mind go through it first-hand.

Overthink And Implicit And Explicit Memory

Central to the problem of overthink and "choking", especially in the context of physical movement and athletic performance, are the concepts of implicit and explicit memory. Without going into great detail here implicit memory is anything that we learn to do through practice and that becomes automatic to us, such as riding a bike or throwing a punch or kick. Implicit memory is a type of long-term memory that doesn't require any kind of conscious thought. It also cannot be described in words alone. Try to explain using just words how to throw a punch and you will see what I mean.

Explicit memory is another kind of long term memory but one which is consciously formed and can also be described in words.

Implicit memory is strengthened through practice and repetition, enabling us to act on autopilot and achieve a state of flow. Choking occurs when you are constantly overthinking your performance (physical or otherwise) by engaging explicit memory, which then causes interference that leads to discombobulation and short circuits the fluidity of your performance.

That's the science behind choking and overthink. But what can we do about it?

Solutions To Overthinking And Choking

In a training context, the single best cure for overthinking is to just relax. Sometimes when I'm training a person they will stand in front of the pad ready to do a strike and the physical and mental tension they exhibit is palpable. They hesitate before they strike and when they do strike the technique is off and usually lacking in power.

You can't consciously think out an entire physical process. There are many parts to a technique and trying to consciously become aware of them all at once will only lead to analysis-paralysis. It's okay to consciously think about just one part of the process and to work at it until that one part becomes instinctive, but not the whole technique at once. Conscious thought will kill the fluidity of your movements. You just have to let the technique happen instead of trying to force it to happen. *Let* instead of trying. (Incidentally a good tip here is when you are doing pad work to have the pad holder flash the pads instead of just holding them out all the time. Staring at a pad that is constantly being held out only leads to overthinking and choking. Having the pad suddenly flash into view leads to a more instinctive reaction, and thus a more fluid one.)

Also check to see if the student is putting themselves under too much mental pressure to perform and get things right. I have observed students who allowed their fear of failure and perfectionist tendencies to inhibit their performance. A student must let these thoughts and anxieties go. Tell them to forget about consequences or how they will be perceived by others and just do. Get them to find their flow.

Students must remember that training is a process. They should be able to see some instant progress, but not expect to get it all and be able to remember it all without spending some time integrating the training. Mastery takes time.

Training is synergistic. So if a student only manages to get one small aspect of it better, this will positively impact other parts of their training. So get them to relax and stop overthinking things.

Finally, try to get your students to stay in the moment as much as possible when training. Personally speaking, I'm never more in the moment than when I am training. It's one of the reasons why I love training so much. Tell your students not to live in the past, thinking about what you as their instructor just asked them to do, but instead trust that they will integrate the previously suggested change along with the new suggestion. Trust that if they get the previous thing wrong, you will let them know, and will help them re-correct that one thing. A little trust and faith goes a long way in training, as in life.

The bottom line is this: Students should not try, but instead *let*.

CHAPTER 24: COMBATIVE MINDSET

The idea of the combative mindset has become something of a cliché in the self defense world these days. But just because it is a term that is freely thrown around, that doesn't make it any less important.

In a nutshell, a combative mindset is just about having the ability the do what needs to be done, come what may. Confidence obviously plays a major part in this, but so too does aggression, violent intent and the sheer will to overcome the odds and survive whatever happens (all backed up by proper training of course).

Again, this is not something which can be directly taught, but is something which is learned and developed over time. As an instructor, you must emphasize the importance of having a good combative mindset from the beginning, and continue to hammer it home in every session. Every time a student practices a technique remind them to do so with 100% focus and intent, giving each rep their all. It is not enough to perform techniques in any way half assed or this attitude will carry over into the street.

When doing drills, this attitude must also be maintained. Try to get the students to engage in the drills with full aggression and intent every time. One way to do this is to simply discount the reps that are lacking in these things. If you ask for fifty reps of a technique, then count only the reps that are done with full power and intent, and also good technique. Any reps that fall short in any of these areas are not counted. This is a good way to insure that students give each rep their all and it forges the habit of doing so. If they don't want to double or triple their rep count then they will soon learn to give each rep everything they've got.

In live drills against resisting opponents, the same attitude should be encouraged. A lot of time the student will not succeed in these drills unless they give it their all. This is especially true in pressure drills and stress inoculation drills, where fatigue is the biggest obstacle to overcome. Obstacles of this kind will only be overcome if the student gets mentally strong and refuses to give up no matter what. This is a mighty important attitude to have in a real situation. Sometimes it comes down to who can last the longest or who can take the most damage and still carry on.

In many ways the kind of attitude we are talking about here can be summed up in a physical sense through the use of forward pressure, or attacking the attacker. In training this means driving forward with strikes against the pads or charging forward into a padded assailant. It is through this type of training, alongside the bolstering of self-belief and the tapping of aggression, coupled with physical forward movement, that the required combative mindset will be cultivated.

If students do this kind of training for long enough and with enough encouragement from you as their instructor, eventually they will begin to feel that they can take on anyone, and that they could prevail against even the toughest of attackers.

In one sense, this kind of attitude is pretty essential if students are going to build up enough confidence so they will be able to use their skills against a real attacker. If they don't believe they will prevail against an attacker then it is unlikely that they will.

So this is why it is essential that the whole combative mindset thing be properly cultivated through good training practices. Students must be allowed to develop good technique that is then tested under pressure of some sort. This goes a long way towards building confidence in a student and allowing them to believe that they could really do it for real if they had to.

All that is well and good, but it is equally important that you know where to draw the line with this stuff. It's a bit like positive thinking. It's impossible to think positively all the time and it is wrong of people to make others believe that it is possible to think positively all the time.

In the same way, just believing that you can prevail against anyone is not enough to enable you to do so and it is wrong of any instructor who tries to convince students that they will win all the time, or that there techniques will work every time.

It is okay building up a student's confidence, but as an instructor you must be very careful not to induce a false sense of security in people. Students must not only know the limitations of the game they are playing (self defense in general) but also their own limitations when it comes to self defense.

Self defense training of itself is not full proof and neither should it be put across as such to naive students. I'm always pointing out the limitations of training to those I teach. It's my job as their instructor to reign them in when they start to get too flushed with success or when they become over confident.

It must always be emphasized to students that there are no guarantees when it comes to defending against violence. No defense or method of attack is full proof. What self defense training is all about is giving people a greater chance of prevailing in a physical altercation, not making them believe they are bullet proof, so to speak.

Trainees must know that they can and probably will get hit. That they will likely suffer some kind of damage to themselves and that there is a fair likelihood they will *lose*, especially if they are up against multiple attackers or facing someone who has a weapon.

In fact, this indoctrination of false confidence is at its height when people are training weapon defenses. I see many people who train knife defenses and disarm techniques and I know by looking at them that they really believe they will be able to pull of these moves for real if they had too.

Everything seems easy and possible in practice, but practice and the real thing are totally different animals, especially when weapons are involved.

It's a bit like a magician who practices magic tricks at home. The magician may get really good at the tricks they practice, but ask the same magician to do those tricks in the same flawless manner in front of a crowd of thousands of people or on TV with millions watching and they might struggle to even keep their hands steady enough, never mind pull of the trick in the same flawless way they did at home all those times.

So you see what I'm saying here? Self defense training obviously does work, but there are many more variables to consider that will greatly affect the outcome of any given situation and this must be impressed upon people if they are to have realistic expectations of themselves and their responses in a given situation. Expectations must be managed, in other words.

To have realistic expectations students must also have a good understanding of what their limitations are, and what the limitations of their training are. They must make an honest assessment of themselves, with your help, which means knowing what they are capable of and what they are not capable of. I may be able to handle myself fairly well for instance, but I certainly don't think I can deftly handle whoever comes along. That would just be folly on my part, not to mention dangerous.

Going back to the forward pressure mentality. How this is trained most often, is that students are taught to press forward as they attack, overwhelming their "attacker" with a barrage of strikes and constant forward pressure. In training this usually means doing so on a fairly compliant partner, pulling your strikes as they helpfully cover up and allow you to force them back. The next level up from this is doing the same thing but to a padded assailant, which allows for a bit more contact in your strikes.

Both training methods have merit in that they do teach the things we are talking about here, the forward pressure mentality etc. but these training methods also have their limitations and it is vital that these are recognized and acknowledged.

Its okay doing all that in the gym, but when you have to try and do it against someone the size of The Rock or some other man-mountain, do you think your tactics would still work then? Maybe, maybe not. The odds in this case would be fairly stacked against you. No amount of believing you can do it will make a difference, especially if that same man-mountain can also fight.

And that doesn't just apply to big guys, that also applies to guys who can really fight. Would your forward pressure mentality easily overwhelm someone who has fought in the cage many times? Or a boxer with a couple of hundred fights under their belt? Probably not!

Students need to be made aware of the fact that they are not and never will be Jason Bourne or have the skills that many of these action heroes have. That's the movies. This is real life we are talking here.

In order for students to really be aware of their limitations, they must first find out what they are. You can help them do this in training fairly easy.

One quick way to test their limitations is to have them spar someone who is more skilled than they are or who is much bigger and stronger than they are. This can be a very humbling experience, believe me. At the very least it will underline to students the fact that there are people out there who are better than them and who can easily beat them, even if under a particular rule set, as in sparring or grappling.

Another good way to test the limits of your students is through pressure testing. There are a number of different ways you can do this. You can have students try to defend against multiple attackers all coming at them at once for instance. Or they can fight one attacker after another, pushing themselves past the point of exhaustion so they can barely fight back anymore. Or you can have them try to defend against an attacker or attackers who have rubber knives and who are really trying to "kill" your student. This is another humbling experience.

I'm sure you can think of plenty of ways to find out what your students' limitations are. The point here is that you should try to be as honest as possible with them (as they should be with themselves) and make an objective and fair appraisal of their abilities.

At least if they know what their weaknesses are they can work on them. If they don't know what is realistically possible in a given situation they will at least not be going in blind or over confident, and thus they will be less likely to be surprised by anything, even if things don't go their way (which will be often!).

SECTION 6| EXAMPLE DRILLS

In this section of the book I want to give you some example training drills that you can use to get you started if you don't already have any drills in mind, or if you want to add more to the ones you already have. Drills are important in combatives. They are the lifeblood of training and they are what allow a student to move away from static practice towards more dynamic practice that is going to help them learn to use their techniques under a variety of different circumstances.

What follows is not an exhaustive list of every drill ever conceived. I've just provided a few example drills for each of the core aspects of combatives. Obviously it will be up to you as an instructor to source as many drills as you can, or even better, to come up with your own drills.

CHAPTER 25: STRIKING DRILLS

1. Engaged Start Drill

This is a great drill for moving student's away static practice to makes things a bit more dynamic and realistic. Very simply have one student as the striker, the other as the pad holder. The pad holder will try to invade the other student's personal space while that student keeps them back using the fence, thus engaging their hands. When ready the pad holder will suddenly flash the pad and the other student will immediately strike with a palm strike or punch.

Another variation on this drill is to have the pad holder try to wrestle the other student's arms down while the student resists. It's like arm grappling. At some point the pad is flashed and the student will strike as before. You can use follow up strikes here as well. It's up to you how you want to develop things.

Often in a confrontation our hands are occupied in some way or other, so this drill will teach students to strike immediately, even while their hands busy.

In terms of how to actually hold the pad, a better way than just raising it up is to actually thrust the pad out towards the striker, with the free hand supporting the back of the pad. Doing it this way will accomplish a few things at the same time. Firstly, having the free hand support the back of the pad will the pad to be held more firmly, thus offering more resistance and a better sense of impact for the striker. Secondly, when the pad is thrust towards the striker, all the striker can really see is the pad, the target in front of them. Holding the pad in the conventional way out to the side, the pad holder is in full view and becomes part of the overall target. It is more realistic to present the target out on its own, taking the holder out of the equation. I hope that makes sense. Lastly, outstretching both arms to present the target will also help the holder get used to having the arms out in front, which as we know is essential for defense and also indexing and striking. So the pad holder will get something out of the drills as well, not just the striker. Apply this method of holding the pads whenever possible.

2. Clearing Obstructions Drill

This drill is all about learning to clear target obstructions. The obstruction could be anything. For this example we will work on the premise that an opponent has covered their head (target area) with their arms. For the drill have one student as pad holder, the other as the striker. Once the striker hits the pads with two or three strikes the pad holder will place the free pad over the pad that is being struck to simulate a cover. The striker will use their free hand (index) to slap the arm away from the pad before continuing to strike, thus clearing the target for striking again.

Like I say, the obstruction can be anything. You could also have someone walk in front of the striker as they are hitting the pads, then the striker must shove the third party out of the striking path before continuing.

This is a great drill for teaching students to solve combative problems and not get flustered by such things.

3. Off-Line Striking Drill

As the name suggests, this drill will work on off-line striking, using the side hammer fist strike. A student will begin to palm strike the pads, either from a static or engaged start. After two or three strikes the pad holder will suddenly shift off-line to the left or right. Rather than turn around to face the pad again the striker will simply use a side hammer fist to continue to strike the pad before transitioning into palm strikes again.

This is an excellent drill for working the side hammer fist strike and for teaching a student to not get flustered when an opponent suddenly moves off-line. They learn to simply switch tactics rather than try to persist with the same tactic.

You can also work this drill with two pad holders, where a student must use the side hammer fist to strike the off-line pad holder. You can play around with different scenarios for this drill. Just use your imagination, but try to keep things as realistic as possible.

4. Create Space Drills

Here are a couple of drills for teaching students how to create space from an attacker so they can strike at full capacity again.

The first drill will use an elbow strike to create the space. Simply have a pad holder aggressively push forward into the strikers space while holding the pad out (one pad held out, the other hand behind the pad for support). The striker will raise their hands to control the space and then, without stepping in any way they will execute an elbow strike into the pad, driving the pad holder back to create space. From there they can follow up with palm strikes to finish.

Another way to do this is for the pad holder to suddenly flash the pad right in front of the strikers face. The striker will then use an eye gouge technique, grabbing the pad with both hands, pushing the thumbs into the pad as they would an attackers eyes and then pushing the pad away from them to create space. From there they can follow up with palm strikes. This is an especially good drill for women, who are generally more suited to gouging than elbowing.

5. Downward Hammer Fist Drill

This drill is fairly simple and will work the downward hammer fist strike. A pad holder will simply thrust a pad out towards the trainee so that it goes towards the trainee's midsection. The pad will be facing up so the trainee can execute a downward strike into the pad. The point of this drill is to simulate an attacker going in for a tackle or front shoot. The trainee must step back to create space and then execute the downward hammer fist strike.

6. Transitional Striking Drill

This drill is all about learning to transition from one strike to another as dictated by whatever target is available. It is about learning to put together combinations but not in the traditional sense of having a set pattern to follow. In this drill, the position and angle of the pad will dictate which strike is used. As an example, a trainee may begin with palm striking the pad as normal. The pad holder may then shift the pad down low, setting the pad to a forty-five degree angle, which will indicate to the striker that they must use a downward palm strike. From there the pad may be turned all the way over so it faces up, indicating to the striker that a downward hammer fist is to be used. After that the pad holder may go down on one knee and hold the pads out in front, facing down, indicating to the striker that a groin kick must be used. The pads may then change to be facing towards the striker, indicating a low knee strike should be used.

You get the idea here. The pad holder can transition from one target to the next as they please so the striker doesn't know what is coming next. In general the sequence should end with a finishing move on the ground.

Again you can mix this up by having two pad holders and executed in the manner of the basic live drill. In the basic live drill you would have a trainee in the middle of the floor with two pad holders either side. The trainee will start with eyes closed and then a selected pad holder will tap them on the shoulder with the pad, indicating the drill has started. The trainee will immediately begin to palm strike the pad until the other pad holder taps them on the shoulder (or cuffs the back of their head), at which point the trainee will turn around and start to strike until they are tapped again by the other pad holder and so forth. This goes on for thirty seconds.

The variation we talked about would be to introduce transitional strikes into the mix instead of just palm striking.

7. Multiple Target Acquisition Drill

The friend and foe drill as it is nick-named is done with multiple partners, and as the name suggests, pad holders will alternate between friend and foe as they please, forcing the trainee to use a bit of judgment.

Basically the drill goes like this: Multiple pad holders form a circle around a trainee (the more pad holders the better). It is the trainee's job to strike the pads with a single strike as they are near. So pad holders will move in and out with the pad held in front of them for the trainee to strike. If a pad holder behind the trainee hits the trainee on the back of the head with the pad, this signifies they are a foe and the trainee must spin round and strike them (the pad). If a pad holder taps the trainee on the shoulder, this signifies they are a friend so must try not to strike them. The whole time, any of the pad holders can latch on to the trainee and hold them back just as a friend might if they were trying to hold you back with good intentions. This will make it harder for the trainee to strike.

Amongst all the confusion, it can be hard to discern who is friend and who is foe, but that is exactly the point of the drill. Quite often in real situations, friends can get involved and hold you back. Without meaning too however, they are making it more difficult for you to deal with the real attackers.

What I like about this drill is that it gives you a sense of how chaotic and confusing such situations can be when there are multiple persons involved and not all of them real threats. After a while trainees may find themselves telling their "friends" to stay back and stay out of it so they can effectively deal with the real foes.

A minute or two is usually long enough for this drill but if you want to go longer then you can do so.

CHAPTER 26: DEFENSIVE DRILLS

In this chapter we will look at a few examples of defensive drills, where a student must defend against an incoming attack against single and multiple opponents. Again, this will not be an exhaustive list, but just a sample selection to get you started.

1. Cover And Strike Drill

This is a basic drill that is used to practice defending against an attacker who is making a frontal attack such as a punch to the head. To begin have one student put on a pair of boxing gloves and stand in front of the trainee. The attacking student will start by throwing slowed down punches to the trainee's head, both straight and hook punches. The trainee will then simply drop down into the covering position as shown in the photos. This is done by dropping down low, hunching the shoulders to make the head less of a target and keeping the arms outstretched in front of the face. Having the arms out in this manner will make it difficult for the attacker to cleanly land any strikes while also enabling the trainee to move forward using the hands to index, control and strike. As soon as the punch comes the trainee adopts this position. At this stage there will be no follow up. This is just about getting used to the initial defensive/offensive position. Once a trainee starts to get used to this position the attacks can be speeded up.

The next stage is for the trainee to practice moving forward into their attacker from the first previous position. The trainee will use their hands to push into the attackers face, disrupting the attack and creating space for follow up striking. A trainee can either simply push forward with the hands or use a piston-like motion as they move into their attacker, rather like a Sumo wrestler would do.

The final stage is for the trainee to strike their attacker while using forward pressure to keep them off-balance. Once a trainee gets used to all this the drill can be done at full speed. For safety precautions use protective helmets. That way both students can attack properly without having to do much pulling of strikes.

A trainee may also close distance with this method without wanting to create space, if it is their intention to grapple or clinch their attacker. I don't really recommend this because it isn't as effective as creating space and striking, but if you want your students to see the differences you can have them clinch instead, pointing out the disadvantages of such a tactic. Strikes are harder to do at close range. It can also get messy when you begin to grapple an attacker or try to choke them. It is cleaner and more effective to create space and use strikes to finish. But show your students both tactics and let them experience them for themselves.

2. Ambush Drills

These drills are very similar to the previous drill, only this time trainees will be forced to completely cover their head until they get orientated to what is going on. Either have a student close their eyes or make them have a conversation with someone first to keep them distracted, then have another student attack them from behind or from the side. The trainee will cover up immediately to minimize any further damage. Once orientated they will turn to face their attacker and go forward with the arms outstretched in the same position as in the previous drill, going on to strike their attacker.

For the next drill you will need two pad holders. The trainee will close their eyes as they are turned in a circle ten times until they start to feel dizzy. This simulates instability and disorientation similar to the effects of being sucker punched from behind.

From here the trainee is let go of as they try to clear their head and as the feeders attempt to close on them with the pads. The trainee will strive to respond as best they can with single impact strikes and priority positioning. If they fall over for any reason the drill should continue and they must now fend from the floor and strive to get up on their feet quickly.

3. Multiple Attacker Drills

The drill requires a minimum of 7 people and a maximum of 15 all wearing focus pads. The trainee defender will be in the middle of the group who will strive to keep them closed in from all directions.

The trainee's objective is too continuously move and cover their head so as to present as little target area as possible. The method used to do this is what is known as the wash your hair defense, or the crazy monkey defense. Simply have the trainee place both open hands on their head and raise their elbows and then move their arms and hands vigorously over their face, head and neck in order to protect this vital area from a continuous assault from the entire group who attempt to slap the trainee from all directions with the pads.

The idea is to keep damage and blows to their person to a bare minimum and the trainee's sole objective is to escape. Find a gap and blast through it verbalizing and striking out as they go.

This drill will quickly show students just how limited their options are in such a situation. Damage limitation is the key as they priorities their escape. This is the only sensible decision in such a scenario.

This next drill is called the cornered rat drill. For this drill a trainee will be placed into a corner and surrounded by a minimum of four gloved up partners so that they have no escape except to go through their aggressors.

On the go signal the trainee's aggressors will lay into them all at the same time with punches. Just like in the previous drill their objective will be to move and cover initially and then blast their way through their attackers so they can run to safety.

For a trainee, trying to strike their aggressors individually will not work here because they are all hitting the trainee at the same time. Doing so will only expose the trainee to head shots which will inevitably put them down or out.

Close and crash through is the best tactic in this situation.

CHAPTER 27: WEAPON DEFENSE DRILLS

In this chapter we will be looking at drills designed to help students learn to defend against weapons attacks, specifically against blunt and edged weapons. With any weapons defense the first priority should be on awareness of the weapon itself. The sooner you become aware of the weapon the better. It is much harder to defend against a weapon that is fully out and in use than it is to defend against one that hasn't yet been drawn or has only been partially drawn. The following few drills will therefore reflect this.

1. Blunt Weapon Defense

A blunt weapon can be anything from a baseball bat to a bottle to a brick that has just been picked up during a confrontation. Regardless of what type of blunt weapon is in use, the defense against them are basically the same.

To begin you can have your students work on their awareness of the weapon itself. In general, most blunt weapons are hard to conceal and unlike knifes they are generally out in full view from the beginning. So you can have students attack their opponent immediately upon noticing the weapon. You could for instance, have someone walk towards a trainee while brandishing a stick and before the person even reaches the trainee the trainee will rush forward to attack, subduing the other person before they even have a chance to swing the weapon.

If the weapon is out and being swung then have students practice closing the weapon down. Have them avoid being hit initially and then as quickly as possible they will rush forward and either strike the attacker hard in the head before they get a chance to swing the weapon again or a trainee may trap the weapon arm first before striking. Try both methods and see which works best.

2. Edged Weapon Defense

Awareness is even more important when it comes to knife defense. In general, the quicker you can determine the presence of a knife the better. Once a knife has been drawn and it is in play it becomes very difficult to defend against it without getting cut.

To begin you can have your trainee's learn to look out for any signs that a weapon is about to be drawn in a confrontation. So have someone conceal a knife on their person and approach the trainee. The trainee must then watch for any suspicious movements, such as the aggressor reaching around behind them or reaching into their pockets or inside jacket. Once this has been noticed the trainee will attack immediately by striking their aggressor in the head. Protective helmets should be worn for this so trainees can strike with impact.

Next, the trainee will try to get a visual lock on the knife. An aggressor may have the knife out but concealed in some way. Again, once the knife is seen the trainee will attack immediately.

The next stage is when the knife has been fully drawn. Again, once spotted the trainee will attack as quickly as possible by striking their attackers head. Secondary to that they will try to control the knife arm if possible.

Knife defense should be no more complicated than that. Forget about chasing the knife arm or trying to trap or lock the knife arm. By the time you do you will be cut to pieces.

You can also get students to practice similar kinds of drills from the ground. It's just the same only from a downed position or in a grappling situation with their opponent.

SECTION 7| EXPANDED TOPICS

In this section I have included a number of further chapters on different topics that are relevant to the main theme of this book, which is teaching self defense and combatives. I didn't include this information earlier in the book because it would have meant going off in a tangent somewhat and taking your focus away from what I was trying to put across. So what follows are several chapters that deal in-depth with some of the subjects and training practices that I have already mentioned in the book so far.

CHAPTER 28: LEARNING THROUGH DEEP PRACTICE

Have you heard of "deep practice"?

Deep practice is a term that was coined by Daniel Coyle in his ground-breaking book, *The Talent Code*

Deep practice will transform the way that you practice. If you train Combatives, applying deep practice methods to your training will make you better and more skilled in less time.

Deep practice is not achieved by merely turning up for practice and going through the motions.

Deep practice, although embodied by many different methods, has what Coyle calls "a tell-tale emotional flavor" which can be summed up in one word: "struggle".

Deep practice, also called deliberate practice, is the form of learning marked by:

1. The willingness to operate on the edge of your ability, aiming for targets that are just beyond your reach.

2. The embrace of attentive repetition.

This is the opposite of "shallow practice". Shallow practice is marked by a lack of intensity, vagueness of goal and/or the unwillingness to reach beyond your current abilities.

Shallow practice is indulged in when there is an aversion to making mistakes, which nearly always results in vastly slowed skill acquisition and learning.

As John Wooden, the American basketball coach says:

"Never mistake mere activity for accomplishment."

So deep practice is about finding your "sweet spot", the zone on the edge of your current ability where learning happens fastest. This zone is marked by the frequency of mistakes, and also by the recognition of those mistakes.

Making mistake after mistake can be trying, but make them you must if you wish to progress beyond your current abilities.

With that in mind, here are some tips that will bring about deep practice and put you in your sweet spot. As an instructor you can use these learning methods to further inform your teaching.

Tip#1: Differentiate Between Soft Skills And Hard Skills

One of the first steps towards building a skill is to sort out exactly what type of skill you are building. Every skill (not just Combatives) will fall into two categories:

Hard, high precision skills are skills which are performed as correctly and as efficiently as possible every single time. They are skills that have an ideal result and which you could imagine being performed by a reliable robot.

Hard skills are about repeatable precision. An example would be a right cross, or a leg sweep or an elbow strike. Any of the physical tricks and skills.

The goal here is to build a skill that functions like a Swiss swatch--reliable, exact and performed the same way every time, without fail.

To quote Coyle:

"Hard skills are all about ABC-- Always Be Consistent."

Soft, high flexibility skills on the other hand are those that have many paths to an ideal result.

Soft skills, such as awareness or verbal de-escalation are about being agile and interactive; about instantly recognizing patterns as they unfold and making smart, timely choices.

To quote Coyle again:

"Soft skills are about the three Rs: Reading, Recognizing and Responding."

Hard and soft skills use different structures of circuits in our brains so different methods of deep practice must be used to develop them.

Tip#2: Become A Watcher

Watch whatever skill you wish to perform, closely and with great intensity, over and over, until you build a high-definition blueprint of it in your mind. This method has been proven to increase your chances of picking up the skill in question quicker and more correctly.

When I wanted to learn how to throw a good pre-emptive right cross I looked to Geoff Thompson, whose short-range punching ability is second to none. I spent a lot of time studying video footage of Geoff doing that punch. I analyzed his every move. Then, when I eventually came to train with him, I got the chance to watch him do the punch right in front of me. Once again I studied his form, his movements. I took note of how relaxed he was when he threw the punch.

All this watching and studying really helped me build a good mental blue-print of what a good right cross should be. I then worked of that blue-print in my own practice of the punch, the result of which was (along with thousands of reps), I developed a killer right cross that could do the business whenever I needed it too.

If there is a particular technique you want to get good at, find someone else who has already mastered it and then study them intensively to see exactly how they do it, right down to the last detail.

Watch their performance over and over until you know every last movement, then try to do the same in your own practice. Even as you watch, try to feel what it must be like to move just like the person you are watching.

To make this technique more effective, watch videos of the person doing the technique you desire to get good at just before you practice and before you go to sleep. This will help imprint the blue-print deeper into your mind.

Tip#3: Be Willing To Feel Stupid

As I've already said, don't be afraid of making mistakes and the feelings of stupidity that comes along with them.

No matter how skilled you are, you should always be willing to improve and push the boundaries of what is possible. The only way to do that is to build new connections in the brain, which means reaching, failing and yes, feeling damn stupid.

I remember when I first started teaching to a class. I felt incredibly stupid standing there in front of all my fellow students, bumbling my way through some technique or other. I made many mistakes as well.

However, after a bit of time I began to feel less and less stupid when I was teaching, and I made less mistakes as well.

Even now I sometimes get those feelings of stupidity, especially when I make some kind of mistake.

But I also understand the process at work, the learning curve that I am on.

I know that if I keep at it, despite what I may be feeling, I'll keep improving.

So don't let feeling stupid scare you too much. The feelings lessen over time.

Tip#4: Be A Precision Engineer When It Comes To Building Hard Skills

To develop reliable hard skills you need to connect the right wires in your brain. That means working slow and being especially attuned to errors. You must work like a precision engineer, carefully building the structure of the skill.

Precision matters greatly early on when you are learning a new skill or technique because the first reps establish the pathways for the future. Neurologists call this the "sled on the snowy hill" phenomenon.

The first reps are like sled tracks on fresh snow. On subsequent tries, your sled will tend to follow those tracks.

Our brains are not very good at dismantling connections once made (hence bad habits) which is why it is so important to get the movements right in the beginning.

It is also important you pay close attention to errors and

mistakes and that you fix them as soon as possible to prevent bad connections forming (bad habits).

This kind of careful practice can seem boring, but believe me, time spent learning a new skill in this way is the most important investment you can make for the future.

Building the right pathways in your brain can save you a lot of trouble down the line.

Tip#5: Be A Daring Explorer When It Comes To Building Soft Skills

While hard skills are best put together with precision engineering, soft skills are built by playing and exploring inside of challenging and ever-changing environments.

By encountering and responding to different situations over and over, you are building a network of sensitive wiring that you need in order to read, recognize and react.

Take awareness, for example. You can't learn awareness skills the way you learn a punch. To learn awareness you must operate within an ever-changing environment and respond to many different situations before you can begin to recognize patterns of behavior and changes of environment ahead of time.

This kind of practice also demands that you coach yourself. When you work on a soft skill, be it awareness, verbal de-escalation or recognizing violence dynamics, ask yourself afterwards: What worked? What didn't? And why?

Tip#6: Ignore The Time

Deep practice is not measured in hours or minutes, but in the number of high quality reaches and reps you make--basically how many new connections you form in your brain.

Instead of saying you are going to train for half an hour or an hour, say to yourself that you will complete 100 reps of your right cross or 50 knee strikes each leg.

This will focus your practice much more. It becomes about doing high quality reps rather than just going till your time is up.

Tip#7: Chunk Every Thing Down

A really simple and effective way to learn any new skill is to break the movement down into smaller chunks, a process which is called "chunking" (don't know what it is about that word but it makes me think of throwing up!).

Chunking works because it accurately reflects the way our brains learn. Every skill is built out of smaller chunks.

To begin chunking, first ask yourself:

1. What is the smallest single element of this skill that I can master?

2. What other chunks link to that chunk?

Practice one chunk by itself until you have mastered it, then connect more chunks one by one until you have the complete movement.

Tip#8: Embrace Struggle

Most of us instinctively avoid struggle. It feels like failure. But it isn't.

Struggle is a biological necessity when it comes to developing your talents and skills.

The struggle and frustrations you feel at the edges of your abilities--that uncomfortable burn of almost but not quite getting there--is the sensation of constructing new neural connections, a process known as "desirable difficulty".

Your brain works just like your muscles: no pain, no gain!

Tip#9: Take Five Minutes A Day Over An Hour A Week

Training for five minutes a day is actually more beneficial than training for one hour a week.

The reason being is because our brains grow incrementally just a little each day, even when we sleep. Daily practice will nourish this process, whereas training once a week will force your brain into playing catch-up.

By training for short periods each day you are also exercising your self-discipline muscles and helping to build a new habit into yourself (which research suggests takes about thirty days).

Tip#10: Practice Alone

A recent study compared world class performers in music with top amateurs. The researchers found that both groups were almost the same in every practice variable except one: the world class performers spent *five times* as many hours practicing alone.

Practicing alone will build self-discipline. It is also the best way to seek out the sweet spot on the edge of your ability.

As the soccer coach Anson Dorrance has said:

"The vision of a champion is someone who is bent over, drenched in sweat, at the point of exhaustion, when no one else is watching."

Tip#11: Slow It Down

When we learn a new technique our instinct is to always do it with as much speed and power as we can muster, also known as the Hey! Look At Me! reflex.

Training this way, especially in the beginning, can lead to sloppiness however, which is why it is a good idea to slow your movements right down.

Super slow practice works like a magnifying glass: it lets you sense your errors more clearly so you can then correct them.

So it's not how fast you can do it, it's how slowly you can do it correctly.

Tip#12: Close Your Eyes

Closing your eyes while practicing is a quick way to nudge you to the edge of your ability.

Doing so will sweep away distractions and provide you with new feedback. It will help engrave the blue-print of a skill on your brain by making even a familiar task seem strange and fresh.

This also why sensitivity drills work so well.

CHAPTER 29: THE IMPORTANCE OF FUN IN TRAINING

"For every Way there's a way of following that Way that's fun"

Combatives (and reality self defense training in general) is a serious business.

Or at least, that's how it comes across. All that talk about violently smashing, pounding, gouging another human being, hurting them, often severely. Occasionally killing them. Talk of do or die, kill or be killed.

It's all very...well, *violent*.

But just because training is based around violence and counter-violence, doesn't mean we can't still have a bit of fun.

And fun is the one thing that many of us (myself included) are sometimes guilty of forgetting about. We forget to have fun.

Just because it's fun we're talking about, doesn't make it any less important, especially in training. Even more especially in your life.

Most people underestimate the importance of fun, as well as misunderstanding what fun is all about.

When we talk about fun, we are talking about enjoying and being excited by what we do, not necessarily mindless fun, or fun for the sake of it (like with two hookers in a Jacuzzi in Vegas kind of fun), but fun in striving to accomplish our goals, in working towards something important to us, important to our growth as individuals (some would argue that the experience of having two hookers in a Jacuzzi in Vegas is vital to ones growth as well...those people may have a point :-)).

The Definition Of Fun

Our definition of fun in this context comes from Mihaly Csikszentmihalyi's work on the psychological state called "flow." His concept of fun has many components to it, including the following:

- The activity matches challenges with ability.

- Focus on the task is required.

- Focus is possible because there are clear-cut goals and immediate feedback.

- The worries and frustrations of life do not intrude.

- There is a sense of control over actions.

- Self-consciousness is absent.

- The sense of self is stronger after the activity.

- The sense of time is altered.

Training can often be grueling and extremely uncomfortable on all levels, and if you were to ask someone after one of these hard sessions, what was your experience of it, they would likely reply, *"Fantastic, just not at the time."*

The implication here is that although the activity was not at every moment totally pleasurable, the overall experience was uplifting. Enriching even.

You may frequently experience pain, extreme fatigue, nagging injuries, or severe disappointment as a result of your training activities, but you go back to them because you find them rewarding overall.

This was a revelation to me when I first discovered this truth. It made doing the hard things easier. I knew the rewards and the positive emotions and changes that I would feel after doing the hard things would be worth the pain of doing them.

Process Over Outcome

This philosophy doesn't just apply to training, it also applies to any activity that you may find difficult in life, but which will yield the most growth for you. I'll give you an example from my own life.

A while ago I started making instructional videos. Making those videos, for me, was an often-times very uncomfortable process. I tend to communicate better in literally rather than verbally (though I'm working on it), so to stand in front of a camera and communicate my ideas in a clear and concise way was quite a stretch for me. The videos I have done so far are by no means perfect, but that's beside the point.

The point is the process. It was in the process of actually making those videos that I gained the most from, not in the actual finished products.

I know I'll get better at doing videos over time because I have faith in the creative process.

But the experience of making them is the real reward, providing me with an uplifting experience that transcends any initial discomfort.

The point I'm making here is that process goals in training are better than outcome based goals when it comes to enjoying what you do and having fun along the way.

Process Goals

Process goals in training include demonstrating competence, creatively expressing oneself, improving one's self-image, feeling the joy of skilled movement, testing one's ability (through pressure testing), and, perhaps most important, experiencing fun.

Fun is a major motivational factor for continued persistence in any activity.

One study has also shown that some people are better able to experience fun than others. This occurs when-as a result of genetics or training-they have better control of their mental energies and are better able to focus their attention on the tasks to be done; they are able to set process goals instead of only outcome goals; they have a higher level of self-confidence and learned optimism; and they are less distracted by physical discomfort.

These are the traits you will want to exhibit also if you wish to get the most from your training.

World class performers recognize the importance of fun in what they do. Look at any top performer and you will see that despite how hard they work, despite how challenged they are, despite how under pressure they often are, they still manage to enjoy what they do-- they still have fun! Probably more fun than someone who has less stress and strain in their life.

The closer to the edge you walk, the scarier it may be; but the more exciting it is and the more fun it is as well.

"When you have confidence, you can have a lot of fun, and when you have fun, you can do amazing things." Joe Namath

(Professional Football Player)

World class performers make having fun a priority. They also know that to have the most fun they have to push themselves and take risks.

However, you can only really push yourself and take risks if you are passionate about what you do, if you *enjoy* what you do.

The discomfort must be worth it to you in some way.

If you enjoy what you do then it is easy to have a laugh and joke during training. When you can do that, learning becomes easier and, you guessed it, more fun.

There is no doubt that we all take ourselves a little too seriously at times. What we should be doing is taking the training seriously and not ourselves. In this way, we will make the most progress and have the most fun.

We are only here for a short time, right? We might as well enjoy it while we can.

To quote from George Bernard Shaw:

"We don't stop playing because we grow old; we grow old because we stop playing."

We'd all do well to keep that in mind at all times.

CHAPTER 30: THREE THINGS THAT MIGHT BE MAKING YOUR TRAINING COUNTER-PRODUCTIVE

In training, as in life, we only have so much time to spend. The time we have at our disposal is not infinite, and this is especially true of our training time. We all lead pretty busy lives these days, so most of us have only so much time we can devote to training (although in saying that, we usually have more time to devote than we think, if we just spend less time doing other less important things, like indulging ourselves in digital media junk). It would make sense then, that your training time should be as productive as possible.

Unfortunately, many people who train in self defense waste a lot of time by indulging in counter-productive practices that don't really get them anywhere.

Here are a few examples of counter-productive training practices and how to avoid them.

1. Not Being Clear On Your Goals

Before you go training you need to remind yourself of why you are training in the first place. Just showing up and doing a bunch of random things, or worse, just going through the motions, isn't enough and such a practice will likely not help you advance in any significant way.

To counter this you need to have an overall goal in mind, a larger objective that will help keep you focused while you train. It could be something like: *I train because I want to be good at defending myself*, or *I train because I want to develop my confidence*.

Having larger goals like these will keep you focused and help you stick to a certain path. It will also enable you to dismiss or filter out anything that doesn't contribute to this larger goal.

When you don't have an overall purpose it is easy to get distracted and get pulled down the wrong paths.

"The rush of unexpected events, and the doubts and criticisms of those around you, are like a fierce wind at sea. It can come from any point of the compass, and there is no place to go to escape from it, no way to predict when and in what direction it will strike. To change direction with each gust of wind will only throw you out to sea. Good pilots do not waste time worrying about what they cannot control. They concentrate on themselves, the skill and steadiness of their hand, the course they have plotted, and their determination to reach port, come what may."

Robert Greene, *The 33 Strategies Of War.*

2. Trying To Do Too Much At Once

Multitasking, however productive it might sound simply isn't. As Leo Widrich explains in his article on the effects of multitasking on our brains:

"People who multitask a lot are in fact a lot worse at filtering irrelevant information and also perform significantly worse at switching between task, compared to single-taskers. Now most studies all point towards the fact that multitasking is very bad for us. We get less productive and skills like filtering out irrelevant information decline."

I see people trying to multitask all the time in the martial arts. You have people who think it a good idea to be training in two, three or four different arts or disciplines at once, rushing from one class to the next and delighting in telling anyone who will listen how many different things they are training in, as if this makes them super dedicated and better than those who choose to train in just one discipline.

When someone tells me they are training in multiple disciplines at once, I get suspicious and I just think to myself, *Why? Why this need to try and learn all this stuff at once?*

Aside from the fact that we live in a world where multitasking has become one of those corporate buzzwords that everyone thinks will help them be more productive (even though it doesn't), I also think that the idea of sticking to one discipline and mastering that before moving on to another is an alien concept to most people. We have lost in our society, the notion of mastery, of knowing a subject deeply and of having the patience, dedication and perseverance to do so.

(I baulk at people who brag about having black belts in several different arts. That denotes a trophy mentality and is just a step up from technique collecting. Besides, all that means is that you are a virtual beginner in the art you were training in. I have more respect for someone who has spent their time studying just one art. It shows dedication and an appreciation for mastery.)

We all want shortcuts, but in reality, there are no shortcuts to mastery. You have to work hard for years--that's the reality.

There's a lot to be said for attaining mastery in one discipline, as opposed to being a Jack of all trades and master of none.

Multitasking triggers certain reward systems in our brains that can make you feel like an heroic over-achiever, when in reality you are just heading for burnout, and burnout is never good.

3. Distracting Yourself With Junk Science And Research Porn

The martial arts and self defense fields are both riddled with junk science.

Junk science is faulty scientific data and analysis used to advance special interests and hidden agendas. Thus we have reams of theory and supposed supporting evidence on pressure points, chi, psychology, power generation etc. etc.

Some of this stuff is interesting no doubt, but most of it has no scientific basis, despite claims to the contrary from those spread these ideas around.

Your thoughts and ideas should be based on experiential evidence, not theory. This means that you base your training on your experiences on the training floor or in real life, not on academia.

Research porn is just like real porn: It feels like you're engaging in something worthwhile but in the end you realize you have just wasted hours of your time with nothing to show for it (quit the sniggering in the back there). It becomes like an addiction.

You can go too far into something, to the point where your efforts become pointless and the many details you are trawling through become just plain irrelevant.

A good example of research porn is studying criminal psychology in depth. Lots of people indulge in this, thinking that knowing what makes criminals tick will better help them defend against them. It won't. If some guy throws a punch in your direction, does it really matter what motivates him to do it? Of

Course not! All that matters is that he did. Your time would be better spent learning how to physically defend against that punch.

Likewise with all the social theory getting bandied about these days. Not only do we have reams of detailed information on self defense law, but we also have floods of information on psychology and sociology and criminology and physiology and biology and too many other -ology's to name.

There is nothing wrong with looking into these areas of study, but you can go too far with it, to the point where it just stops becoming useful and only serves to drag you into a state of technical lock.

That's the result of too much detailed research. Your training and your way of thinking becomes myopic and you lose sight of the bigger picture, of the reason why you are involved in self defense or martial arts in the first place.

Too much information can be counter-productive. When information no longer serves any practical value, it merely becomes academic and stops serving your cause. You cross the line between research and research porn.

Self defense should be as practical as it gets, given what it is needed for. It doesn't need to be cluttered with junk science and pointless research. To maintain the integrity of your self defense it should be kept as pure as possible, with no filler.

Instead of looking outside of yourself for answers all the time, in the form of endless research and other people's ideas, try looking inward the odd time and figure some stuff out for yourself.

You don't need much to be good at self defense, but you need to be good at using what you have.

So a more productive strategy would be to spend time deep

practicing the skills that you have already and working on yourself. Such a strategy involves work and lots of deliberate, focused practice. Maybe not as interesting at times as the shiny new ideas on your laptop screen or in the pages of a book, but such practice will improve your skills quicker and afford you a deeper understanding of what you are doing.

Then you would be truly advancing your cause.

CHAPTER 31: ERROR RECOVERY—TRAINING FOR FUCK-UPS IN A FIGHT

"By failing to prepare, you are preparing to fail."
— Benjamin Franklin

I've always said that there are no guarantees when it comes to self defense, but that isn't strictly true. One thing is guaranteed in self defense, and it's this:

You will almost always fail in some way.

This can't really be helped. Due to the often highly chaotic and unpredictable nature of violent altercations, it is very easy for things to go wrong-- and they almost always do.

No one, no matter how experienced, consistently performs like the Jason Bourne-type operators seen in Hollywood movies. If ever there is a time when fuck-ups cannot just happen, but are almost *guaranteed* to happen, it's when you are in a fight.

Obviously, the more experienced you are in fighting-- the more fights you've had-- the less chance you have of fucking up, but that doesn't mean external factors can't fuck things up for you.

There are so many variables to consider that you couldn't possibly hope to plan for, or control them all.

Shit is going to happen, that much is certain. Its how you deal with it that counts however.

So how do you deal with fucking up in a fight?

The answer is simple enough: The same way you deal with the fight in general-- you train.

If you know that errors can occur and unexpected things can

happen, then it makes sense to plan for these, by introducing errors and unexpected variables into your training also.

You train to fail, in other words. But more importantly, you also train to *recover from said failure and get back on course.*

Doing rep after perfect rep under ideal conditions all of the time is not training for reality. Of course any self-respecting practitioner will try to achieve perfection of technique, but equally, any self-respecting practitioner will also train for times when that technique will fail them, not necessarily because they did the technique wrong (although that can definitely happen), but because an attacker has made it difficult to do it properly, or because some other variable has come into play which thwarts a person's efforts at defending themselves-- like another attacker, or something on the floor that disrupts their balance.

I don't think I've ever been in a fight were something hasn't happened to make things difficult for me. More than once I've paid the price for my mistakes or my failure at the time to deal with the unexpected.

You learn from your mistakes however, and one of the ways you learn is to plan a bit better for when things do go wrong.

So how do you do this?

Disrupted Striking Training

One way is to do some disrupted striking practice. The way to do this is to have the partner holding the pads to suddenly move backwards or forwards as you throw your strike, to simulate a miss or an obstruction of some kind (which happens more often than people realize). Either way, you will fail to execute the strike properly. The important thing here is not that you fail, but that you immediately recover from the fail and launch into another strike, which will of course be on target this time.

Another way to do this is to have the partner holding the pad wear a boxing glove on the other hand. As you go to strike, the pad holder will punch you in the face, as if your attacker was quicker of the mark. Again, you will recover as quickly as possible and execute another on-target strike.

The pad holder should make things unpredictable in these drills by varying the timing of the fails, which will make things more realistic.

Other ways to include errors are: having another person suddenly slam into you as you go to strike (as will often happen, especially in crowded places like nightclubs); have someone throw something at you (again, can happen); or even simulate slipping and falling as you move to strike (which can obviously happen). Your imagination is the limit here.

You don't have to practice failure all the time. You certainly don't want to condition it. Just introduce it occasionally, practice recovering from it, enough to keep you on your toes.

Wrestling With An Attacker

Recovering from failure is about having the ability to flow from one thing to the next. Another good way to practice this is by simulating a real fight. You'll need protective equipment if you are going to include striking. If you don't have the equipment then you just practice grappling, which is often how fights end up anyway if you fail to put the other guy down with strikes. Really go for it with this and do so with plenty of aggressive intent. To make things more interesting, you can introduce the same type of variables as the ones in the disrupted striking drills. This kind of drill is excellent for teaching you to flow and how to recover from mistakes made.

Plan For Failure

Errors in performance are a fact. We all make them, even more so in high pressure, unpredictable situations like violent altercations.

Plan for them. Train for them. Learn how to recover from them. At least that way, when you make a mistake for real, even though you will still be surprised by it and it may still throw you, at least you will have a better chance of recovering from it and carrying on.

CHAPTER 32: INDEXING FOR BETTER, MORE ACCURATE STRIKING

Here, I'd like to discuss the concept of indexing, and how it relates to pre-emptive and follow-up striking.

What Is Indexing?

It is certainly not a new concept. In fact, you probably do it already to some degree. Watch a typical bar-room brawl and you will probably also see the participants index before they strike.

In simple terms, to index is to use your free hand (non-striking hand) to make some sort of contact with your attacker, usually very near where you are going to strike.

In essence, indexing gives you a visual and tactile point of reference that you can use to make a more accurate and effective strike, pre-emptive or otherwise.

Think for a moment just how difficult it can be to land a good solid shot on someone who is constantly in motion, who is agitated and changing distance all the time. Then think about how under pressure you are in a typical confrontation, how adrenalized you are, how scared you may be.

Add all those things together and you have a difficult job on your hands trying to land a good enough shot to take down your attacker.

This is the thing with pre-emptive striking. It is made out to be an easy thing to accomplish, knocking out an aggressor with a single shot.

It isn't however. It is actually quite difficult in most circumstances, due to the amount of different factors that have to be right for this to be achieved.

Here's Mick Coup on this, from his article on indexing for Black Belt Magazine:

"Hitting something requires a fair degree of proficiency to get any tool right on target with actual stopping power - just consider all the on-going calculations such as judging range to the target, gauging the orientation of the target to yourself, assessing your available 'reach' etc. - and this is only for a static shot! Start moving the target, just in one plane, and these calculations become more involved - now move it erratically in every plane and it becomes near-impossible - no wonder people miss!

Firing off a punch to the head, for example, relies on a visual point of reference before any of these conscious/subconscious calculations can even be attempted, and plenty can happen before the punch lands, requiring constant re-evaluation and adjustment - even in the split-second time-frame involved. Often the difference between a knockout or not is down to the target's instinctive shift away from the incoming blow to the head, this can be minuscule - not even a true 'flinch' as such but enough to negate the desired effect. Sometimes the head movement is dramatic - people just don't want to get hit I reckon! - making landing solid, finishing, blows hard using just visual reference, and this is an understatement as anyone knows who has tried it."

Verbal Tricks

After much re-evaluation, I've also come to the conclusion that the old trick of using some sort of distracting dialogue before delivering a pre-emptive strike will not work as well as some people advocate (and I'm as guilty as anyone here).

Asking a question before you strike has become like dogma in the self protection field. It's a tactic that has been advocated for many years by many well-known instructors, and because of this, it has been accepted at face value like a lot of other things.

Here's the thing about distracting dialogue though: It will only work if someone is still in a calm and reasonable state.

It will not work against someone who is highly aggressive, completely adrenalized and really determined to carry out their threat of ripping your head off your shoulders.

As anyone would know if they have ever faced a growling, highly aggressive person, nothing you say to them makes a difference to their state. Your words don't compute because they have gone beyond words. Their focus is only on carrying out their threat of hitting you.

So by bothering with this distraction tactic you are only wasting your time, and in actual fact, you are only distracting *yourself*, not them, which kind of defeats the point, doesn't it?

This tactic was used primarily by quick-fisted bouncers in the days when you could hit anyone indiscriminately and get away with it (not so now). So if a punter refused to leave when asked they were immediately lined up, distracted and then knocked out. They never saw it coming usually.

The victim was not adrenalized, therefore still able to think and process thoughts, which left them open to distraction tactics. They never stood a chance, in other words.

The point here is this: If the other person is still open to a two way dialogue, why not carry that on and attempt to de-escalate rather than knock them out?

So if violence is truly your last resort you will carry on with de-escalation until it becomes obvious it isn't working. Your aggressor has shifted into a highly aggressive state. Now you are justified in striking them.

You may still need a distraction before striking though, and this is where indexing comes in.

(By the way, distracting dialogue can still work in certain instances, but you must be comfortable and confident in your use of such tactics for them to work, and like I said, oftentimes, they will still not work anyway. Using verbal in this way is more a spur of the moment thing rather than a pre-thought out strategy.)

Indexing For Distraction

Indexing is a better option when it comes to distracting a would-be attacker. It requires less thought to simply reach out and put a hand in your opponents face than it does to start thinking about and firing of verbal that may not work.

The tactic works the same from neutral or fence positions. You simply use your lead hand and place it on the side of your aggressors head/face, preferably allowing your thumb to cover one of his eyes. Once in place, you then strike with the other hand.

We are not grabbing here, we are simply placing the hand in position, allowing the fingers to "stick" to your opponents head/face and no more.

The beauty about this movement is that it is completely non-telegraphic. Your opponent will not see it coming. Even in practice, if you ask your training partner to prevent you from touching his face, they won't be able too. They are never fast enough.

And remember, all we need is a second to strike. By the time your opponent reaches to take your hand away you will have already hit him.

This to me is a much better distraction tactic than using verbal tricks. It's more reliable and it improves our position in other ways.

Indexing For Better Striking

The simple act of reaching out with the lead hand will turn your body nicely, cocking your rear hand for a full power strike that will hopefully do its job and put the other guy down.

Striking just from a fence position you don't get the same torque behind the strike. There is also a tendency to over-obsess about not telegraphing the strike. In reality, at the close range we are talking about, telegraphing is a non-issue.

Even if you don't get the knock-out you were looking for after the first strike, by keeping your index hand in place, you are giving yourself an excellent point of reference for your follow-up strikes.

It is so much easier to strike accurately when you have this point of reference. It can be quite difficult to strike with any accuracy when you don't have this point of reference, especially when you are under pressure, or when you are trying to see in low light conditions. In such instances, having a lead arm index can be a godsend.

Having one hand placed on your attacker's body will also improve your overall structure for striking. It prevents you from following through too much and going off balance, plus it creates a more integral structure that is better able to withstand the recoil of your strike.

No doubt, your striking is greatly improved while indexing.

There is also the issue of control. It is easy to turn your index into a control mechanism, where you grab a hold of your opponent or use the hand/forearm to press forward, driving your opponent back as you strike.

And if the other guy starts to cover against your strikes (as will happen- no one likes getting hit, after all!) you simply use your indexing hand to clear the obstruction and continue striking.

Support Skill

Indexing is just a supporting skill, and as such it is not an integral part of your overall game plan. You can still get the job done without it; no one is saying you have to use it. You can take it or leave it.

Me personally, I always use indexing wherever possible. There are too many advantages and benefits not too.

And the more you work with and practice this skill, the more you learn about it, the more you get out of it and the more useful it becomes to you.

If haven't tried indexing yet, I really suggest you do so, especially if you want to improve your striking and give yourself a better chance in a physical confrontation.

And indeed, why wouldn't you want those things?

CHAPTER 33: HOW A SIMPLE SHIFT IN MINDSET CAN DRAMATICALLY IMPROVE YOUR COMBATIVES TRAINING

You're probably sick of hearing about the whole combative mindset concept. It's become something of a cliché in Combatives/SD circles these days. Yet despite the fact that the phrase is kicked about like an old football, few if anyone bothers to explain exactly what a combative mindset is, nor how to get it.

We all know that in basic terms, a combative mindset is one that is supposed to help us out in a physical altercation. It allows us to take action and do what has to be done to the other guy so we can hopefully prevail in whatever situation we're in. It's a forward drive mentality, backed up with aggression and the will to prevail no matter what the odds.

That's all fine in theory, but how does this concept translate into practical terms? In training and in practice, how does one get this mindset, what does it feel like and exactly how does it affect our performance?

The Inner Animal

Tapping into the inner animal is most people's idea of taking on a combative mindset, though I am here to tell you that this may not be the best part of yourself to tap into when it comes to dealing with physical violence.

Tapping into that part of yourself may have its benefits in certain situations. The state that it brings about is made up of raw emotion and boundless aggression. Coupled with a real sense of ferocious resolve, you can create an energy that is very powerful and difficult to stand up against, which is why it is normally the go-to state for most people who train in self defense. It's an energy that can make you feel like a juggernaut powering into your opponent.

When you are in a tight spot and your back is against the wall so to speak, this kind of mindset and ferocious energy can prove very useful, even lifesaving depending on the circumstances. If you need to give it all you've got, then tapping into the inner animal will certainly help you do that.

The main problem with this approach however, is that the inner animal can prove to be very hard to control. Once you unleash the beast from the cage it tends to stick to its nature and proceed to go ape shit. Whatever is in front of it is going to get eaten, no matter the consequences.

The thing is though, most of the situations that you will likely encounter will not require this kind of overkill mentality. In most situations, you can likely afford to be a little more controlled about things.

Once that animal has been released from the cage it tends to do what it wants, which means the danger exists that you will go overboard with your response. You may not even stop after you put the other guy down. You may even kill somebody.

Quite a few times I've seen people fly into uncontrolled rages that they can't bring themselves down from. We've all seen the guy that has to be pulled off the other guy before he kills him. *You* may have even been that guy in the past.

When powerful emotions are in the driving seat you are just along for the ride.

I don't know about you, but I'd like to have a bit more control than that, especially when it comes to inflicting violence, where one wrong move can have disastrous consequences.

The other downside to using such strong emotions to fuel your actions is that they can drain you of energy very quickly. Your actions also become quite frantic in nature, almost like an act of desperation on your part and this will inevitably lead to a pronounced degradation in your technique. Stress compression will kick in and your movements will drastically shorten, making them less effective. I also have found that mentally speaking, your stress levels will go up quite a bit as well.

So if you are on the battlefield or if you're in a real tight spot, unleashing the inner-animal is the way to go if you want to survive. For most other situations, the common ones that most of us will likely face, we need a different approach, and one which allows for more control.

The Professional Mindset

A much more beneficial mindset to cultivate in training is one that I like to call the professional mindset. The professional mindset is not based on emotion, but on measured and deliberate action. Aggression and violent intent are still very much present, but the difference is they are not in the driving seat, you are. To do this, you need to be able to detach yourself from the situation and allow a cold mechanical efficiency to take over. The inner-animal will stay locked in the cage. The cold, hard professional will take over instead.

I'm aware that this all sounds very Jason Bourne, this idea of being a cold and clinical fighting machine, but let me assure you that fantasy has nothing to do with this. What I'm talking about here is completely practical and can easily be demonstrated in training, as the video below will show.

To get this professional mindset you need to learn to switch off your emotions, not completely, but enough that they don't have any control over you. The idea is to keep those emotions below the surface where they belong, fuelling the engines rather than operating the machine.

In practice this means cultivating self-control. Training should be all about control anyway. The point of putting in so many hours of practice is that you try to gain control over yourself and your actions. If that wasn't your goal in training there wouldn't be much point to it. You don't really need training in order to unleash the beast, you just need an emotional trigger (and what is a fight if not an emotional trigger?).

So the professional mindset starts with self-control. It requires detachment and deliberate action. With the inner-animal in control, your actions are not very deliberate and they verge on desperate and frantic. Amateurish in other words.

For the professional mindset to kick in you first need to detach yourself from the drama and emotion of the situation. This is the first step.

When I was bouncing, one of the things that I quickly learned how to do was detach myself from whatever situations I encountered on the job. Once I realized that I had a job to do, this enabled me to stay detached and professional (most of the time–we are only human after all!) and to keep personal feelings and emotions out of the situation. Once I started to do that I found this shift in mindset made a significant difference in the way that I handled things. I felt calmer for a start because my emotions where kept fairly in check. And as a result of feeling calmer and less desperate just to end things my actions became a lot more deliberate, which in turn made them more effective. The extreme discomfort and unpleasantness still remained. That never really goes away, but it is easier to deal with when you are bit calmer about things.

Bottom line, I had a job to do and that was that. Any professional doing their job will experience the same thing. Look at doctors, paramedics, military operatives and others who work in high stress professions, even criminals. They all learn to cultivate the same calm and professional mindset that allows them to just get on with their job.

If you want the same professional mindset, you have to start thinking in those terms, like fighting is just your job. Fighting obviously isn't your job, but if you approach it like that anyway you will find it much easier to remain detached and in control of yourself.

Your inner dialogue will go from, *Shit, this is a nightmare, I don't want to do this*, to *Shit, this is a nightmare, but I'm going to handle it because I have too.*

Training The Professional Mindset

Actually training this mindset is fairly simple. It just requires you to be a bit more focused and a bit more deliberate in your actions.

When doing pad drills, for instance, don't just unthinkingly lash out at the pad with full aggression, almost tripping over yourself to get the next shot in. Be a bit more deliberate about what you are doing. Try to choose your shots carefully and force yourself to take your time.

I find with a lot of people when they are doing pad drills, they often rush things too much, to the point where they shorten their movements too much and also end up clipping or missing the target a lot. Footwork also suffers and they stumble rather than move precisely forward.

Remember that the goal in training is to practice your techniques in a way that will allow you to do them with full effectiveness and efficiency, both of which tend to suffer when you allow unthinking emotion and the tendency to rush things to take over.

You have more time than you think! The consensus in self defense circles seems to be to attack as fast as possible at all times. Speed obviously matters, but not to the detriment of power and technique. What's the point of rushing forward, throwing all these strikes, if none of them are having much effect?

To combat this urge to rush things you have to slow down a little and focus more on your target and on what you are doing. This will feel counter-intuitive at first because you will feel like you are giving your opponent the chance to recover, but we are only talking about a nano-second here, just enough to allow you to be more deliberate in your actions, but not so much that your opponent can exploit the time gap.

The effect of being more deliberate in your actions is that your technique will improve. Your movements will become more expansive and thus your techniques more powerful and much more accurate. Internally speaking, you should feel a lot calmer as well, less stressed.

So when you're practicing your strikes, be a lot more deliberate in your actions and try to focus and remain mentally detached. Cultivate an inner calm. The more you do this, the better you will get at it.

The same applies when it comes to doing live drills against resisting opponents. These kinds of drills are always a lot more frantic and pressurized than normal pad drills, mainly because the stress levels are higher and you are often up against others who are trying to hit you back. It can be difficult to maintain a level head and inner-calm in these circumstances, but you must try. It is in these kinds of situations that you need the professional mindset the most. All it really takes is again, being a bit more deliberate about what you are doing and consciously trying to remain calm and in control of yourself. You will of course fail often at this, but eventually you will get better at it.

Should you find yourself in an altercation on the street, a cool head is not only important during the altercation, but also afterwards as well. You never know what you have to do afterwards. You may be required to deal with the law, help someone who is injured or even prevent another altercation from starting. You can't really do any of these things if you are running around like an enraged animal, unable to come down from the strong emotions you are feeling.

This is something that also needs to be practiced in training. After every live drill and pressure drill you need to immediately check your state and consciously bring yourself down to a calmer state where you can think clearly again.

Deep Practice

All this requires not just practice, but deep, deliberate practice.

Stay mindful in training. What you do in training, you will do outside of training.

Self Defense Solutions

INTRODUCTION

This is a book for serious combatives practitioners—for those who train on a regular basis and who want to improve their skills. It's also for those who don't shy away from a little thinking and who don't mind working some things out for themselves.

I've written this book for those who would like to change and improve their approach to training (and self defense in general). How you approach your training can make all the difference. If you approach things the wrong way then you will not get the results that you are looking for. So this is a book that will help you refine your approach to certain aspects of training so you can hopefully improve upon the results you are currently getting.

Read through the book and take out of it what is useful to you. The information you are about to read is a representation of my own approach to self defense and combatives training. It's an approach that has taken a lot of learning (on my own and under other instructors in the field) and a lot of hard work to formulate.

This book is not representative of all aspects of combatives or self defense, but I have included what I think will be most useful to you—stuff that will have a broad effect on your overall training and attitude to training.

This isn't a technical how-to book either, but you will find many practical tips in these pages. You will also find things in it that will hopefully trigger in you a desire to examine your own training and to possibly explore different options and ways of doing things that will end up improving upon the results you are getting at the moment.

I say that not to devalue the worth of your current training. I don't know what it is you do, but with everyone, there is always room for improvement.

Study the information in this book, but also be sure to apply it in your own training. That is the only way you will know if there is any practical value in the information I am offering here.

Test things out, don't just read about them.

There is always more to learn and discover. My hope is that this book will help you in that regard. I don't have all the answers (does anyone?) but I can certainly point you in the right direction.

There is no particular order to the chapters in this book. Realistically, you could start reading whichever chapter you want first, for they are all stand- alone. At the same time, each chapter is a piece of a bigger theme—that theme being how to improve the results you are getting from your training by altering your approach to certain aspects of it.

Strive for truth and honesty in your training and you won't go far wrong.

CHAPTER 1: TARGET HARDENING

Before we get to talking about combatives training and the physical side of self defense, I thought it a good idea to spend this first chapter of the book talking about target hardening. In other words, how to protect oneself against unwanted attention and violence in the first place.

Even though I have talked about this aspect of self defense at length in my first book, I feel this information bears repeating. Your goal, when it comes to self-protection, should be to avoid any kind of trouble in the first place by implementing awareness and avoidance strategies into your game plan. So in this chapter I will discuss some of the ways in which you can do that. We will start with a website called Quora.

Quora is a bit like Yahoo Answers in that people ask questions on a whole range of different subjects and other people give their answers to those questions. One of the categories in Quora is self defense, which I like to check out now and again just to see what people are talking about. During one of my visits to the site I came across this question:

"What is the best form of self-defence for a woman who is very small (shorter than 5'3)? "

A friend of mine has confided in me that she is not just cat-called on the streets, but that creepy older guys have actually walked up behind her and whispered sexual things in her ears, and guys have even driven up to her on motorcycles and groped her before driving off.

What could she do to protect herself in these situations? Scream loudly? Carry a knife? Taser? Pepper-spray? Learn martial arts?

A few people answered this question, but by far the best answer was this one, from a woman called Bianca, who is a nurse:

"The first and best self-defense weapon for a small woman is your voice. PERIOD.

"I'm not even 5 foot tall and have worked in a dangerous field for almost 20 years. I've worked in a forensic psychiatric hospital and now work in a drug rehab. All men, usually. The psych hospital housed murderers, rapists, child molesters, etc.

"We were trained in self-defense, yes, but my voice is what saved me from injury far more than any self-defense classes would.

"People don't want a lot of noise when they're committing a crime and YES, men driving up and fondling you IS A CRIME.

"YELL. If a creepy old man is walking behind you, especially if he's close enough to WHISPER IN YOUR EAR, YELL!

""GET AWAY FROM ME! I DON'T KNOW YOU!"

"Calling attention to the situation will generally make that person get away from you. They don't want to go to jail. They don't want others to notice what they're doing.

"Aside from that, keep your phone with you at all times. Call 911. Call the authorities.

"The situations you've described are UNACCEPTABLE! I'm not placing blame on your friend but WHERE IS SHE HANGING OUT WHERE THESE THINGS ARE HAPPENING THIS FREQUENTLY?

"She needs to walk with confidence. Show no fear. Men don't DO things like that to me and I'm not disgusting or anything. I think they just know better. I walk with confidence. Perhaps even an ATTITUDE.

"I can hear it now, "That little thing just THINKS she's safe" but I've spent YEARS swimming with sharks. How you carry yourself speaks volumes to criminals.

"If it makes you feel better, carry some pepper spray. Take some self-defense courses. A knife is a bad idea, in my opinion. You have to be pretty close to someone to use a knife and they don't do the damage you really hope for in a struggle. You might not even get to use it. Perhaps the perp will even take it from you.

"All I carry with me is a HUGE voice, an awareness of my surroundings, and an attitude problem. It's served me well."

Great answer, right? It highlighted a few problems that people often have when it comes to self defense, such as a lack of awareness and no situational control skills.

But the issue brought up here that I am most interested in is how you put yourself across to other people, and especially those people who you really don't want anywhere near you, such as the undesirables described in the Quora question.

Target Hardening

Target hardening, the concept of making oneself a hard target for criminals by fortifying yourself against their advances, is massively important. If you have no defenses in place that will repel those who would seek to take advantage then you are just a walking open invitation to anyone who feels like messing with you. In other words, you will exhibit a *victim profile*, just like the woman described in the Quora question.

How you carry yourself and how you interact with other people speaks volumes about the kind of person you are. Those who have made it their business to seek out and victimize other people know just what to look for in a potential target victim. They know the profile: lack of confidence in the way someone carries themselves; lack of assertiveness; overly polite and willing to let strangers into their personal space; easily controlled and manipulated—the exact opposite of a hard target.

I discovered a long time ago that the way you carry yourself in public has a massive bearing on how other people treat you. If you carry yourself with confidence, in general you will attract less trouble.

In my experience, the quieter that confidence is the better. Cockiness and arrogance can still attract trouble. I've always found that people are more respectful of someone who is quietly confident and not too overbearing.

A quiet confidence comes from having the attitude that you have nothing to prove. Arrogant and over-confident people quite often come across like they have something to prove, and usually there will be someone there who will challenge them on that. I don't know about you, but I don't need that kind of attention. I like to be left alone when I'm out and about.

Having a quiet confidence will still communicate to have-a-go dickheads that you are not an easy target, without having to broadcast this fact every chance you get and risk aggravating the wrong person or persons.

I've been out before with some very extroverted people who didn't know how to keep their mouths shut. They would challenge anyone at the drop of a hat. Inevitably they would end up scrapping with someone. One night a friend and I found ourselves being chased by a gang of twenty lads over the head of such a person (that was a fun experience, especially once they surrounded us!).

You don't need to be an asshole to protect yourself. In fact, being an asshole will have the opposite effect and will attract trouble *to* you.

Be confident, be self-assured, but remain relaxed and try to keep your needy ego out of the equation.

Increasing Your Confidence

But how does one get this kind of confidence? How would the woman described in the Quora question get this kind of confidence?

That's not a particularly easy question to answer. Suggestions of self defense lessons, carrying pepper spray or some other weapon are just one part of the equation. A number of other factors contribute to forming a real sense of confidence that can be felt by others.

Bianca, who answered the question above, is obviously a confident woman, but I'd say most of that confidence came from her job as a nurse and having to deal with all sorts of difficult people day in and day out. Time spent in that kind of environment will naturally increase anyone's confidence.

There is no quick fix for growing your confidence, despite what many self-help gurus will tell you.

To increase your confidence you have to put yourself in

situations that demand confidence from you.

For many people, this means doing challenging jobs, dealing with problematic people or having to cope with difficult situations on a regular basis.

Working as a bouncer helped me grow my confidence when it came to dealing with difficult people and demanding situations. After a while I got used to it and found ways of being comfortable (or as comfortable as one can be) with such situations. This in turn gave me a sense of confidence that I could carry into other areas of my life.

In terms of making yourself a hard target, the starting point would have to be making that initial decision in your own mind that *you will never be anybody's victim.*

If a person is being victimized on a regular basis it is because, most of the time, they allow themselves to be victimized. They invite trouble upon themselves in some way. That may be a bit of a blanket statement, but if you think about it, it's true.

Whatever you have in your life you have invited it in in some way.

What signals is a person putting out that cause them to attract the people who do these acts? Why are they chosen over another?

In some way, they fit the victim profile.

You therefore make the decision to no longer come across as a victim.

Then what?

Then you begin to fortify yourself against any attacks on

your person. You begin to practice assertiveness. And yes, assertiveness needs to be practiced if it doesn't come naturally to you.

Practice saying no to people, but not in an arrogant way, rather in a quietly confident way. People will soon begin to respect you a lot more. They will also realize that they can no longer treat you like a doormat because you simply won't stand for it.

At some point you must stand up for yourself or forever remain the victim.

Using Your Voice

Bianca drew attention to the fact that she used her voice a lot to project her confidence and authority. Your voice is a powerful tool when it comes to communicating your intentions. Not so much what you say, but *how you say it matters most.*

I read somewhere that 10% of conflicts are due to a difference of opinion and 90% are due to wrong tone of voice. That statistic serves to highlight the importance of how you use your voice in a conflict situation.

Exactly how you use your voice will depend on the situation. Different circumstances will demand different responses. If you're a woman being followed or accosted by some creep, using your voice loudly and with a commanding tone will work better than using your voice in a quiet, pleading manner.

Similarly, if you are a man who is facing another man who is trying to start an argument with you, using your voice in a calm and levelled manner will de-escalate things quicker than using your voice in a loud, arrogant or accusatory way.

Sometimes it is better not to use your voice at all, and to just listen. Other times, for your own protection, you have to make full use of your voice.

And let's not forget the accompanying body language, which must match the tone of your voice. If there is a mismatch you will give away your lack of congruity and confidence. To be truly assertive, everything about you has to communicate the fact that *you are* assertive. Without this congruent state your communication will not be as powerful or as effective as it should be. You may fail in your attempts at persuasion. If a threat is not convinced by your actions they will not stop what they are doing.

A threat has to be convinced in some way that you are not worth pursuing or the conflict will continue.

It can be difficult being assertive if you are not used to being so. But everything is difficult at first. And like everything else, it gets easier. Eventually it will just be a natural part of who you are.

Physical Self-Defense and Target Hardening

Self-defense only works if you have all that other stuff in place. Without that bedrock of confidence and assertiveness you will not be able to use physical self defense in an effective manner. You will simply allow yourself to be bullied and manipulated to the point where self defense is no longer any use to you. It will be too late to use your physical skills. The game will be long over.

Physical training will obviously contribute to your overall confidence and self-esteem, but it can't be relied upon to give you everything that you need to survive in the big bad world.

Not all self defense situations call for physical responses

anyway. Situations where someone is being more subtly attacked, as in the case of sexual harassment or verbal assault, demand a different kind of response, one that can only come from an innate sense of confidence, assertiveness and the belief that you will not be bullied or victimized by anyone.

Living a life that is relatively trouble free, one where you don't attract the unwanted attention of every dickhead you come into contact with, requires more than just a few (or even many) self defense lessons or the purchase of pepper spray or even a gun. It's not as simple as that. People who do martial arts and self defense still get bullied, they still get victimized and they still get beaten up on occasion, but that is mainly because they are lacking in the essential qualities that we just discussed—those of confidence, assertiveness and even social intelligence.

Physical self defense training is only part of the solution when it comes to making oneself a hard target. The rest of the solution lies within you. It's up to you to bring that power out so that you can learn to use it.

CHAPTER 2: SOME TRUTHS ABOUT COMBATIVES

One of the things I have observed about many of those who train in combatives is the tendency to feel superior when they compare themselves to those who train in other martial arts systems. I have been guilty of this myself at times. Combatives training, with its emphasis on "real fighting", tends to make its practitioners believe they are superior street fighters, or more physically capable than those who train in regular martial arts.

This is blatant nonsense of course. The vast majority of those who claim to train in RBSD systems are, in reality, no more capable than the average martial artist or sport fighter. Indeed in many cases, I'd say a lot of those who claim to be more capable in fighting terms *just aren't*. They are, in fact, *much less* capable than many of those who train in combat sports like MMA.

Obviously the individual in question has a lot to do with it, but in the main, MMA fighters—with their generally superior fighting skill and conditioning—would likely annihilate your average combatives practitioner in a fight.

This is why I get annoyed when combatives guys try to downplay MMA for self defense, claiming it is only good for competition. Sure, MMA guys train for a different context, but fighting is fighting when it kicks off. A person who has fought against many fully resisting opponents in the cage (opponents who don't hold back and fight as hard as they possibly can) is bound to be more capable in a fight than some guy whose only experience of fighting is against a compliant partner in a padded suit who is barely trying.

The point I am trying to make here is that too many combatives practitioners view combatives training itself as infallible and beyond any kind of reproach. Combatives training can give a person a good advantage when it comes to self defense, *but only if the training is right*. Even then, combatives training can still have its downsides which must be addressed if practitioners are to get the most from it.

So here, for the sake of balance, we will look at four downsides to combatives training and what can be done to address those downsides.

Combatives training can increase people's paranoia and feed their insecurities.

To my mind, one of the main benefits of combatives training is that it can greatly increase a person's confidence and self-esteem. I've observed this effect in many of the students I have trained over the years and it is great to see.

On the other hand, I've seen combatives training have the opposite effect on some people. I've seen some individuals get more paranoid and insecure the longer they continue to train.

Here's martial artist Matt Thornton concurring on this:

"One would think that by training in "street" orientated martial arts, or combatives that emphasize the self-defense aspects of martial arts, to the exclusion of what they deem to be "sports" training, that these types of individuals would gain more confidence, more peace, more happiness, and become more comfortable within themselves as their skills at 'self-defense' grew. Unfortunately, it has been my experience that the opposite seems to be true. Individuals that come to strictly "street" oriented martial arts, that were already prone to feelings of inadequacy, shame, physiological fear, and paranoia, tend to have those qualities magnified by such training, rather than eased."

If a person is generally led in life by their ego and they suffer from insecurity and a degree of paranoia, then combatives training can exacerbate these traits. I've seen it happen quite a few times.

Combatives often attracts a certain type of individual, and these individuals can suffer from an excess of psychological fear. The training, with its focus on extreme violence and outward aggression, does nothing to alleviate this fear in the individual. It just makes it worse.

As the scholar Robert Thurman put it:

"Once we are prone to hate and rage, we project around us a field of paranoia and all people become our potential enemies. We feel destructive towards them, and we assume they feel destructive towards us."

Thus you have guys walking around thinking that everyone is out to get them. To combat this feeling of paranoia they often adopt a very aggressive persona that is quick to violence.

The fact is, some people just aren't ready for the type of training that combatives offers. These people are better off going into combat sports where they can learn some humility and get a handle on their insecurities.

Combatives training is not meant to make a person quick to violence. It is supposed to shape a person into one who is aware of themselves and their environment, one who has the confidence to try other methods of problem solving in a conflict situation before resorting to violence.

To quote Thurman again:

"When we become cool, we don't project enmity on

others; we can observe them more objectively, and if they are in fact out to cause trouble, we can quickly act to avoid it."

Combatives training is just a tool at the end of the day, and in the right hands it can be a very effective tool. But just like a gun, in the wrong hands combatives can be dangerous, for the individual practicing and for those around them. It is up to instructors to make sure they are not creating a monster out of certain people.

Many so-called combatives systems are fantasy based nonsense.

The above statement may be a strong one but it is nonetheless true. Quite a lot of the combatives and modern reality based self defense systems around today are based more on fantasy than on fact. Don't believe me? Take a quick browse through YouTube and look at some of the videos that people have put up in the name of "real" or "reality" self defense. What becomes clear when you watch many of these videos is that the people in them have no grasp of the issues involved in self defense, nor any understanding of what constitutes a proper self

defense technique.

So when I meet people and they tell me they "do combatives" I don't immediately think that this person must know what they are doing when it comes to training for self defense. Instead, I reserve judgment until I see for myself what it is they do. There are so many bullshit systems out there with the combatives label attached that just saying you train in combatives isn't enough. That no more qualifies you in self defense than saying you're a black belt qualifies you as a good martial artist.

The proof is in what you do, not what you say you do.

For a combatives system to be worth a damn it has to be based on truth, not somebody's version of the truth. The techniques have to be based on sound physics and they must also have been tested repeatedly in the real world, not just once or twice. Just because you managed to pull off a jumping spin kick outside the pub one night doesn't mean that technique is now a valid self defense technique that should be taught to everyone.

Many combatives systems also operate on the premise that problems should be made to fit solutions instead of the other way around. So you have these techniques being taught that are only good for a problem that has been made up in the gym. Thus we see silly attack scenarios that would never happen in the real world, just so the people training can use the awesome technique they made up for the imaginary attack!

In some of the more commercial combatives systems we also see a lot of fantasy based stuff like weapon disarm techniques and defenses that are straight out of a Jason Bourne movie.

The truth about most "combatives" systems is that they are deeply flawed and only cater to the fantasies of those who train in them. Good combatives systems are few and far between. The systems that contain stuff that actually works a high percentage of the time are often considered boring or lacking in material, due to the fact that they are based around only a handful of techniques. Such criticisms, however, are based on ignorance and a wilful blindness to the truth. The kinds of people who propagate such ignorant nonsense are the kinds of people who pay good money to have their fantasies indulged on a regular basis (kind of like visiting a brothel twice a week), and are the reason why you can't trust a system just because it is labelled combatives.

Instinctive fighting skills are not worked enough—if at all—in many combatives systems.

Most combatives systems are based around two things: pad drills and scenario training. Both of these training methods are perfectly valid if done correctly, but in my experience neither of these training methods are enough on their own to make someone into a half-way decent fighter.

Pad drills are essential in combatives training. I'm in no way denying that. The best way to learn correct technique, body mechanics, power generation etc. is by utilizing pad drills to isolate and work the different components that make up the fundamental combatives techniques. I'll be going into detail on pad training in a later chapter.

Scenario training can be useful if done correctly. Unfortunately, most scenario training in combatives involves the use of a padded suit and unrealistic scenarios and attack sequences.

What tends to be missing in many combatives systems is what falls in between these two training methods, and that is the development of instinctive fighting skills. By that, I mean developing the ability to think on your feet, to react spontaneously to the demands of the situation and to use the techniques that are most effective in response to whatever your opponent is doing.

To an extent, fighting instinct *can* be developed through pad drills, *if* the drills themselves are correctly designed. But in my experience, pad drills will only get you so far. Fighting with a live opponent is a different matter and it requires practice in that very situation, not through hitting pads.

In general, if a fight goes beyond a few seconds in length

then it will turn into some kind of brawl. Most pad drills are designed to help a trainee practice finishing a fight in the first few seconds. The thinking goes, if you don't finish the fight in those first few seconds then you are doing something wrong. This may be so, but in reality some situations do develop into protracted brawls and if you are not used to tussling with an attacker in this way then you will likely freeze as you will not know how to handle it.

In a sense I am talking here about specialist fighting techniques, things like wrestling and grappling skills, takedowns and even boxing. When you go beyond the fundamental combatives techniques, these are the type of skills you'll be moving on to learning.

One way to practice these is to pad up and go for it with a partner. Slug it out or move in to wrestle and grapple, which more often than not happens anyway. Just knowing how to manipulate the other person, knowing how to handle someone at that range, is very useful. The only way to learn that is through live fighting. It's not like normal sparring exactly, because you are sticking to the fundamental techniques you have learned through pad drill training, but you can also utilize wrestling and grappling techniques to manipulate your opponent into a better position so you can strike them. I'll deal with this aspect in more detail later in the book.

Combatives shouldn't be all about pad drills and scenario training. Utilize the kind of live fighting I just talked about, even normal sparring as well. It all helps mold you into a better fighter.

The wrong mindset is often instilled in combatives.

The kind of "combative mindset" often instilled into

trainees of combatives is the kind of mindset that means you go ape-shit on whatever threat is in front of you.

All threats are not the same however. To ramp up your aggression levels and go nuts on anyone who dares confront you is unwise, in my opinion. Not every situation you will find yourself in will demand the same response. Indeed in some cases, if you tap into your inner animal and beat the hell out of someone, perhaps going too far, you may find yourself in jail, which these days is a very real possibility.

Too many combatives instructors advocate the whole macho, kill-or-be-killed attitude when it comes to self defense. There is a certain usefulness in cultivating such an attitude, as long as you temper it with a little common sense and self-restraint. Personally, I'm not a fan of such blind aggression. I prefer to take a more detached attitude to things.

In my previous book I talked about the professional mindset, which is a combative mindset based on detachment and cold, controlled aggression. Admittedly this is an ideal that is hard to reach sometimes, especially in situations where emotions are high. The closer you can get to this mindset, however, the more control you will have over yourself and the situation you are in.

Tapping into the inner animal, going ape-shit on your attacker is fine if your back is really against the wall and you have no other options. In my experience though, most of the situations the average person will find themselves in are not life or death and can be dealt with without recourse to too much violence.

You have to at least *try* to maintain control of yourself in these situations, for your sake as well as the other person's. Advocating a lack of control through unbridled aggression is not the way to go to achieve that, yet many combatives instructors and systems do just that.

So combatives training isn't perfect. It does have its downsides like everything else. The purpose of the rest of this book is to show you how you can minimize those downsides by taking the correct approach to your training. We will start in the next chapter by looking at pad training.

CHAPTER 3: PAD DRILL TRAINING

Pad drills are an integral part of combatives training. If you are training in a system that revolves for the most part around striking, then you need to be able to properly utilize pad drills in order to practice those strikes.

When I first started training in combatives, the pad drills that I used were fairly basic. They mainly involved striking the pad while it was held in a completely static position. This may be fine for initially learning the basics of a particular technique, but in terms of actual application and being able to use that technique in a more "alive" manner, your pad drills have to evolve to meet the demands of a real situation.

It wasn't until I met Mick Coup and saw the kind of pad training that he was doing that I realized I could get a lot more value from pad training if I put more thought into the questions of what pad drills are for and how you could get the most from using them.

Like any kind of self defense training, the goal should be to make the training as realistic as possible. By that I mean that, whatever you do in training, the training should hold some kind of relevance to the type of situations you are going to be facing in the real world.

Going back to static pad drills – where the pad holder stands, usually half asleep, holding the pad aloft like a stop sign, basically passing time while he awaits his turn to strike – what relevance does that have to a real situation? When was the last time an attacker stood perfectly still in front of you and allowed you line up and fire off a shot without any resistance or attempt to avoid the strike? If that happened then the person didn't deserve to be hit in the first place.

Completely static pad training should only be used when you are first beginning to learn a particular technique. At this early stage you are not worried about application or performing the technique under pressure; your only goal is to learn the movements of the technique itself. You can't do that when the pad is moving around or other stuff is happening at the same time. So having a fixed target to strike means you can concentrate solely on body mechanics, accuracy and power generation. It also allows the pad holder or your instructor to evaluate your technique and give feedback more easily, since they are not having to worry about doing other stuff, like utilizing another pad or firing off strikes themselves.

Once you get a good handle on the fundamentals of your techniques then it is time to move on to more complex drills and movements, and this is where the real creativity and innovation comes into play because you now have to think about the kinds of problems you will most likely be up against in a real situation. This brings us on to how to formulate the drills themselves.

How to Create a Pad Drill

When creating pad drills you have to start with a problem-solution mindset. Think about a typical attack scenario that might take place. What kinds of things happen in such a situation in terms of fighting? What does the other guy do? How do they attack? How do they make it difficult for you to attack them back? These are the types of questions you should ask. Look deeply at different attack scenarios. Think about your own experience or any fights that you have witnessed. Ask yourself how you can best relate your current pad training to what actually happened in those situations.

Let's take a basic highline strike—a palm strike or a right cross, it doesn't really matter. Your goal is obviously to land that strike on your attacker's head somewhere, and to do so as many times as it takes to end the situation. What might prevent you from doing that? Might your opponent throw their arms up in front of them in defense, making it more difficult for you to land a clean shot? Might your opponent move around a lot? Might he move his head so you can't hit him? I'd say that's a safe bet, wouldn't you? People don't like to be hit and they will do all they can to avoid that happening.

So we've established that the other guy is going to move around a lot and possibly flinch his head away from your strike. Wouldn't it be a good idea to practice hitting a target that doesn't want to be hit? Now we formulate a drill where the pad holder suddenly moves the pad when you go to hit it. He may pull the pad back slightly to simulate a head flinch. He may move the pad off-side to simulate an evasion. He may also move the pad towards you to simulate a distance closure. Or he may just cover one pad with the other one to simulate a covering of the head. Does that ever happen, do you think? It's a pretty safe bet that one or all of those things will happen in a real fight.

Now you are throwing shots at a pad that doesn't want to be hit, just like a real person. The level of realism and relevancy just went up considerably. Now you have to find a solution to the problem of a moving target. How can you hit a target that keeps moving? Simple really—you move with it.

If an opponent flinches their head back in reaction to your strike, you throw another one as you advance forward. Or you quickly move around to the side because your opponent has moved that way. Or you could throw an off-line strike. You are learning to track the target wherever it goes, no matter what way it moves. You are also learning to keep up offensive pressure, even if some of your strikes are far from good or even if you miss the target altogether. This is error recovery, which I talked about in my last book. You make a mistake you don't stop. You keep going. There is no resetting in a real fight. You get what you are given.

Let's look at some other examples. Would your opponent ever try to hit you back, even as you are trying to hit him? Of course he would. So how do you simulate that in a drill? Quite simply, you get the pad holder to throw shots at your head with the free pad. You will cover or block the strike and then immediately strike back again. Have the pad holder vary the timing of the shots and also the type and amount of shots thrown. You could also bring in the moving target drills to combine with this for even more realism and difficulty.

Another example. Has an attacker ever reached out and grabbed you in some way, or held you back with their free hand while trying to hit you with the other? Then have the pad holder do the same, either grabbing your shirt while you strike the pad, or shoving the free pad into your chest to keep you at a distance while you continue to strike the target pad. Again you can mix this up by having the target pad move around a lot.

How about creating space to strike, like when an opponent has completely closed you down, perhaps in an attempt to take you down or just to prevent you from striking them any further? How could you simulate this in a drill? You could start by having your partner grab a hold of you, hugging you almost. You must now find a way to create enough space so you can use your highline strike again. You could do this in a number of ways. You could simply push back off your opponent to create space that way, or you could employ elbow strikes or head-butts to force them back instead, both of which can be practiced on the pads. Either way, you will finish by highline striking the pad again.

Maybe you want to up the pressure in these drills. You could do this by bringing in two or more pad holders. Stand between the pad holders with your eyes closed. The go signal is when you are tapped or slapped by one of the pads. You will open your eyes and immediately respond to whatever the pad holder is feeding you. He may be feeding you one of the drills we mentioned earlier, perhaps moving the pad away as you try to strike. You just keep trying to hit the moving target with as many good shots as possible until you feel yourself being tapped by another pad holder. Immediately turn around to face whatever the pad holder is feeding you. This time you may be faced with the pads very close in and you will have to create space some way, just as we discussed earlier, with elbow strikes, head-butts or simply pushing them away before reverting to highline strikes.

Keep at it until you are tapped again and you have to turn around to face another pad situation. The more the pad holders mix up the problems you will be faced with the better. Not knowing what's coming next will only add to the pressure of the drill which will make it hard to think. You may even freeze sometimes as you work out what to do. This is nothing to worry about. It's normal for that to happen. You will freeze less the more you practice the drill. The whole drill should go on for a minimum of thirty seconds, but you can go on for as long as you like. Extending the drill to a minute or two minutes will add an element of stress to it as well as you struggle to keep going even though you are fatigued.

There is a myriad of ways that you can make your pad drills more relevant and more realistic. The methodology is to build the drills up in layers, adding in one component at a time. You can make the drills as complex as you like, just as long as you stick to the rule of thumb that you relate the drills to what actually happens in real situations. There is no point adding in stuff that isn't going to happen in a real situation. Always keep the end goal in mind, which is to learn to properly apply your techniques in a variety of circumstances and under various levels of pressure. The more you can do this, the more competent and prepared you will be for a real situation.

Take the time to put some thought into your pad training. There is somewhat of an art to it, especially when it comes to actually working the pads for a partner. You won't do your partner any favors by just moving the pads around in a haphazard fashion. A good pad holder will visualize the situation they are trying to create in the drill and they will use the pads to mimic as closely as possible the movements of a real person. A pad holder must therefore fully engage with the drill just as much as the striker.

We have only scratched the surface of pad drill training in this chapter. You could probably fill a book with the different combinations of drills it's possible to do. The important thing is that you understand the goals of pad drill training and the fundamental principles involved. Once you grasp these, you should be able to come up with your own forms of pad training.

CHAPTER 4: IMPROVING YOUR STRIKING

The highline strike is one of the most fundamental strikes in combatives, as it is in fighting in general. It sits firmly in the high percentage bracket and as such it can be firmly relied upon to help get you out of trouble.

Think of all the fights you've ever been in. Consider all of the sport fights you've seen and those street fight videos on YouTube.

How many of those fights were finished with a highline strike?

The vast majority of them, that's how many.

It is therefore in your interests as a self defense practitioner to work hard on your highline strikes, and to make them as powerful and as effective as they can be.

When I say highline strike, I'm talking about a strike to the head, either with closed fist or open hand. Personally, I like to practice both. Despite all the discussions about closed fist techniques being bad for your hands, I still like to practice them.

Often when you are under pressure, you will default to closed fist strikes whether you want to or not. It's just one of those things. Punching seems to be a conditioned response in most people.

Whatever your preferences, the practice methods will be the same. This is what we are going to focus on in this chapter: How to practice your highline strikes so you can get maximum benefit from the practice.

Practicing With a Partner

Solo practice for striking is okay, but I believe to get the most from your practice you need a good partner to give you feedback.

Feedback is essential if you want to correctly gauge how effective your strikes really are. Partners can also spot flaws in your body mechanics that you may not even be aware of. And as we are about to see, a partner is essential for creating a *feedback loop*, but we'll get to that in a minute.

First I would like to talk briefly about the much vaunted "10,000 hour rule", which states that in order to master anything you must invest at least ten thousand hours of practice time.

While this rule seems to be true, by and large, it is only half the story. The other half of the story is that, if during those hours of practice the movements you are practicing are full of errors, you are wasting your time repeating them. You are just instilling errors into your technique and performance.

Anders Erricson, the psychologist whose research helped to spawn the aforementioned rule, has stated:

"You don't get benefits from mechanical repetition, but by adjusting your execution over and over to get closer to your goal."

"You have to tweak the system by pushing," he adds, *"allowing for more errors at first as you increase your limits."*

The *quality* of your practice is therefore very important when it comes to mastery and making improvements.

That's the first key to proper deliberate practice.

The second key is adding in a *feedback loop*, which, as we have said, must come in the form of a coach or partner who knows what they are doing and what to look for.

The cornerstone of effective practice is therefore engaging in that feedback loop while working with someone who has an expert eye.

Learning to Concentrate

It sounds simple. Just concentrate. Not always easy for some.

Concentration requires that you get good at controlling your attention and focus.

The only thing you should be focusing on is the task at hand, which is practicing your highline strike and focusing on whatever aspect you need to focus on. That may be getting the right recoil, or following through more, or improving your accuracy, whatever aspect of the strike needs working on.

Nothing else should be in your head at this time.

Nothing.

You should be completely in the present moment.

Daniel Goldman says:

"Paying full attention seems to boost the mind's processing speed, strengthen synaptic connections, and expand or create neural networks for what we are practicing."

So forget the rest of your life and what's going on around you (although if people are talking loudly in the background while you are trying to train you have my permission to throw a kettlebell at their heads).

Learning to concentrate is an important mental skill, and not just for practice, but also in live self defensc situations. The more switched on you are in a given situation, the quicker you will notice things and the quicker you will react to them.

Learn to focus fully on the task at hand. Your practice will improve when you do.

Establishing a Baseline for Impact

What I mean by establish a baseline is that your partner should tell you when you have hit the pad correctly, with either palm strike or closed fist.

Too much bounce on impact will result in a weak strike.

From the pad holder's point of view, there will be no penetration felt. The energy of the strike just seems to fizzle out into the pad.

Too much follow-through will also result in a weak strike because the focused impact will not be there.

From the pad holder's perspective, it will feel like the pad is being pushed or "patted" instead of struck.

For your strike to be effective, it's crucial that you get the balance right between recoil (bounce) and follow-through.

When the balance is right, the strike will feel solid. The impact should penetrate into the pad to the point where it almost hurts the hand of the pad holder.

The pad holder should be able to feel the impact on the palm of their own hand.

That's the baseline for your impact.

Your partner should tell you when the impact is there by saying *yes* or *no* after each strike.

It is up to you to get as many positive responses as possible, which will require you to concentrate.

In doing this you are practicing very deliberately, striving towards the goal of delivering correct and maximum impact each time.

It's deliberate practice with an inbuilt feedback loop.

Not Overthinking the Body Mechanics

Correct body mechanics are clearly important when it comes to striking, but sometimes I see people get so caught up in the finer points that they stiffen up through trying too hard and thinking too much about what they are doing.

Don't fall victim to overthinking.

The basic goal of a highline strike, in terms of body mechanics, is to get as much of your body weight behind the strike as possible. That's it in a nutshell.

How you do that is really up to you. Most people get how to use the hips to generate torque. It's not that hard.

Measure the effectiveness of your strike by how much impact you deliver with it, not by the body mechanics you use to deliver that impact.

If you focus more on hitting the pad correctly, as we discussed previously, the body mechanics will more or less take care of themselves.

Of course you can tweak certain movements, but only if it makes a significant difference to the effectiveness of your strike.

You are trying to hit hard. That is all.

Spending too much time on tweaking body mechanics probably isn't wise when you could be focusing more on delivering impact and learning to apply your technique in different situations. Technical lock can set in, which is where you get bogged down in tiny details to the point where you begin to lose all perspective. You lose sight of the real purpose behind doing the technique in the first place, which is just to learn to hit a target as hard as you can. If you want to spend hours on the minutiae of body mechanics, then go ahead. It's your practice time.

One further tip here is to exaggerate your movements and fully load up before you strike. This will help to counteract stress compression.

Stress compression is when your movements get shorter when you are under any kind of pressure (such as in a real fight).

If you keep your movements long in practice there will be less compression when you find yourself having to do them under pressure.

Using Your Head

It is possible to increase the power of your strikes by learning how to use your head correctly when striking.

In basic terms, you simply lead with the head by throwing it forward first (as you would when throwing an object), with everything else following behind.

Doing this seems to lead to greater impact and more bodyweight going into the strike since the head pulls the rest of the body with it, creating more momentum in the process.

You will need to try this out yourself to understand it fully.

Not Being Afraid To Fail

Just about everyone I have trained has had a tendency to be overly critical of themselves and their performance, to the point where it sometimes leads to them getting depressed and losing confidence.

This can happen if a person continually makes errors in their practice or if their strikes aren't measuring up to whatever standard they have set for themselves.

No good can come from this type of negative thinking.

You can't be afraid to fail.

You can't be afraid to repeatedly mess things up, especially in the beginning when you are just learning this stuff.

Proper deliberate practice is about working on the edge of your abilities. On that edge lies frustration and the potential to make many errors, errors that you must learn to recover from.

That edge is also where you need to be if you want to improve.

No one ever improved while remaining inside their comfort zone.

If your strike doesn't measure up for whatever reason, don't stop and go into a slump and start saying things like, *"Damn..."* like it's the end of the world.

Just do the next strike!

Forget about your previous mistake and move on immediately.

Sometimes I would ask a student to do three or four strikes in quick succession. They do the first one right and the next one would be off for whatever reason, and then they would stop and start cursing or apologizing for their perceived ineptitude.

Why?

Keep going, even if you do mess up the first couple.

Just keep hitting!

You most likely will make similar mistakes in a real situation, so you'd better get used to carrying on regardless and adjusting course if necessary.

You can't reset in a real fight.

Keep your self-talk under control as well. Banish any type of negative thinking.

See your mistakes as bringing you closer to your goal.

Don't dwell or overthink.

Learn the lesson in the mistake and then move on.

Using Your Internal Energy

I'm not talking about using chi or any similar nonsense when I say use your internal energy.

I'm talking about firing up your central nervous system just before you strike and using aggression and intent in your delivery of the strike.

If you focus, you will get a visceral feel for this energy. Usually it starts in the core and travels out from there.

Learn how to conjure this energy up from inside of yourself and direct it into whatever target you are hitting.

This internal energy will help to increase the explosiveness of your strikes. I will talk more about intent and internal energy in the next chapter.

Slowing Down

Another very common mistake that I see people make when striking is that they try to do so too fast, to the point where they almost trip over themselves.

The best way to counter this is to fully focus on what you are doing and concentrate your attention on making every movement as deliberate and as effective as possible.

Your strikes will improve significantly if you can do this.

For a more detailed explanation of this, see the chapter on taking your time.

Approaching Your Training Like a Pro

If you really want results from your training then you have to take a professional approach to it.

Taking a professional approach you will put the required time and effort into your training and you will always strive to improve.

With an amateur approach you will train only when you feel like it (which won't be often) and when you do train you will hold back from giving it your all because you just can't be bothered and you think you are good enough already.

Here's Daniel Goldman again to sum up these two approaches:

"Amateurs are content at some point to let their efforts become bottom-up operations. After about fifty hours of training — whether in skiing or driving — people get to that "good-enough" performance level, where they can go through the motions more or less effortlessly. They no longer feel the need for concentrated practice, but are content to coast on what they've learned. No matter how much more they practice in this bottom-up mode, their improvement will be negligible.

"The experts, in contrast, keep paying attention top-down, intentionally counteracting the brain's urge to automatize routines. They concentrate actively on those moves they have yet to perfect, on correcting what's not working in their game, and on refining their mental models of how to play the game, or focusing on the particulars of feedback from a seasoned coach. Those at the top never stop learning: if at any point they start coasting and stop such smart practice, too much of their game becomes bottom-up and their skills plateau."

Apply these things to your practice, along with everything else in this book, and you will quickly start to see improved results.

CHAPTER 5: INTENT

An important concept to be aware of in combatives training is the concept of intent, or *violent intent*. Intent is what fuels your actions and powers up your techniques. Without it you would be performing empty movements and there wouldn't be much point in that.

Intention itself starts with a thought and that thought leads to action. However, in the context we are discussing here, there is slightly more to intent than that.

Violent intent is having the intention to do harm to someone. In a self defense scenario that would be your attacker. You can be certain that your attacker will have a lot of violent intent behind their actions so you need to have the same.

In fact it is this intent to do harm that often gives away a potential attacker's game plan. One of the key tenets of awareness is being switched on enough to sense or spot that violent intent in a person before they get the chance to follow it through with violence of action. The quicker you can pick up on a person's violent intent, the more time you will have to formulate a response to it, which could mean avoiding that person, pre-empting them or, at the very least, being ready to counter their attack on you.

In a training context, intent is important because it will make your techniques much more effective if you can learn to use and channel that intent and convert it into a violent action. But how do we do this? How do we learn to stir up and channel something as intangible as intent?

Like I said, intent starts in the mind. Every time you perform a technique, a highline strike say, you should be thinking in your mind about what kind of effect you want that strike to have. This will be a split second process for most. The longer you have been training, the quicker and easier it will be for you to form your intent. In the beginning, it may take a little longer as you familiarize yourself with the process.

Every time you strike a pad you should be intending for that strike to be as effective as possible, which means hitting with full power and speed. Without a certain amount of intent behind your movements you will not reach full effectiveness with your strike. This is why intent is so important. It will help you dig deep and tap into more of your potential.

The type of thoughts that you formulate in your mind so you can stir up that intent are up to you. Do whatever works for you. The whole point of the initial thought process is to trigger your emotions. This is what thoughts do. They trigger emotions.

Have you ever found yourself dwelling on certain thoughts, only to find yourself feeling a certain way soon after? That's because your thoughts stirred up those emotions.

This is also why it is so important to keep a handle on what thoughts pass through your head, especially in self defense scenarios. Psychological fear in these situations can trigger very debilitating emotions that will greatly hamper how you perform in such situations.

Be mindful of the thoughts you are thinking. You don't always have to engage with them. Try to let them pass by like clouds. This is isn't always possible when you are under duress, but at least if you are aware of the process at work, you stand a greater chance of getting it under control.

In this case, however, we don't want to stop our thoughts; we want to create them so we can trigger certain emotions and bodily reactions. To be honest, I'm not sure what goes on in my head before I strike. The whole process has been reduced to just a feeling and an explosion of energy. Somewhere in my mind, though, there are thoughts of doing harm and thoughts of bad intention, or else nothing would be triggered in my body. Experiment with this yourself. Find out what kinds of thoughts trigger the most intense reactions in you and stick to those thoughts.

So what kind of emotions and bodily reactions are triggered by these thoughts and intentions? Well to me it is all just energy. That's how I think of it—internal energy. For the sake of clarity, however, I'll try to pinpoint some of the emotions that make up this energy.

For sure, one of the main sources of this internal energy is aggression. This is something many people struggle with, females especially. Anytime I have trained a woman in self defense the biggest stumbling block to progress has been their reluctance and seeming inability to tap into and use their aggression. It's just not a natural thing for most females, which is why they often struggle with it. In saying that, I have trained plenty of males who struggled just as much with the same thing. Usually though, in both cases, once we got the thought process right, the rest would fall into place.

In terms of bodily sensations, you should feel that explosion of energy somewhere in your core. Intention itself is creating something from nothing. That's what you are doing when you form an intention: you are creating something that doesn't currently exist. It is the same with aggression. The aggression itself isn't there yet. You must create it in order to bring it into being.

You can practice creating this energy just by forming intention over and over, each time feeling that energy rise up inside of you. Make like you are going to strike but don't actually perform the full movements. Hold back from striking but feel the energy that materializes inside of you, and then feel it dissipate as you relax again. This is a good way to get a feel for what is going on inside of you, and a way to practice bringing that energy – that aggression – into existence with just your will alone.

Take this a step further by practicing on the heavy bag. Do your strikes in bursts of three in rapid succession. Do so with as much violent intent as you can muster. Practicing your strikes in this way really brings out your aggression. You'll be surprised by just how much.

The more you can make yourself aware of this process of energy creation, and the more you practice it, the better you will get at controlling it. That's really what it's all about, controlling that energy so you can turn it on and off at will.

I can't stress enough the importance of being able to form this kind of violent intent. If you don't have it, especially in a real situation, your strikes will not be anywhere near as effective as they should be.

In almost all self defense scenarios, you will need a good amount of violent intent to get you through them. Without that energy to carry you through you will be overwhelmed by the energy of your opponent, which, as I mentioned, they will likely have in spades. Criminals and street thugs are experts at using bad intent to get what they want. They are experts at turning it on and off like a tap.

Think about your average mugger or street thug. They will casually approach their victims, seemingly very relaxed and not showing any signs of overt aggression. Then, at a certain point in the interview, they will suddenly explode into violence and drop their victims like a stone before the victim even knows what hit them. Then the criminal will switch off the violence again and casually flee the scene. Violence and violent intent are tools to these people and they know how to use those tools to good effect.

You may be saying that not every situation will require you to have full violent intent. I'm not saying you should behave like a psychopath or a violent, out of control animal. I am saying, though, that you need to be able to go for it when you have too and give it all you've got.

Consider the fact that most people will not end up in very many violent confrontations and when they do it is because they have been left with no choice but to use violence to counter the threat. You aren't going to hit anyone unless you are left with no choice in the matter. If the situation is serious enough that you have to use violence to contain it, then it is serious enough for you to not hold back with whatever countermeasures you use. If you are going to do it, then do it right.

The first few altercations I ended up in when I started bouncing were an eye-opener for me. I held back somewhat when I had to hit anyone and consequently my opponents didn't go down as quickly as they should have. In fact, they came back at me even more forcefully. So an experienced bouncer I was working with at the time pulled me aside and said, *"This isn't like in the gym. If you are going to hit them don't hold back because they won't hold back on you."* His language was a lot more colorful than that but that's what he was trying to get across. He was talking about violent intent. He was telling me to hit with violent intent, which is what I'm telling you now.

So when you are in the gym and you are practicing your strikes, make sure you hit with full violent intent each and every time. I think of it as a form of nastiness. I often tell my students this: Be nasty when you hit, but also keep it controlled.

Controlled nastiness.

If you are practicing highline strikes on the pads, don't think about hitting the pad, think about trying to break your partner's hand as they hold the pad. If you are practicing a thigh kick on the pads, then it's the same thing. You are not just simply hitting the pad; you are trying to break your partner's leg. That's being nasty. Not that you will break anything, but the point is the intention is there and that intention will make your strikes more potent.

To misquote Bruce Lee: *"Be nasty, my friend…"*

Now let's move on to look at support skills in the next chapter.

CHAPTER 6: SUPPORT SKILLS FOR BETTER OFFENCE AND DEFENCE

An important support skill in combatives is the ability to use the hands and arms in a tactical manner that involves more than just striking.

Your arms are your first line of defense when you get attacked, and as such they can be used in different ways before any strike is thrown. You can also continue to use your hands in various ways to set up your strikes.

Even before an attack happens, the arms are used to control space between you and whatever threat you are facing, as in the fence concept.

What I want to talk about here is the continuation of that fence concept even after an attack has begun. It is one of the things that I always try to emphasize with students, the need to always keep the arms out in front in a fluid guard position. From that position, a number of different applications will flow, which we will look at now.

The Initial Guard Position

There really isn't much more to say on this that hasn't already been said a thousand times before, though the importance of this guard position cannot be over-emphasized. It's your first line of defense between you and your attacker. Without that defense in place, a difficult situation can get even harder if your personal space is invaded and the other guy is on top of you, so to speak.

This position is also important because it will help you to

underscore your assertiveness. As I've discussed in my previous books, it is important to control the pre-fight phase by drawing a metaphorical line in the sand for your opponent. You must communicate to your aggressor with your body language and choice of words that if they step over that line they will not do so without consequences.

Drilling this initial guard position is easy enough. Just have a partner try to invade your space and use your hands to push back off them while stepping back or around. No need to try to hold your ground unless you can't move back for some reason.

Also, the higher your hands, the harder it will be for the other person to hit you, and the quicker you will be able to pre-empt should you need to.

Defensive Movements

If your opponent should attack first in any way you need to be able to use your hands/arms to defend against the attack. I'm not talking about blocking here, at least not in the traditional sense. To all intents and purposes though, this is what you are doing, blocking the incoming attack and preventing it from hitting you (too much).

The most effective ways to do this seem to be based upon an initial flinch reaction. Again, much has been said about the so-called startle-flinch reaction but it is nothing more than your mind saying, "HOLY SHIT!" and your body following suit by flinching away from whatever attack has come.

There are quite a few different variations on this flinch reaction and which one you use will be up to you. I'm sure it's possible to make them all work with practice.

I'm not fond of anything that involves covering by clamping the arms around the head (although sometimes this may be necessary, especially in the case of multiple opponents). I'm not saying this isn't a useful tactic, but I prefer to keep my arms out in front of me whenever possible, allowing the lead arm to absorb most of the attack. I'll flinch away and throw my lead arm up and out, so in the case of a punch, it will mostly hit my arm. If more punches come I keep both arms moving out in front so I can deflect, block, parry or trap my opponent's punching arm.

The main reason I do this is so I can quickly strike when I get the chance. This isn't so easy when your arms are clamped to your head.

What I have discovered about defending against attacks like punches is that there are no real fixed techniques to use. Under pressure, it is a case of flinching and blocking/covering. This process tends to pan out differently each time, depending on the type of attack and how good or bad your reaction has been. Sometimes you fail and get hit. Put the full contact gear on and you will soon discover this.

What is more important than how you initially deal with an incoming attack is how quickly you go on the offensive afterwards.

Regardless of what shape your startle-flinch reaction took, you must be swift in moving forward with your own attack, otherwise you are going to end up on the back foot, losing ground until you are overwhelmed.

In terms of drilling this, you can start by having a partner simply try to hit you with a pad so you can practice whatever defense you are working on, be it blocking with the lead arm out or by clamping it to the side of your head before you strike back. I suggest you also practice defense with safety helmets on so you can both go hard. Your partner should attack hard and you should try to get on the offensive as quickly as possible before they get the chance to throw any more strikes.

I find working full contact in this way helps develop your fighting instincts much more. We will discuss this aspect of fighting drills in a later chapter.

Indexing, Checking, Grabbing and Controlling

As I've said, it's important to keep the hands out in front throughout the duration of the fight whenever possible.

If an opponent is moving in towards you (as they will be as they are trying to hit you) you also need to be able to utilize your lead arm to check, grab, control and index.

Indexing as a concept you should already be familiar with, especially if you have read my other books. To recap, indexing is using the lead arm to give you a reference point so you can strike with accuracy. If you can touch your opponent you can also hit him. Indexing will also help your body mechanics, helping to form a solid and stable structure from which to strike.

This is why I like to keep my arms out in front and moving fluidly, because you are always feeling out the space and always indexing to back up your strikes.

Beyond indexing we have checking, which I always find very useful. You don't want any attacker in on top of you, so checking them as they come in is a very effective way to keep them at bay or to redirect them off-side.

Often an attacker will use their own lead arm in a similar

way, keeping it out front as they strike. In that case, you can slap their arm down or away from you, which will make it easier for your strikes to get through.

Grabbing and controlling are two other aspects that can prove useful, depending on the circumstances. I tend to utilize these more when I am in close and I want to get a grip on my opponent.

It's hard to say exactly when you will use these applications in a fight. In the main they are used spontaneously.

A good drill though is to have a partner attack you with boxing gloves on or else wear the protective gear. Have them come forward and attack while you practice using your arms to check, grab, control, index and strike or whatever the circumstances require. Practice creating gaps, clearing paths and getting some sort of index to strike. This kind of practice will hone your fighting instincts so that these support techniques come naturally to you after a while. Again I'll discuss this further in a later chapter.

Alternatively, isolate the different components and come up with different pad drills to practice them. Follow up the pad drills with the full contact drills so you can practice applying them under pressure.

CHAPTER 7: THREE MAJOR FLAWS IN COMBATIVES TRAINING AND HOW TO FIX THEM

When it comes to combatives training, not all roads lead to Rome. In fact, some of the roads people tread lead to nowhere at all in terms of getting good results. To get good results, combatives training has to be structured in a certain way. The problem is that many people who profess to train in combatives don't know what that way is.

Much of what passes for combatives and self defense training is marred by ignorance and indulgence. Many people are just unable to resist the gratification that comes from indulging their whims and desires. Consequently, an awful lot of combatives "systems" out there are just a total mess, ungoverned by either rhyme or reason.

For some reason, in this industry people think it is okay to do what they want and teach what they want without even considering if what they are doing is correct. And by correct I mean does what they are doing lead to tangible results? Can they prove that their training is effective? In a lot of cases, the answer is no.

If you took the people who train in these faulty and indulgent systems and you put them in a professional environment where they had to use their "skills" (such as law enforcement, security, military roles, even street fighting) they would most likely fail miserably in trying to implement their training into these environments. This is because the training methods and objectives are way off in most cases, which leads to the wrong outcomes.

It would take another book to detail all the ways in which combatives and self defense in general are incorrectly taught and trained, so in this chapter I'm going to highlight just three major flaws that I see in a lot of combatives training out there. These flaws are big enough that they effectively mess up everything else, rendering most training useless. So let's look at these flaws now.

Too much emphasis on role-play and padded suit drills.

This is one of the biggest flaws that currently exist in combatives training. Think about combatives and the image that will most likely pop into your head is of a guy wearing a padded suit with a huge helmet on his head as he "attacks" some trainee.

On the surface, scenario training with padded suits seems like a great idea, but in reality this is rarely the case. Think about the way in which most of these drills are done: The padded man ambles up to the trainee mouthing some nonsense like, *"What the fuck are you looking at? You want some, do you?"* before launching into the worst attack you've ever seen. The trainee, meanwhile, launches their own (often sloppy and uncoordinated) counter attack and the padded assailant makes a show of being overwhelmed by the ferocity of the trainee's attack, helpfully backtracking as the trainee bangs that huge helmet with a few largely ineffectual palm strikes or pulled punches. Afterwards everybody claps and pats themselves on the back like they are at a Tony Robbins seminar. *"What a rush! That was so real!"*

No! There was nothing real about that scenario! It was all pre-planned and it looked like a fight scene from a really bad action movie. Nothing about it was realistic. Yet everyone involved thought it to be the height of realism. There may have been some kind of buzz involved, some minor adrenaline rush, but that doesn't make the drill any less unrealistic. It was a feel-good drill, an ego massage, that's it. Would such a drill make you a better operator, a better fighter? Not likely.

Unfortunately, this is how quite a lot of people in combatives train. They take a few techniques, drill those techniques for a short while (usually wrongly) and then "pressure test" them against the padded suit guy before going home, certain that they are now fully prepared and ready for action if they ever find themselves in trouble.

It takes more than a few ill-conceived and sloppy pressure tests to make someone operational. And by the way, I use the terms "operator" and "operational" not in a tactical tourist sense (please) but in a purely practical and functional sense. I don't like the term "fighting" as it has too many negative connotations and it also implies dueling, which is not what combatives is about. Combatives is about learning to operate and use your skills in different situations, hence the term "operator". It's a much more apt term for what we are trying to achieve through training. Just don't go all Jason Bourne when you hear the term, for God's sake. Anyway, moving on…

In the same bracket we have the whole scenario training thing where you have to method act your way through some made up situation. Instructors will say things like, *"Okay, you're tired, you're just home from work, you haven't been feeling well all day and you get home to find six guys there waiting for you… "* or *"You're in the cinema and an old lady jumps you from behind because she's pissed at the sound of your popcorn munching… What are you gonna do?"*

Okay, maybe not quite as ludicrous as that last one, but not far off it! Between the padded suit drills and these silly scenarios, people have wandered off into fantasy land again, haven't they?

These drills can certainly *feel* very realistic in the training hall, but in the training hall you can bend reality whatever way you like it. People do it all the time. So the fact that these drills feel real in the gym does not under any circumstances mean they are viable training methods. In most cases they are simply a feel-good buzz for the participants.

This is not to say that full contact drills cannot be useful. Force on force training can be useful of course (as we will see later), and indeed it is necessary at some point. Trainees need to feel what it is like to go up against a fully resisting opponent. They also need to experience the feeling of shock and awe that comes from being thrust into a sudden-violence situation. Most padded suit drills fail to meet these two criteria. The attacker doesn't usually offer much resistance and there is too much build up for any shock and awe to occur.

For shock and awe you need to look towards Mick Coup's Live Drill, where two participants clash head on and GLF (Go Like Fuck!), as Mick would say, for just a few seconds before being pulled apart again. There is no dialogue exchange or squaring off, just sudden violence that ends just as suddenly (like most real world scenarios).

With other force on force drills you can have two (or more) participants start in various different positions and go from there, for instance, one person on the ground, the other standing, or both in a standing grappling position. Both participants would obviously be going as hard as their equipment will allow; pretty much full contact. Throughout, an instructor would provide coaching, very much like the way an MMA fighter is coached from the side-lines.

That's two examples of how to make good use of your padded suits and also your training time. Both these methods are far more preferable and far more useful than the whole *what are you looking at?* one-sided affairs that pass for pressure testing and scenario training.

To be honest, your training time would be much better spent training the fundamentals, doing simple pad drills that are based on occurrences in actual fights and leaving the full contact stuff until the fundamental fighting skills are firmly enough grasped. But more on that shortly. Let's look at the next major flaw first.

Not enough repeat and/or deliberate practice.

It's quite simple really: The sharper your tools are the more effective they are going to be. Dull tools don't do a very good job.

To have effective tools (effective techniques) you need to sharpen those tools on a continuous basis, which means doing countless reps of each technique. Most martial arts and self defense practitioners already know this, but still very few actually do it.

There could be many reasons as to why the fundamental techniques are not practiced enough. It really doesn't matter. You only need to know one thing: *If you want results from your training you have to go beyond the norm when it comes to how you practice.*

You have to practice as *deliberately* as possible. It's not just a matter of banging out a few hundred reps of a technique. It's a simple matter to do that. What is harder, and what is far more effective, is to try to make each rep as perfect as you can make it. This means that each rep must be focused, powerful and correctly formed, as efficient and as effective as you can make it. What's more, you should be aiming to do each rep with as little conscious thought involved as possible. There is no room for overthinking. Each movement should be instinctual almost, not labored and over-thought. The goal is to get better all the time and to instil the technique as deeply as possible.

Many people avoid this kind of practice because they don't see it as being sexy enough. They want the cool stuff, not the boring stuff. Well, you know what? It's the boring stuff that makes you good. The cool sexy stuff just makes you useless, that's all there is to it.

If you understand the nature of what you are trying to achieve in your training then you shouldn't run away from simple, repetitive practice. If you avoid this kind of training then you obviously don't want to *be* good, you just want to *look* good; you want to feed your ego and your fantasies—or you're just too damn stupid to recognize bullshit when you see it. As you're reading this, I'll assume you don't fall into the latter category.

Remember also that repetitive practice of single techniques is just a part of the overall process of training. Once you have fully grasped the fundamentals of a technique then you must work on being able to use it in context. But even with this type of contextual practice, the rules of repetition still apply. You can never practice these things too much, even drills, either live or with pads.

The goal of repeat practice of the fundamentals is not to turn you into a mindless robot, but into someone who knows how to use their tools effectively in varying circumstances. Keep the bigger picture in mind as you train and know why you are doing what you are doing.

This is purposeful practice. To quote Matthew Syed from

his book, *Bounce*:

"The practice sessions of aspiring champions have a specific and never-changing purpose: progress. Every second of every minute of every hour, the goal is to extend one's mind and body, to push oneself beyond the outer limits of one's capacities, to engage so deeply in the task that one leaves the training session, literally, a changed person."

This kind of purposeful practice begins with repeat practice of the fundamentals. It does not entail practicing some move a few times before moving on to the next one. Purposeful practice is how professional athletes train. It is how you should train as well.

Not using systemized training methods.

If you have ever tried to write a novel then you will know how important having an outline is, a basic structure to follow. Try to write a novel without an outline and I guarantee you will fail miserably. Your novel, if it even gets finished, will be all over the place. It won't make much sense. It will be full of holes. A good read is one thing it won't be.

When it comes to self defense and combatives training, most people approach it like someone trying to write a novel with no outline or pre-thought out structure. In short, the training is all over the place. As a result, most people who train this way are also all over the place.

If you wanted to build a machine would you hastily cobble together a load of random parts and hope the machine worked in the end? Of course not, you'd draw up a blueprint first, decide exactly what parts you will need and then go about assembling those parts in the correct order and in the correct way. Following this approach you will end up with a fully working, efficient and effective machine, capable of doing the job it was built to do.

This is the same approach you need to take to your training as well. You need a system that is going to build a good operator. The system must make logical sense and it must be based on truth. It also must produce tangible results, results that can be measured to a large degree.

I'm not going to get into details here on what should be in this system (read my *Combatives Instruction* book for basic guidance in this area). Suffice to say, a system is not a collection of someone's favorite techniques. That's going back to the random machine building again. A true system requires a bit more thought than that.

And actually there it is, the fix for any training flaw you can think of: *Put a bit more thought into it!*

Now staying on a similar vein, let's look at bad training habits.

CHAPTER 8: FIXING BAD TRAINING HABITS

Quite often in training we can develop bad habits that negatively impact our performance in some way, not to mention slow down our progress. Such habits can also bleed out into real life.

A habit that I had for many years was unthinkingly closing to grappling distance when someone attacked me. This came from years of Jujitsu training, which, in general, is all about closing down an opponent. This tactic seemed like a good idea in training, because you are not only closing down the attack but also getting control of your opponent.

When I started working doors, however, it quickly became clear that this tactic wasn't always the most effective response. I may have closed down the attack but things often got very messy after that and a lot of the time I ended up on the floor with people, struggling to get back to my feet again. If I hadn't been so quick to close distance in the first place I wouldn't have ended up on the floor.

So pretty quickly I realized I had to change tactics. Not only is it bloody exhausting wrestling with someone, it's also risky. A few times I was very lucky not to get badly hurt (from third parties) when I hit the deck with some guy. Eventually I learned to keep my distance and strike if I had to, rather than go rushing in. It wasn't easy breaking that habit. My entire approach to training had to change in order for me to do that. (Being completely honest, it is still a habit that is there, but I am more aware of it now and better able to control it.)

That's an extreme example of a bad training habit. Most unwanted training habits are small things, but small things that can have a big impact on the way that you perform. If you want to be at the top of your game then these negative habits need fixing.

So in this chapter I'm going to outline a three step process for finding and fixing any negative training habits you might have. It's actually a very simple process, but one that will require a bit of work on your part.

Step 1: Identifying the Problem

Obviously we have to start by identifying the problem. You may be aware of your bad training habits by now, or you may not. A lot of the time we are indeed aware of many of our bad habits but they are so low down on our awareness spectrum as to be hardly there at all, at least in our own minds.

We tend to wilfully ignore our bad habits. The only time we take note of them is when they play a part in messing up a drill or when they emerge at the wrong time in a fight. Then we vow to iron the problem out, but we rarely do. And so the cycle repeats itself.

If you know about your bad habits but aren't doing anything about them then you need to look at why this is. Do you think they will clear up over time or even go away by themselves, as if by magic? Or are you just not bothered by them that much?

In the latter case, I'd be bothered by them if I knew they were affecting my performance in some way. Like I said in the previous chapter, the point of training is to progress and get better, so why wouldn't you want to fix the problems that are likely hampering that progress? If you are serious about your training then you should resolve to fix those problems and habits that are having a negative impact on your performance and progress.

In the former case ... come on. These things aren't going

to clear themselves up are they? They aren't going to magically disappear at some point. They will remain with you always until you do something about them.

It is, of course, slightly daunting when you first consider trying to work out and change a bad habit; all that work and frustration, the hours of conscious and deliberate practice. It can be a little off-putting. But it has to be done. If you are staying true to your intentions of wanting to get better then you will face the discomfort and get to work.

If you have already identified your bad habits, you can move on to the next step. If you haven't fully identified what needs correcting then you need to look at your training, examine it until you find something that needs fixing, something that is hampering your performance and something that, if fixed, will have a positive impact on your training.

You usually won't have to think too hard. Most of us have plenty of bad training habits, probably more than we would care to admit. Find one that's going to have the biggest impact on your training if corrected. That's the one you are going to work on. If you are having trouble finding your most pressing bad habit, just ask your instructor. They no doubt will have a long list!

One example of something that I worked on is left/right transitions while striking. Like a lot of people, I was in the habit of striking predominately with my right hand. Consequently the left hand often got neglected in practice. So if I was doing pad drills and I was striking off the right, when the opposite pad was suddenly presented, quite often I would just jab with the left hand instead of changing my feet so I could strike off the back hand. That was the habit I needed to change, jabbing with the left instead of utilizing footwork to strike off the back hand. Nothing really wrong with lead arm strikes per se, but you get more power off the back hand. So that option should take preference whenever possible. Plus, such drills are also about taking you out of your comfort zone (striking comfortably of the strong side all the time), so practice of this type does you good.

Step 2: Deciding How to Fix the Problem

Whatever you're bad habit, problem or weakness is you must decide how you are going to fix it. This begins by first being conscious of the problem. You must be aware of it while you are training and try to correct it or prevent it at all times. Sometimes this isn't enough, however, especially if the habit is deeply ingrained and has become automatic. In that case, you will need to drill down a little deeper to isolate the problem itself.

An easy way to do this is to simply come up with a drill or form of practice that allows you to only work on the specific problem. A weakness for many people is working off the left side as I said, so the solution to that would be to simply force yourself to practice a lot more off the left side. Of course this will feel awkward and frustrating, but if you keep practicing you will get better. If you can do a few hundred reps of a technique in one session, counting only the reps that are spot on and discarding the rest, then you will quickly see a significant improvement in your technique. Your goal then would be to schedule regular practice sessions like this until you get comfortable and competent working off the left.

The process isn't much different for any other bad habit or problem you might have. Simply isolate it and consciously work on changing it. Eventually you will have to think about your movements less and less and the new way of doing things will become the norm. It's just mindful practice.

Another example I can give you would be using your index hand to grab the pad or the wrist of the pad holder while striking. This often happens when people try to index the target but end up grabbing it instead. I do it myself sometimes. It is not a good habit to have since you will not be able to grab an attacker in the same way, so it doesn't make sense to grab the pads like that. It's unrealistic.

So how do you fix such a habit? Again, just be conscious of it first of all, and then come up with little drills that isolate the problem. In this case you might simply practice indexing a pad or some other target, over and over, making sure only your fingers stick to the target and that you don't grab it. After that you might drill slowly, indexing and striking a target. All this will slowly ingrain in you the new habit of sticky fingers rather than grabbing. Finally you will move on to full-on pad drills to test if the new way of doing things has stuck. You will still try to be conscious of what you are doing to an extent. If you catch yourself grabbing the target just resolve not to do it again and continue trying to use just sticky fingers to index. Eventually the new habit will be ingrained and you won't have to think about it at all.

You may not have that problem. Your problem or habit may be different, but the process of fixing it is still the same. You will still need a plan to fix it.

Step 3: Fixing the Problem

This is the simplest step and also the hardest because it requires a good deal of work and effort. Once you have worked out how you are going to fix your problem you must then go about fixing it. This means doing the drills, putting the practice time in, maintaining mindfulness during practice and sticking at it until the bad habit, weakness or problem is ironed out.

As well as being mindful of your own practice you should also enlist the help of a training partner or instructor to provide you with feedback (remember how important to progress this is?). Sometimes they will see things that you miss or let you know when you have fallen unconsciously back into the bad habit again.

Trusting the Process

Bad training habits can be changed but you have to be honest about them first and acknowledge that you have them. Then you have to come up with the right plan to change them and stick to executing that plan. Trust the process and you will eventually iron out whatever problems you may have.

It comes down to deliberate practice again. Purposeful practice can be frustrating but ultimately it is this kind of practice that will improve your training and get you better results.

So say it: *Purposeful, deliberate practice will get me better results.*

Keep repeating that until it is burned into your brain.

And don't forget to actually practice—often.

CHAPTER 9: LIVE FIGHT TRAINING AND DEVELOPING FIGHTING INSTINCTS

One of the major problems in self defense training has always been the problem of how to go from pad drill training to live fight training whilst still trying to retain some semblance of reality. The major problem with this is how to conduct the fight training without letting it descend into ordinary dojo sparring, where two opponents face off and then begin to dance around each other and feel each other out, every now and then moving in to attack. The attack parts of these drills are fine. It's the dancing around in between that is the problem. In a real street fight, very rarely do two people dance around in that manner. It's usually just a clash of fists with each opponent trying to put the other down as quickly as possible.

In self defense training, there needs to be some kind of live fighting, that much is certain. If the only experience of fighting that a trainee has had is striking pads then they are going to be at a severe disadvantage if they have to face someone outside the gym who has fought in the street many times.

There are things about fighting that you can only learn through fighting, such as what it feels like to have someone try to hit you or wrestle you to the ground, or how hard it is to hit a moving opponent. Those are things that can only be experienced by going up against a fully resisting opponent.

So the question is: How can we conduct live fight drills that don't contain all the pointless dancing around and feeling out that exists in traditional dojo sparring? And also how can we insure they are not one-sided affairs?

Some instructors have done a good job in answering these questions and have come up with innovative ways to meet the above criteria. You have Mick Coup's live drills, which I talked about in my last book and also Southnarc who conducts similar force on force drills in his Shivworks system.

I have worked on this problem myself and I have come up with a couple of different ways to conduct live fighting that I have found to be quite beneficial when it comes to getting students used to the pressure of a real fight.

The drills that I use are primarily designed to work on developing a person's fighting instincts, something that I touched upon in an earlier chapter. The shock and awe aspect is therefore a secondary concern in these drills. My main concern in formulating the drills was to allow participants to work on their spontaneity while under pressure.

There are a few ways in which you can start these drills. Experiment and see what works best for you. Some suggestions might be for you and your partner to face each other with eyes closed – upon the go signal, you will both immediately attack one another – or you could begin by standing back to back. The point of starting like this is to prevent any kind of squaring off which is what would happen if you started the drill like a normal sparring bout.

Once the drill begins, the point is to keep attacking your opponent (both of you), trying to land as many shots as possible before the allotted time is up or before you get pulled apart. I suggest keeping the bouts to just a few seconds to create a sense of urgency. If it goes on too long there will be a tendency for both of you to start dancing around and feeling each other out. That's not really what we want from these drills. We want to create the pressure of having to end things quickly, just like in a real fight.

In saying that, you can also extend the length of the drills.

In that case you wouldn't be worrying too much about ending things quickly. This would be more of an opportunity to practice your fighting skills, such as controlling your opponent, capitalizing on openings and mistakes made by your opponent by putting in strikes wherever possible and also maybe applying takedowns and chokes if the opportunity presents itself. If the fight goes to the ground then you both continue until time is called or one gets the better of the other and finishes the fight in some way, even if that means getting up and escaping.

I find these extended bouts to be an ideal opportunity to practice your close-in skills. Normally, after a few seconds there is a clash and you will both end up in grappling range. Not that you have to grapple, mind you. You can also strike from that range or try to create distance again so you can land better strikes.

Another scenario you can begin with is for both of you to start on the ground, perhaps with one of you holding down the other. Upon the go signal, you will both begin to fight from that position, trying to land strikes and create an opportunity to get back to your feet again. This drill isn't really about grappling as such, although you can practice getting to a position from which to strike or control your opponent while you get back up again.

Like I said, these drills are basically very short sparring drills without the dancing around. They are an opportunity for both partners to practice using their skills in a pressurized environment, and also practice fighting in a brawling context if things did get that far in a real situation, which it often does. Ideally you should finish a real fight in just seconds, but for various reasons that doesn't always happen. If a clash happens and brawling begins it is good to know how to handle that kind of situation.

The other main goal of these drills is so you can practice your techniques in a spontaneous manner, which you will have to do in a real situation anyway. Trying to land strikes against someone who is also doing the same and who is moving around a lot isn't easy. You can only practice this aspect of fighting so much with pad drills. With the fighting drills we are discussing here, you will find the whole experience of trying to land good shots a lot more difficult and frustrating. This is why it is good to do these kinds of drills on a regular basis.

These drills can also show up holes in your game. If you continually find yourself freezing when in close then you know you need to work more on fighting from that position. Maybe you need to work on elbow strikes more to drive your opponent back, or maybe you need to work on controlling your opponent better at that range. Whatever is lacking, your instructor will see it and tell you if you don't know yourself.

Remember that these drills represent just one aspect of training. They are not the be all and end all of combatives training. Be sure to balance such drills out by doing plenty of pad work and dedicated technique work. If you don't take the time to learn the fundamentals of fighting and good technique, these live drills won't do you much good. You'll be a mess under pressure. Use the drills at the right time, when the fundamentals have been firmly enough grasped.

CHAPTER 10: REALITY DYSLEXIA

I read an article once in which the author was talking about punching someone on the nose. He gave a very detailed and eloquent description of this: the instant pain, the explosion of blood from the nostrils, the watering of the eyes, the force of the blow causing the recipient to stagger back, both hands clamped over their injured appendage, groaning as blood seeped through their fingers, the fight gone out of them.

This same author then went on to state that such a reaction is pretty much par for the course when someone gets whacked on the nose, like the above reaction is guaranteed.

Regardless of whether the author of said article was overstating his case or not (and I think he probably was), his assertion that a blow to the nose will *always* have the same effect only draws attention to a more widespread and insidious malaise that permeates the vast majority of the reality self defense scene.

I'm talking about reality dyslexia. Not my term, regrettably, someone else's. Regardless of origin, the term is still very apt and perfectly describes the thinking and outlook of many people, especially those involved in 'reality' self defense.

The aforementioned article is a good starting point from which to discuss this condition. Why?

Because only reality dyslexia would cause someone to say that if you hit a guy in the nose they will always react in the same way, therefore you can always rely on this to happen.

That's a bit like saying that it's okay to swim in shark infested waters because if you punch a shark in the nose it will always swim away and leave you alone. Care to guarantee that one?

Dyslexic Reality versus Real Reality

The fact is, you can't assume anything when it comes to fighting and self defense, most of all how your opponent is going to react when you hit them.

An assumption like that creates a dual reality: *Dyslexic Reality* and *Real Reality*.

In the dyslexic version there is how you would like or how you suppose a person would react to certain techniques. In this version, every punch would have a devastating effect on your opponent; every hit would be a perfect knockout. Every strike to the eyes would be eye-wateringly incapacitating; every kick to the groin would have your opponent flying back onto their knees in agonizing pain. Similarly, things like throws and joint locks would work just the way they do in the gym.

In the other version of reality, the one that most people in the world inhabit, things would go quite differently. Not every strike would have a devastating effect and every punch thrown would not guarantee a knockout. Eye strikes would not result in your opponent staggering back with their hands over their eyes and screaming, "MY EYES! MY EYES!" Throws and joint locks would hardly get a look in.

When you put it in those terms, it can seem quite unlikely that anyone would think like that, but many people do. Reality dyslexia has a way of creeping in almost unnoticed.

Before you know it, you start to believe that your techniques are going to have the same effect every single time. They might do, but the chances of that being the case are slim to none.

The fact is that people in fights absorb so-called devastating blows all the time like they are nothing.

Pre-emptive strikes don't always result in immediate knockouts and attacks to 'vital points' like eyes, throat and groin often have no discernible effect against a fully adrenalized and determined opponent (we will discuss vital points in the next chapter).

So how do you counter this faulty thinking? What's the cure for reality dyslexia?

Beliefs and Assumptions

Firstly you must look at the beliefs and assumptions you hold regarding your training. When you find out what they are, ask yourself the following question:

Are my beliefs and assumptions about my training based on solid fact, and have those facts been proven?

If one of your beliefs is that your techniques will work perfectly under all circumstances, what proof exists to back this up?

Have you tested all of your techniques under all circumstances?

Can you even assert with proof that when you punch someone in the nose they will react in the same way every time?

The answer to both those questions is obviously going to be no. So on what basis do some people hold these beliefs to be true?

Think of the techniques that are taught in most self defense classes. How many of those techniques would stand up to the kind of scrutiny we are talking about here?

What proof exists that these techniques do as advertised? What proof exists that these techniques work even some of the time?

Usually none in both cases.

Yet people teach them and train them like they are rock solid truths, without a shred of evidence that this is the case.

When you consider that there is potentially a lot at stake in the situations these techniques are supposed to be used in, I don't think I'm being unfair in asking for a little proof that they do what they say on the tin.

I'd say the efficacy of a technique is a pretty big prerequisite when it comes to self defense training.

The stuff has to stand a chance of working for most people, otherwise what is the point?

But back to dangerous assumptions…

What happens when you have been training for a one punch knockout and then one day you use it and the other guy doesn't go down?

If you haven't trained to immediately follow up on that punch then you are going to freeze and a very pissed off opponent is going to hit you back really hard, ironically maybe knocking you out in the process.

Generally speaking, you should of course have a certain amount of faith in your abilities and in the techniques that you use.

If you don't have that level of confidence in yourself and your abilities then you will struggle against an adversary who does have that confidence and faith in their abilities.

Remember that most predators and thugs have had a lot of practice doing what they do and using the techniques and tactics that help them take down their victims as quickly and as brutally as possible. For that reason, you had better make sure that your shit's really together.

But that doesn't mean that you should make dangerous assumptions about yourself, your skills or your abilities.

Sticking to the high percentage techniques is a good start when it comes to avoiding reality dyslexia.

Train the stuff that has actually been proven to work and resist the temptation to go down the path of whimsy or indulgence.

Unlike scientists, who actively set out to disprove their own theories, many people in the reality self defense game do the opposite, and set out to *prove* their own shaky theories and assumptions.

People can convince themselves of anything given enough time.

If a large portion of the world population can convince themselves there is a god who created the universe and who looks out for all of its inhabitants, and do so without any concrete proof whatsoever, then it's no surprise that many self defense practitioners can convince themselves of the efficacy of certain techniques without any proof whatsoever.

Reality dyslexia pervades the martial arts/self defense worlds like a sickness.

When you objectively examine what actually works a high percentage of the time in a self defense situation then you have no choice but to acknowledge that the majority of what is taught as self defense simply isn't self defense, and is instead self-indulgent and ignorance/ego based nonsense.

When I look at a self defense technique I don't care where it originated from or which celebrity instructor 'invented' or teaches it.

The measure of a technique is not based on where it came from or who teaches it, but on what it can do. End of story.

The minute you allow concessions based on favoritism of some kind, assumptions begin to creep in and suddenly you have a bout of full blown reality dyslexia on your hands.

After all, if you have no concrete proof that something works (beyond working on compliant partners in training or less than worthy opponents in a real situation) then you are forced to make assumptions instead.

Assumption replaces proof.

How different would the world of science be if that where the abiding philosophy? Every crack pot theory in the world would be held up as fact.

But that doesn't happen in the scientific community. Instead, scientists posit the most likely theory, which is based on much testing and examination, before going on to try to find an even more likely theory.

Nothing is set in stone in science. If the facts change, so do the theories.

In the self defense world, even if the facts change, the

theories stay the same.

Objective reality doesn't come into it.

Self-defense should only be based on what is known to work a high percentage of the time. Assumptions shouldn't come into it.

As the saying goes: Assumption is the mother of all fuck-ups.

Those are words that should be written on the wall of every self defense gym in the world.

Now staying along the same lines, let's examine the beliefs surrounding the so-called vital attack points.

CHAPTER 11: VITAL ATTACK POINTS

Vital attack points are those areas on the human body that are deemed to be most vulnerable to attack. They are weak spots on the body – that's how they are put across anyway – areas such as eyes, throat, ears, nose, groin etc., etc. The thinking surrounding vital attack points is that, no matter what size your attacker is, they will still be vulnerable to attack in these areas.

I'm not doubting that these areas on the human body are indeed vulnerable, but does that automatically make them the best areas to attack?

Not necessarily, in my opinion.

Let's take the eyes. You will often hear advice like, *"Go for the eyes! If he can't see, he can't fight!"* or *"He may be twenty stone of muscle, but he doesn't have twenty stone of muscle in his eyes! "*

Fair enough. Let's take the first point of you can't see, you can't fight. If you have ever done blindfolded drills, you will know that it is perfectly possible to fight without sight. As long as you have some kind of index like a hand on the other person, you can fight almost as well as when you can actually see.

As a quick test, close your eyes and index a pad, then hit the pad. You will hit it every time. This is because you don't need to see what you are doing; you only need to *feel* what you are doing.

Taking away an opponent's sight is a good tactic, but only as a temporary measure so you can distract them long enough to line them up for a strike to the head.

As for the second point, the eyes are indeed quite soft and

vulnerable. But they are also surprisingly resilient and can take a remarkable amount of punishment before they start to get really damaged. I've never gouged an eye out of its socket, but I'd wager it isn't as easy as some people think. I'd also wager that most people who talk about gouging out eyeballs from their sockets wouldn't have the internal capacity to do so.

For attacking the eyes, the common attack is to use the thumbs to press into the eye sockets. From a standing position, most people will struggle their way out of this eventually, which is why eye gouging is better used as more of a transition technique rather than a finishing move.

It's an excellent technique when someone is right in on you and you need to create space in order to strike, but that's about as far as it goes. Of course it is possible to inflict real damage to the eyes if you know what you're doing, but for common fight situations, it's unlikely that you will need to inflict permanent eye damage on your attacker, unless you don't mind getting done for GBH.

The throat is another surprisingly resilient 'weak spot'. The old web hand strike is often cited as being the best way to strike the throat. Again though, such a strike is unlikely to stop a determined opponent. Indeed, enough people have tested this technique by now that we know it isn't nearly as devastating as some believe. As such it is only useful as a set up strike.

But in saying that, why do it at all? Why not just go straight for the head? A full force punch to the throat may be a different matter and could potentially be very damaging, perhaps even lethal. But why use such a strike, unless the other guy had a knife or similar lethal weapon? It could land you in jail.

How about clawing techniques that attack the eyes and

throat? Unpleasant, I'm sure, but hardly enough to stop a determined attacker. Only useful as distractions or for creating space so you can transition into more forceful techniques.

Moving on to the groin. Is a kick to the groin a fight finisher? You would think so, but it usually isn't. We've all heard enough times about people absorbing such blows easily. How many times have you caught a kick to the groin in sparring and still managed to fight on? I've lost count of how many times this has happened to me. Now factor in adrenaline and the will to survive in a real situation and you can easily see how groin shots can be ineffective. I'm not saying you shouldn't use them; they can still prove useful if preceded or followed by other strikes elsewhere.

There are many more so called vital attack points as displayed on one of those posters that used to hang on the wall of every dojo back in the day, but the fact is you'd be wasting your time with most of them. Trying to target specific and small areas on a person's body in the franticness of a fight is difficult enough. It is even more difficult to do so with any real effect. Perhaps you could do so if you were supremely skilled and highly experienced, but the average person isn't any of those things.

Targeting these areas on a compliant partner in the gym can make attacking such areas seem effective. But when you factor in adrenaline, sheer aggression, possibly alcohol and drugs, plus the fact that the other guy doesn't give a shit about what you are doing to him and will absorb any and all pain that you inflict on him, these vital attack points don't seem as deadly or as effective anymore. They are merely distractions at best, and at worst a way to further antagonize the other guy.

So what's the alternative? Ironically it is to attack another vital point on the body, and the biggest one at that—the head!

364

It has been proven over and over again that hitting your attacker in the head is the most efficient way to finish a fight. Everyone knows this from their own experience, and if not from experience, then from the thousands of fight clips on YouTube. Out of all those fights caught on camera, how many were finished by one of the participants attacking any of the vital points we have talked about here? I haven't seen a single example yet. That should tell you something.

And staying on the topic of hitting heads, let's talk further about this in the next chapter.

CHAPTER 12: CREATE SPACE OR CLOSE DISTANCE?

Let me ask you this: During a physical altercation, is it better to close distance with your attacker or create space between you and them?

Your answer to that question will depend essentially on how you train for such situations. Some people train to close down an opponent when they are under attack so they can get to grappling range. Others train to create space between themselves and their attacker so they can strike more easily.

But which strategy is best? Which one will offer you the most advantage and give you the greatest chance of prevailing in an attack situation?

The purpose of this chapter is to answer that question by looking at the advantages and disadvantages of both strategies to see if one is better or wiser than the other.

Closing Distance with An Attacker

The main advantage to closing distance with your attacker is that you are taking away their ability to strike. Most people need space, as well as grounding and torque in order to fire of an effective strike. Closing distance will take those things away from your attacker, leaving them all but helpless.

Apparently most people don't know what to do when their space and ability to strike effectively has been taken away from them. But if you are the one closing the distance then you will know exactly what to do, which, according to some, is to start using quarter beat strikes in conjunction with "shredding" the other guy to overwhelm and incapacitate him, or to initiate some kind of takedown technique.

Tactically speaking, this seems like a sound approach until you consider a couple of important factors. The first one is that, by taking away your attacker's ability to strike effectively, you are also, by default, taking away your own ability to strike effectively. Yes it is possible to strike from that range, but not so effectively. Quarter beat striking seems fine in theory and in a training environment when your opponent is wearing a protective helmet, but against a fully adrenalized attacker? Do you really think a quarter beat palm strike or a close in elbow strike is enough to put someone down? I doubt it.

You only have to look to MMA to see why this is true. Often in cage fights you will see two guys clinch and begin to use short range punches and elbows on each other. These strikes might be painful, they may even cut the other guy (in the case of elbows), but I don't think I've ever seen anyone get knocked out or even go down due to being hit by these short range strikes. You could argue that MMA fighters are used to such punishment, but so are many street fighters and criminals, and when you add in alcohol and drugs to the mix, you have an attacker who isn't going to feel much pain, much less hit the floor after you rap his head a few times with your palm. So against a determined attacker (and what attacker isn't determined?) quarter beat striking is all but useless and will not only stir up an attacker's aggression even further, but will also give them time to recreate the space that you just took away from them.

Of course I realize that these strikes are done in combination with techniques like the infamous Shredder. But is the Shredder really that effective against a real, slavering, highly aggressive and determined attacker? Is it enough to completely stop an attacker? I'm not so sure. Face rubbing and scratching an attacker's face would cause discomfort no doubt; I don't think it would be enough to stop someone, however. And remember, we are talking about a fully adrenalized attacker here, not some role playing participant in a training environment. There is a big, nay *massive*, difference.

But what about attacking the eyes? That's part of the Shredder strategy. For sure, attacking the eyes can be a good tactic, but not really in the way that the Shredder does it. The Shredder presents a superficial attack to the eyes and not much more. If you want to attack the eyes then you have to attack them right. Use the thumbs to properly gouge the eyes—to actually strike into them—not just scratch or press on them. That would be more effective than any amount of scratching or face rubbing.

The other elephant in the room here is that effective self defense techniques are supposed to work for even a person of average attributes and abilities. Given that the Shredder relies upon a person getting their opponent to a chest to back position, how is a smaller person – say a 100lb woman – supposed to get a larger man into that position in the first place? Against a fully resisting opponent, this can prove difficult for even a skilled fighter. And to then go on to "shred" their larger attacker's face? It's just not going to happen, I'm afraid.

Back when I was bouncing I used to close people down a lot, but that's mainly because I wanted to control and restrain them, not hit them. Hitting them would have been much easier, believe me. Trying to get even a small person chest to back if they are really resisting you can prove very difficult unless you are significantly bigger and stronger than most, which I wasn't.

Which brings me to my next point. Getting in that close, things can turn messy very quickly. Not only are you yourself open to punches to the head from your attacker (they mightn't knock you out but they aren't going to be pleasant either), but also biting and gouging. You take away someone's ability to hit and they will resort to savagery out of pure instinct. A wrestling match will often ensue at this distance as well. An attacker will hold on to you and if you try to take them down you will often go down with them.

Bottom line is that, for a small person, closing distance with a bigger attacker is suicide for they would just be playing right into their attacker's hands.

The other stated tactical advantage of getting in so close is the "psychological invasiveness" of doing so. Most people get very uncomfortable when you invade their space and get in their face, so, psychologically speaking, they are now cowering and you are at an advantage because you are used to working within such confined spaces.

This is debatable as well. Some people may feel a sense of panic when someone is that close to them, but enough to significantly affect their determination to hurt you? I doubt that. More likely it would push them into savagery, which in my experience is what happens when you get that close to a psyched up attacker, they resort to biting, gouging and clawing out of instinct or a sense of panic. The last thing I want in a fight is to get bitten. It's happened to me before when I closed a guy and ended up on the ground with him. It wasn't a pleasant experience. Neither was the tetanus shot I got the next day.

Creating Space in an Attack

So now let's look at why I consider creating distance to be a better option in an attack than closing it.

As I've already stated, by creating space you are giving

your attacker the advantage of being able to use their strikes at full capacity, this is true. But you also have the exact same advantage, which is what many distance closers seem to forget. It then becomes a question of who can capitalize on this advantage the most and in the quickest time.

If you know how to set someone up to strike them and you know how to strike properly, this isn't actually much of a problem. It is certainly an easier proposition than trying to manhandle your attacker and finish them with face rubbing, face scratching and quarter beat strikes that have next to no impact potential. Again, for a smaller person against a larger person, this would be even more preposterous.

Same goes with grappling and wrestling techniques. Aside from the damage you may receive trying to get in close enough to grab your attacker, it can prove very difficult to take down a determined opponent. The chances are high that you will also end up on the ground with them. Tactically speaking, this wouldn't be a good move.

The fact is that the best and most effective way to stop an attack is to stop the attacker. The most effective way to do that is to *hit them on the head*, either knocking them out or hitting them enough times that they go down, at the very least giving you the chance to escape the situation.

None of that is possible when you close distance. You can't knock someone out with the Shredder and if things go sideways and you end up in a grappling match, how much harder is it going to be to escape then? If you are a woman being attacked by a sexual predator, your attacker will have you right where they want you—in their grasp!

All else aside, let's not forget about the single biggest

contributing factor here: that of real world evidence.

The tactic of striking an attacker to the head to affect a knockout and finish the fight has been a proven one since time immemorial. We've been finishing fights like this since we lived in caves. Even chimpanzees fight like this; they batter their adversaries into submission (or death). In the history of fighting, striking the head has been the single biggest cause of victory. As a tactic it's as high percentage as you can get.

Now consider the Shredder. It was conceived of within the last twenty years or so and within that time I have never heard of anyone even trying to use it in a fight, much less successfully. If it was really that effective then everyone would be using it, would they not? And it's not like no one knows about it either. Anyone who trains in self defense knows about the Shredder. The only people who claim to have used it are those who just happen to also teach it. I say this not to cause an argument, but only to point out that, for all the marketing and claims of effectiveness, there is little or no evidence to support these claims.

The same goes for BJJ in self defense situations—lots of talk but no proof.

Just because a few select people can make a tactic or technique work for them doesn't make that tactic or technique effective in a broader sense. We all have techniques that only seem to work for us as individuals, but that doesn't mean we should expect them to work for everyone else as well.

When it comes to self defense, whatever techniques are taught need to be high percentage techniques in that they will have a high chance of working in most situations. Not only that, they also need to work for the average person, not just for someone with superior strength, size or skills.

As a final point, you might argue that this all just a matter of personal preference. Some like to close the gap; others like to create a gap. Some like to grapple or shred; others like to strike. That's fine, all things being equal. If you have similar attributes to your opponent (equal size, weight, skills) then that argument might wash. But how often is this actually the case? How many women are the same size and have the same strength as their male attackers?

Few if any, which is why specialist or low percentage techniques can't be relied upon to get you out of trouble. To stand the greatest chance of getting out of trouble you need to use techniques and tactics that have been proven to work over and over again, not techniques that have no proof to validate them.

You feel annoyed after reading this. That's okay. It isn't my intention here to cause upset; I'm just dealing with the facts as they relate to self defense. If someone can come along and prove to me different, then I'll happily listen.

CHAPTER 13: FORCE DISPARITY AND CONTROL AND RESTRAINT

Force disparity is a very useful concept that was introduced to me by another combatives instructor. Force disparity occurs when the level of force between you and your attacker is disproportionate. So if you try to respond to a high level of force with a lower level of force there will be a force disparity and your response will be too inadequate to stop your attacker, who is using a higher level of force.

This force disparity also applies when a small woman, for instance, is being attacked by a significantly larger man, or when you are faced by an aggressor with a weapon like a knife or a gun. The point is that there exists a reality at play here that many in the self defense game don't want to admit exists. In some situations, where the odds are significantly stacked against you, the chances of you prevailing are slim to none, no matter how good your response to the situation is. In this context, many people out there who train in self defense tend to suffer a bout of reality dyslexia and get to thinking that they can still prevail in circumstances where significant force disparity exists.

Where I find this concept most useful, however, is when you think about situations that involve family or friends. Over the years I have been unlucky enough to be involved in more than a few situations where close family or friends have kicked off at a social event and I have had the displeasure of trying to sort the situation out.

No doubt you have been in similar situations yourself. Perhaps you've had to witness a close relative at a family gathering drink too much and suddenly decide that anyone who comes within two feet of them is going to get hit. It doesn't matter what anyone else there does to try and calm the person down; the enraged and very drunk relative now sees everyone there as their enemy and has no qualms about hurting anyone who tries to calm them or restrain them.

The first couple of times I was involved in such a situation I tried to slip into bouncer mode and restrain the person who was causing all the trouble. Was I able to nicely restrain the person and calm them down? Hell no! What I got for my trouble was smacked in the face! Eventually I was able to take the other person down, but have you ever tried to hold someone down who doesn't want to be held down, and on top of that, is possessed of more strength than usual thanks to alcohol and adrenaline and red mist (rage)?

It isn't easy and you holding them down does nothing to calm them; it just makes them more enraged. Eventually you will have no choice but to let them back up, at which point they will kick off again and attack whoever is in their immediate vicinity, or they will seek out the person who they perceived to piss them off in the first place and try to attack them.

It's easy to see how these types of situations can get quickly out of control. I also find that, when family and friends are involved in such altercations, emotions tend to be higher since everyone knows each other so well. We tend to reserve the most rage for the ones we love.

The general consensus amongst martial artists and self defense practitioners is that control and restraint is the only option in such volatile situations, and this consensus remains for two main reasons.

Firstly, it is thought that family and friends should be treated with respect and not hit. We'll discuss this in a moment.

Secondly, it is thought that because someone is trained in martial arts they should be able to control anyone without hitting them. Both of these viewpoints are ridiculous in my opinion and only serve to show the lack of experience of those who spout this naïve nonsense.

Let's take that first point that family and friends should not be hit and should instead be restrained. Aside from the difficulty of restraining people who don't want to be restrained (which I'll discuss shortly), let's examine the circumstances that usually surround these kinds of situations.

Generally, when relatives or friends decide to kick off it is in a social setting, usually surrounded by a gathering of other family members and friends. When Uncle Jack suddenly flies into a rage and starts to fight with someone or everyone he is immediately putting everyone else in danger. In my experience, anyone who gets too close to a person who is enraged and under the influence is putting themselves in harm's way. They are going to get hit or worse. Plus, innocent bystanders may take damage in the process as those fighting may fall into them or worse. Anything could happen, and often does happen.

Now here's the thing. Uncle Jack, in deciding to kick off, has, in my opinion, relinquished any right he has to be treated softly or even with any respect. Knowingly or unknowingly, he has put everyone else in danger by his actions and he needs to be dealt with in whatever way possible. If he is hitting anyone who gets too close to him or endangering people in some other way, he has lost the right to be treated with kid gloves. The only priority now should be to stop him from endangering everyone else and that should be done in the quickest and most efficient way possible, without further endangering anyone else. If that means knocking Uncle Jack out, then so be it.

That second point – that martial artists should be able to restrain anyone – is also rubbish. Having spent a good number of years working doors I know how difficult it can be to restrain even the smallest of people if they don't want to be restrained. And let's be honest, who *does* want to be restrained? No one likes being manhandled and they will resist with all their might most of the time. There is also the force disparity issue that I mentioned at the start of this chapter. You will be trying to use a low level of force against someone who is using a much higher level of force, which is where the disparity comes in. That just isn't going to work. To have any hope of prevailing against someone who is using a high level of force, you must match that force.

I'm not saying control and restraint doesn't work, but it takes a certain amount of skill and experience to pull it off and it always helps if you are bigger and stronger than the person you are trying to restrain; the other way around doesn't work very well. Restraint is best done as a group, by multiple people swarming in and surrounding the person. That kind of team work is very effective. But are you really going to see that kind of team work at your average social gathering when probably no one else there knows what they are doing?

And what if you do manage to restrain Uncle Jack? Does that mean he will instantly calm down and stop struggling? In my experience, no, he won't. He will become even more enraged. People who have adrenalized themselves into high levels of aggression find it very difficult to come down from that. I remember a fight that kicked off between two of my close family members and I spent a full hour trying to restrain them both because I didn't want to hit them at the time. I had no help. As soon as I restrained one, the other would rush in and try to kick the person as I held them. This went back and forth for, as I say, a good hour. It only calmed down when one of the offending family members left the scene. That was a lesson learned for me.

What is that lesson? That in the situations described, the only good control and restraint is unconsciousness. That may sound macho or callous to you, but until you have been in one of these situations you will not understand. The quickest way to sort these people out when they kick off and the quickest way to prevent them putting others in danger is to hit them or choke them out. There will be no force disparity anymore. The situation can be ended quickly – and, hopefully, cleanly – and no one else can potentially get hurt.

Force disparity is certainly a concept you should keep in mind, for it will help to define your approach to certain situations. Even when you are training, it can help to consider the kinds of situations you might be using your techniques in.

An example of that would be when you are training highline strikes. As much as I like palm strikes, and as effective as they are, there are some situations where I wouldn't consider using them if a significant degree of force disparity existed. For instance, if I found myself facing a larger opponent who looked like they might do a lot of damage given the opportunity, I would choose to strike with my fists from the outset if a violent response was needed. Punches do more damage than palm strikes and damage is what is needed against a significantly larger or stronger or more capable opponent. I have more confidence in my fists than in my palms when all is said and done. So when I train my punches, I do so with those kinds of situations in mind. This helps to focus me as I practice.

The same goes for a situation where multiple opponents exist, or if an attacker has a weapon of some sort like a knife. Those odds represent a significant force disparity and whatever your response is, it has to be high up on the force continuum.

To put it in more blunt terms: *In situations where a large degree of force disparity exists, you can't afford to mess about. You have to go in hard and fast and stay on the offensive or you will get beaten. It's as simple as that.*

I also imagine that the force disparity concept might be a useful one to pull out in court should you find yourself in a position where you had to justify your actions in a certain situation. I'm not sure what difference this would make to your case, but I've no doubt that if you can articulate your actions in those terms—and as long as your actions where indeed justified in the first place—it certainly wouldn't harm your defense.

CHAPTER 14: SELF DEFENCE PSYCHOLOGY AND MENTAL TRAINING

In the self defense world much has been made of the "psychology" behind self defense itself. Ask many instructors what they think is most important when it comes to self defense and there answer (after awareness) will likely be the psychology of it all, or having the mental skills to be able to deal with and use violence when necessary.

While there is some truth behind this, in the main, the psychological aspects of self defense are vastly over-emphasized. It's an area that allows for the indulgence of all manner of theories and "head-work" techniques that at the end of the day, can't be shown to have any real value as far as teaching people how to protect themselves.

None of it can be proved because it exists only on the mental plain. Indeed the many theories and hypothesizes that exist concerning self defense psychology, for the most part can't be proved to have any affect in the real world. So we are expected to take the word of the people who put this stuff out there.

There is no doubt it makes for interesting reading at times, but that's about it. I've yet to come across any psychological theory pertaining to self defense that could be said to be anyway useful to the average person who wants to get better at handling violent conflict.

The problem with most of the psychology stuff is that it is based on subjective experience and therefore can't be objectively evaluated. There are no studies to back anything up, only anecdotal evidence backed up by the often dubious authority of the person putting the stuff out there.

I have tried to put across the psychological aspects of self defense myself in the past (read my first book) but I have always made it clear that it is just my subjective opinion on things. It is okay to put across your own experiences so people may learn what they can from those experiences, but to put those experiences across as if they should apply to everyone would be wrong and not very scientific or objective.

Much of what passes for self defense psychology is the result of research porn. What happens is that a person gets really into a certain subject like self defense and they let their whims and indulgences carry them off to places that there is just no need to go. For instance, just because you study self defense doesn't mean you also have to make an in-depth study of the criminal mind by exploring criminology and sociology. When the chips are down, what possible use could such information have? None, I'm sure.

The same applies to "violence dynamics". Again there is this apparent need to "understand the enemy". From a pre-contact point of view I can see why some people feel there is a need for this sort of classification. Some attackers may have to be handled differently, but common sense and intuition should alert you to this anyway. Classifying attackers based on their motives complicates things more than is needed.

I can't really get behind the notion that the enemy must be studied and classified like animals in a lab. The only "enemy" that exists out there are people, and to a very large degree–on a base level– people are all the same. Sure we all have different personalities, different attributes etc. But does this really matter when it comes to defending yourself against violence from another?

There are thousands of books and studies and research papers out there that seek to study and classify people who use criminal and violent behavior to get their own way. And while some of this research is certainly interesting, do I really need to know every nuance of the average criminal mind? Do I need to know what motivates your average thug? Will knowing what motivates an attack on my person help me stop it? Professional law enforcement groups don't even delve that deep when they train people, and these are guys who deal with criminal's day in and day out.

The fact is, if I'm being attacked by someone, I don't really care what is motivating their attack. All I know is that I'm being attacked and I need to defend myself—that's it, the bottom line. The psychology of my attacker matters not.

Why violence is perpetrated is much less important than *how* it is perpetrated, at least in self defense terms. It seems that we all have to know exactly what group a violent individual belongs to now; we have to know the motivation behind their particular brand of violence. Are they Monkey Dancers, Status Seekers, Resource or Process Predators? So many different classifications for what amounts to essentially the same thing: a violent cunt!

In the case of predators, I don't care if they want my money or my head in their fridge. My response will be the same if I am physically threatened. I will fight back.

Sure, if someone threatens me with a knife and demands my wallet, I'll give them the damn thing. That's just common sense. That's being socially intelligent and understanding the type of situation I am in and how it can be resolved.

I've been a member of society long enough now. I don't need academic classifications to help me function around people or in society in general.

Teaching violence dynamics is a bit like teaching

awareness, in that you are trying to make academic what is already intuitively felt. With awareness, you are either switched on or you aren't. With violence dynamics, either you know people or you don't.

Reading about people and hearing someone else talk about people is not going to help you deal with them any better. I could read books all day long about life in prison and the culture that exists in prison and how people act in prison. Does this mean that if I end up in prison that I'll be able to expertly classify and handle every person in there? Of course not. The only way I'd survive in prison is by getting to know the place and its inhabitants first hand, not by reading a book on it.

It's all very interesting this criminal psychology stuff, but in the end, most of it is no more than research porn—pointless reams of data that only serve to complicate the issue at hand.

What so-called interpersonal violence comes down to is that there is someone in front of you that wants to hurt you. The circumstances surrounding this should be obvious to anyone with half a brain. If someone demands my money or car then I know what they want. If someone jumps me in a dark alley then I know what they want. If some dick in a bar tries to pick a fight with me then I know what they want. In each case, I will respond accordingly, using my intuition and common sense.

Whether you face a mugger, a serial killer or some weekend warrior, in the grand scheme of things, it doesn't matter. Your response will be the same in that you will do whatever it takes to stop that other person from hurting you, no matter what their motivations are.

At the end of the day, what is going to help you most in a self defense situation is not what you know about the psychology of your attacker, but the training you have done to learn how to stop him.

It is proper training that will give you the tools you need to protect yourself in a self defense situation. Even if you are lacking in confidence or are struggling with the fear side of things, good combatives training will help you overcome those limitations.

You must also remember that we are all individuals with our own particular strengths and weaknesses. Training of any kind does not guarantee the same results for everyone. Combatives will not help you fix every personal issue that you have, nor is it guaranteed to make you into this confident, highly assertive person who is capable of handling any self defense situation.

Often you will have to take the bull by the horns and work on your personal problems outside of training. Combatives isn't some cure all. It is designed to teach people how to use certain tools and tactics in particular situations. It does not offer magical solutions to all your problems.

I can tell you what it is that I do to make myself mentally stronger, or I can tell you about some of the mental processes I might use to help me handle difficult situations better, but that doesn't mean those things will work for you. You have to find your own way of dealing with things. Sorry if that doesn't equate with some of the solutions and shortcuts offered by some, but that is the reality.

People are desperate for these quick fix solutions to their problems. They say they shit themselves when faced by an attacker and ask how they can overcome their fear. You don't! The reality is, almost everyone shits themselves when faced by someone who wants to hurt them. That's life. This is something you must learn to accept instead of agonizing over solutions that don't exist. There is nothing out there that will make a person fearless, except snake oil. The only solution to that particular problem is to try and harden yourself to the feelings associated with conflict, and you can do that through training. Training will help certainly, but training can only do so much. That's just something you have to accept.

My advice (and I'm speaking from experience here) is to forget about trying to find quick fixes and easy solutions to complex problems. Quit drinking the snake oil. Concentrate instead on your training and work hard to get results from it. Over time you will get most of what you need just from training. The rest you will have to find for yourself. It is naive to think that everything will be handed to you on a plate.

While we are on the subject of training and mental skills, let me end this chapter by talking about yet more snake oil that people can't help drinking.

At one point I spent months researching so-called "mental toughness" and "mental training" techniques because I planned to write a book on the subject as it related to self defense. I read numerous books, articles and research papers on the subject of raising your game by improving your mental game.

When I started the research I felt sure that it would be possible to take my training (and that of others) to the next level. This belief was based not only on my intuition that mental training alongside physical training made complete sense, but also on the fact that so many high profile athletes talked a lot about the importance of the mental game and how "90% of their game was mental".

Well after all that research, what I found was that so-called mental training techniques are mostly bullshit. In the main, what passes for mental training techniques are actually just NLP (Neuro Linguistic Programming) inspired nonsense and have little or no value at all when it comes to raising your game.

The whole field of sports psychology in fact appears to be based on a lot of bullshit pop psychology and shaky research. Despite the claims made by those who call themselves sports psychologists, the techniques and practices that are used in this field to try and raise the mental game of athletes appear to make very little difference to an athlete's performance at the end of the day.

This is none more truly than when it comes to applying this stuff to self defense, and also to law enforcement and the military. There is a lot of anecdotal evidence to suggest that it makes a difference, but little in the way of any concrete evidence to prove that it does.

With any study conducted, there is always going to be "evidence" that is biased towards proving the validity of the study itself. You only have to look at the mountains of research done on human paranormal abilities. Many studies claim to have proved the existence of such abilities and there is much anecdotal evidence to suggest that they have, but amongst all that evidence there is still no concrete proof that human paranormal abilities even exist.

I found the same sort of thing with mental toughness techniques and mental training techniques. Any evidence is based solely on subjective hearsay and not much else. The sports psychology field seems to be no different from the NLP field in that it is populated by pseudo-scientists and confidence tricksters, telling people what they want to hear and backing up there outrageous claims with dubious science and shaky psychology.

Certain aspects of the mental game can be improved

upon—I'm not saying this isn't possible. Techniques like visualization are useful, as is learning to concentrate and focus better, and learning to stay calm under pressure. With a bit of conscious effort, these things can be improved.

In the main though, mental toughness and learning to control your mental game can only come through playing the damn game all the time and gathering as much experience as possible. The more you play and practice the better you will get at controlling your own mind. It's as simple as that.

But that isn't enough for some. It wasn't enough for me when I started my research. I had visions of designing a complete program of mental skills training to run alongside the physical programs. Then I saw what was actually on most these mental programs.

All of the mental training programs that I studied where made up of what can only be described as self-indulgent rubbish. These programs where made by people who were desperate to justify the need for such programs, and also to justify the role they themselves were playing, the role of sports psychologist or mental training coach or whatever title they went under.

Almost all of the techniques in these programs where based around NLP concepts, which in itself should be cause for concern because NLP is nothing more than bullshit packaged up as cutting edge science and "neuropsychology". It has no scientific basis and it is propagated by confidence tricksters who like to prey on the weak-minded.

So to base an entire field of psychology on this nonsense? Hardly a base for credibility is it?

The fact is people at the top of their fields get there because they work hard and they work smart. They understand everything there is to know about what it is they do, and they practice the hell out of every part of their game. They are also experienced players who learn from every game. They already know how to get the most from themselves, they don't need a load of silly mental training techniques to increase their confidence or help them do better.

They get that from training and applying themselves in whatever way they need too so they can get results.

In the end, either you have game or you don't. No amount of bullshit psychology or mental training techniques are going to change that.

For self defense it's no different. If you can't get what you need from training or from your own experience then you will never get it.

Your time will be far better spent by being consistent with the fundamentals. Every master of their field works this way. They spend their time doing the things that will have the greatest impact on their performance and development.

Avoid the snake oil. It will just poison you eventually.

CHAPTER 15: TAKING YOUR TIME

I'd like to end this book by talking about something that is very rarely mentioned in relation to self defense – even though it is vitally important to getting good results – and that is the value of taking your time.

Once upon a time people used to serve apprenticeships. They would spend five to ten years learning some kind of trade from a master tradesman. The goal of such a long apprenticeship was so the apprentice could master every skill involved in their trade and eventually become a master tradesman just like their mentor. To get to that level of mastery though, the apprentice had to put in many thousands of hours of practice, showing complete commitment and dedication to what they were doing.

That level of commitment and desire for mastery still exists to some extent today in society, but I am not sure that it exists in the self defense industry so much. Usually when someone talks about learning self defense they talk about learning it in a matter of weeks or months at the most, sometimes even *days*. There are organizations out there who promise to make anyone an instructor in self defense in just two or three days! That is obviously marketing and greed gone too far, but it characterizes the general view in the industry that self defense can be learned by anyone almost overnight.

Clearly this viewpoint is nonsense. While it may be possible to teach people a few basic techniques over the course of a few weeks—techniques that they *may* be able to put to use if it came to it—it is certainly not possible to train someone to a high level of competence in self defense, nor indeed qualify them as an instructor.

If it is your goal to become highly competent in

combatives and fighting in general, then you are looking at five to ten years' training at least. The thought of committing themselves for so long would no doubt horrify a lot of people, which is why so many go for the quick fix and walk around afterwards kidding themselves that they know what they are doing when it comes to fighting and self defense.

I am a big believer that if you are going to do something then you do it right. Commit to whatever it is you are doing and make your goal nothing less than mastery. Otherwise, what is the point in doing it at all? Why do something if all you are going to be is mediocre at it? Mediocrity in all its forms should be deeply offensive to you. Why? Because being mediocre at something means that you could be better if you worked at it more. It tells people that you are not committed enough to be any better; that you are just passing time without expending too much effort.

Don't go for "just alright". Strive for awesome!

If you are training in combatives then I assume that you are expecting good results from your training, otherwise why do it in the first place, right? So how much time and effort are you putting in to getting those results? Are you in it for the long haul? How do you feel about putting in five to ten years of solid training and study? These are questions you should ask yourself. If the idea of committing yourself to such an extent is too much for you, then perhaps you should find something else to do where you *can* commit yourself to that extent because you are not going to get anywhere near results if you don't.

Getting good results from your training is largely based on your ability to take your time and not rush the process. Obviously the type of training you do matters as well, but assuming everything else is in place, taking your time will ensure you get the results you are after.

And remember we are talking about mastery here. We are talking about knowing your subject inside and out, in great detail; we are talking about having superior physical abilities and intuition. Those things take time to develop.

Taking Your Time in Training

If you have ever been in a fight then you will know what a panic move is. It's one of those moves that you do without thinking, in a panicked state. Nearly always these kinds of moves turn out to be very ineffectual. An example of a common panic move is to lash out unthinkingly in the general direction of your opponent as you try to land a strike on them. Invariably, the strike will have little power and the accuracy will be way off. In fact you'll probably miss your target completely due to the fact that you didn't really focus on a target—you merely blindly lashed out hoping to hit something.

Another example of a panic move would be if you were taking a lot of hits from your opponent and you blindly rushed forward in a panic to close distance and grab hold of your attacker, half hoping that this will end the punishment they are dealing out to you. Now you would find yourself in a wrestling match, probably still getting hit. The fight would go to the ground and more panic moves would follow.

I remember going to the ground with a guy one time and, in a panic, I gripped his throat and held it. I didn't do anything else; I just held it, even though there were plenty of other targets open to me for striking. I stayed that way for what seemed like a long time before waking up and getting back to my feet. That was a panic move—pointless and fairly ineffectual as it turned out.

These kinds of panic moves are understandable under the

pressure of a real fight. None of us are so experienced that nothing fazes us or we never get surprised by things that happen in the fight. It is natural to blindly react and lash out at times under those kinds of circumstances. And to be honest, that's the way it will always be when the shit hits the fan. To what degree this occurs will depend on your training and level of experience in such situations.

Panic moves under real circumstances are forgivable. Where they are *not* too forgivable is in training. I have observed in many of the students I have worked with, especially at the beginning of their training, the tendency to default to panic moves when they are under even the smallest amount of pressure.

As an example, I might ask a trainee to perform a highline strike on the pad and then follow that strike up with three more. Invariably the first strike will be fine but the three follow up strikes will be rushed, performed in a panic and consequently far from adequate in terms of power and effectiveness. The trainee sometimes nearly trips over himself in an effort to quickly do those three strikes. The dead give-away is when the student slaps at the pad instead of striking it if they are doing a palm strike. This is nearly always an indication that the student is in panic mode, which comes from not being centered enough as they strike.

If this habit of falling into panic mode is not soon corrected it will become instilled in the student and they will find it hard to break the habit. As time goes on and the student is put under increasing pressure through various drills, the panic moves will become more and more of a hindrance to their overall performance and they will not achieve the results they desire from their training.

The Antidote to Panic Moves

So what is the antidote to panic moves? The solution is to make your moves assured. You want to be doing assured moves instead of panic moves. The terminology might not have the best ring to it, but it nonetheless sums up what I'm trying to get at when I say that your moves should be assured.

Assured movements are controlled, focused and powerful—the opposite of what a panic move is. Acquiring this kind of assuredness in your movements requires that you learn to take your time when performing techniques, as much as possible anyway under whatever circumstances you are in. Obviously, the more pressure you are under, the harder this will be.

To make your moves more assured, and to avoid falling into a panic every time you have to hit the accelerator, so to speak, you will have to learn to take your time with things. This means you will have to learn how to focus and also center yourself. It will involve reigning yourself in and not letting your mind take control of your body. If your mind thinks there is a panic to get something done then your body will soon concur, which results in the panic moves we talked about.

Making your strikes and overall movements more assured is a simple process. Purposely relax and tell yourself that you will not rush and that you have plenty of time to complete the given task. By doing this *you* are taking control of your mind first of all and telling it that you are in control. Focus and breathe easy. Get a calm center. Make sure that your mind is detached from the outcome you want to achieve. If you allow your mind to focus too much on the outcome your mind will think there is a lot at stake and panic won't be too far away. Just be confident and assured and know that you have the ability to do what you have to do. Then simply do your strikes on the pad. You should find yourself taking your time more, which will result in more effective striking.

This is very simple. I don't want to make it seem like there is some complicated mental process involved. There isn't. It's just a matter of checking yourself to make sure you are centered before you do what you have to do. That's it. That's usually all it takes. You just need to do this every time before you do your drills.

Start with the simple drills to get used to the process. It should become instilled after a time and eventually carry over into the more pressurized drills where you won't have as much time (or any time) to consciously focus. This is why the habit of getting centered and focusing needs to become subconscious and automatic. The only way to ensure this is to practice, and to cultivate the habit of making your movements as assured as possible.

Keeping a Level Head

Try to take a Zen-like approach to your training. Don't invest too heavily in outcomes; focus more on the process. Investing too heavily in outcomes will lead to needless pressure and disappointment when you don't perform the way you would like. Keep a balanced mind. Nothing that happens in training – good or bad – should illicit in you any kind of high emotion. Keep yourself in check always, whether you make a big mistake or whether you do something great. Either way, don't make a big deal out of it because it probably isn't.

Keeping yourself in check in this way, keeping the panic moves to a minimum and the assured moves to a maximum, will greatly improve the results you get from your training. You are controlling that instinctive need to panic and cultivating a sense of assuredness in everything that you do. It's a conscious growth process.

Of course, the more pressure that you find yourself under, the harder all this will be. Don't despair when you fall apart sometimes and resort to panic moves. Sometimes, if the pressure is great enough, this is all that we can do. Accept that it happened and resolve to do your best to prevent it from happening again.

One of the goals of hard skills training is to effectively make someone into a machine who does precise machine-like movements. That's fair enough. Remember, though, that we are also human and as such can be infallible at times, prone to failure and mistakes. Don't let this aspect of human nature get to you. Accept it and strive to get better at minimizing it.

AFTERWARD

I hope you enjoyed reading this book. Like I said in the beginning, my purpose in writing the book was to get you to think about your approach to your training and to consider whether or not you are getting the results you desire from that training. If those results fall short, applying the things I talked about in this book will definitely improve them.

The real trick to getting desirable results is to become more conscious about what you are doing. You need to make yourself aware of the real issues involved in self defense training and the purpose behind the things you do in it.

If you have no clear idea of why you are training or of the kinds of situations you are training *for* and the problems involved, you will not be able to come up with suitable answers to those problems. You'll be groping blindly in the dark.

This is why it is very important to gather as much information and experience as possible, and to learn as much as possible from others who are more experienced than you. If you can train under the right people, your game will improve considerably.

Combatives isn't just about copying what others are doing though. To get the greatest level of understanding and competence you have to think for yourself as well. Knowing things on a surface level isn't enough if you want to attain any level of mastery.

The kind of understanding I am talking about takes time however and you must be patient and prepared for that. Your patience and dedication will pay off though when you reach the point of really knowing your stuff and of having a clear understanding of the issues involved in training and the kind of solutions that are required to resolve those issues.

You will always be learning of course. As much as I know now, there is still a lot that I don't know yet. That's the process though. That's what the journey is all about.

Train hard.

Train honest.

Question everything.

Think for yourself.

And don't forget to have fun along the way.

Neal

P.S. I'd be grateful if you would consider leaving a review of this book on Amazon or wherever you bought it from. Reviews are important for letting other people know about the book and I'd also love to hear your thoughts on the book—good or bad!

Thank you!

ABOUT THE AUTHOR

Neal Martin is a writer and martial artist with over thirty years training experience. His specialty is combatives and self defense. He lives in N.Ireland with his wife and daughters.

Contact via email: neal.martin@hotmail.com

Website: www.combativemind.com

Printed in Great Britain
by Amazon